Judith Schlehe, Michiko Uike-Bormann, Carolyn Oesterle,
Wolfgang Hochbruck (eds.)
Staging the Past

D1565000

Historische Lebenswelten in populären Wissenskulturen
History in Popular Cultures | Volume 2

Editorial

The series **Historische Lebenswelten in populären Wissenskulturen | History in Popular Cultures** provides analyses of popular representations of history from specific and interdisciplinary perspectives (history, literature and media studies, social anthropology, and sociology). The studies focus on the contents, media, genres, as well as functions of contemporary and past historical cultures.

The series is edited by Barbara Korte and Sylvia Paletschek (executives), Hans-Joachim Gehrke, Wolfgang Hochbruck, Sven Kommer and Judith Schlehe.

JUDITH SCHLEHE, MICHIKO UIKE-BORMANN, CAROLYN OESTERLE,
WOLFGANG HOCHBRUCK (EDS.)
Staging the Past.
Themed Environments in Transcultural Perspectives

[transcript]

Gedruckt mit Unterstützung
der Deutschen Forschungsgemeinschaft

**Bibliographic information published by
the Deutsche Nationalbibliothek**
The Deutsche Nationalbibliothek lists this publication in the Deutsche Nationalbibliografie; detailed bibliographic data are available in
the Internet at http://dnb.d-nb.de

Cover layout: Kordula Röckenhaus, Bielefeld
Cover illustration: Michiko Uike-Bormann,
Huis Ten Bosch/Japan, 2008
Proofread by Judith Schlehe, Michiko Uike-Bormann, Carolyn Oesterle,
Wolfgang Hochbruck
Typeset by Carolyn Oesterle, Michiko Uike-Bormann
Printed by Majuskel Medienproduktion GmbH, Wetzlar
ISBN 978-3-8376-1481-7

CONTENTS

TRANSHISTORICAL ACTION:
PERFORMANCE AND SOCIAL EXPERIENCE

Introduction: Staging the Past

WOLFGANG HOCHBRUCK/JUDITH SCHLEHE

In global processes of identity formation, the present is anchored in socially constituted histories and meaningful pasts (Friedman 2008: 89). The production of histories of the self and the negotiation of alterity takes place in many forms and formats – not just in academic historiography. In popular contexts, the practices of theming and staging communicate certain versions of the past that are consumed and appropriated by immense numbers of people. And obviously they enjoy it! But what accounts for this attraction and how may it be assessed?

The origins of this transdisciplinary volume of essays, which the editors hope will serve as an introduction to the field of themed environments and staged pasts, can be traced to a conference in Freiburg, Germany, in 2009.[1] It was the first gathering of scholars as well as practitioners from various fields participating in the creation and study of the current wave of themed and theatrical representations of history as can be discerned in widely separate parts of the world. Researchers in cultural studies, archaeology, anthropology, tourism studies, military history, literature, living history, theatre, museums, media education and pedagogy present their research results and experiences in this book, in a series of writings as diverse as their transdisciplinary approaches.

It is the aim of this volume to go beyond the established patterns of thought within disciplines and to explore the field and its considerable variety of forms and formations in several cultural contexts.[2] The articles seek to explain how history became not only a popular cultural pastime in the second half of the 20th century, but a theatrical venue, a commercial asset, and a hobby for multitudes – without losing its political significance.

---

1   The editors would like to thank Victoria Tafferner and Coman Hamilton for their valuable work in proof-reading this volume.

2   To this end, the DFG Research Group 875: *History in Popular Cultures (Historische Lebenswelten in populären Wissenskulturen der Gegenwart)* has received funding from the German Research Foundation since 2007.

This volume will enhance a deeper understanding of how particularly the spatial and the performative turns in cultural theory and practice have affected, and are continuing to affect, our perspectives on the various popular representations of history that we encounter in theme parks (Joy Hendry, Judith Schlehe/Michiko Uike-Bormann, Noel B. Salazar), music, the theater, living history programmes and experiences with reenactments (Martine Teunissen, Mark Wallis, Vanessa Agnew, Carolyn Oesterle), tourist sites and places of pilgrimage (Cornelius Holtorf, Amos S. Ron), as well as in historiography and literary fiction. (Re-)Constructions of history have become popular pastimes that not only amuse audiences but influence and instruct beyond their historical range (Regina Loftus/ Paul Röllke/Victoria Tafferner), construct new formations of social fabric among participants (Gordon L. Jones, Anja Dreschke), and even gradually leave the realm of bounded space and time allotted to them to become ubiquitous and pervasive as consumer-oriented lifespace (Scott A. Lukas). The title of this volume acknowledges the two main components of themed environment and theatrical reenactment that enable and empower individuals and independent groups as well as museums and other *appareils d'etat*, but also private, commercial and multinational corporations to create their own versions of history. These versions unfold their meanings only when seen in their specific cultural contexts and from a transcultural perspective. It is crucial to understand that what is staged in themed environments is either the creation of a history of a nation, region, or ethnic group, as an offer to the visitor for imaginative identification, or it is the creation of a seemingly timeless exotic Other, juxtaposed to the Self and serving to stabilize and position it in the global world. In order to reveal the meanings of these versions of history in the context of identity politics we suggest extending cultural studies to encompass an inter- and transcultural studies approach which will also focus on global cultural entanglements and particular social positions. It is of great importance in this context that analyses are grounded in empirical field research. When regarding theming and performance of pasts as meaningful social practices, our goal is to critically explore which uses people make of these practices in specific present-day contexts.

Themed Environments

The shifts of power in the media from the word to the image, and from the image to the simulacrum (cf. Ron in this volume), have also affected transmissions of historical knowledge both in terms of the media used in the process and in terms of structuring the acquisition process. Reading and viewing are gradually being replaced by multi-sensory experiences, the active role of the reader/recipient, and the passive consumption of viewing merging in the guided activity of experiencing spatially and thematically structured arrangements of historical knowledge. Themed environments,[3] this volume argues, are not only a device for materially transforming architectural presents world-wide according to individual or collective taste, but have also become a ubiquitous way of experiencing *pastness*, to borrow from Cornelius Holtorf. *Pastness* is here used to describe the practical results of all sorts of themed environment constructions that refer to events, themes, topics, and persons that are perceived as historical by visitors and which have been instrumentalised to cater to the apparently increasing urge to authentificate identities based on individual and/or collective histories: "People are interested in constructing authentic relationships with a particular retelling of the past, and that past assists in the construction or reaffirmation of a sense of identity" (Rowan 2004: 263).

Bringing together disneyite forms of Imagineering (Imagineers 1996) and the reconstructive impulse of historical open-air museums from Swedish Skansen to Plimoth Plantation in Massachusetts and to Taman Mini in Indonesia, theming provides the basic instrumentarium of spatial arrangements necessary to create simulacra that appear to circumvent the obvious irretrievability of the past. Not that this irretrievability had ever kept scholars, politicians or other parties interested from researching, (re-)writing and realigning their impressions of the respective pasts with current affairs, needs, and insights, usually in the form of traditional historiography. The turn towards spatialising history in four permanent dimensions as themed environments, however, is (relatively) new. Its impulse appears to have three roots; one, the theming visible in amusement parks (traceable to the Bakken park which opened already in 1583 at Klampenborg near Kobenhavn, DK) and in the early ethnographic spectacles in commercial venues and in imperial and colonial expositions (Stanley 1998), two, the regional and historical theming of open-air museums where the three-dimensional manikin-based tableaux start walking and talking simultaneously with similar two-dimensional efforts in the field of cinematography, and three, the theming in other architectural environments such as shops, malls, and restaurants (Gottdiener 2001, Wood/Munoz 2007). Several contributors to this volume also mention the transgression between themed and everyday envi-

---

3   The definition of themed environment here follows Gottdiener (2001: 5): "[...] themed material forms that are products of a cultural process aimed at investing constructed spaces with symbolic meaning and at *conveying* that meaning to inhabitants and users through symbolic motifs" (cf. Ron in this volume: 120).

ronments. Theme parks are not necessarily bounded liminal places anymore, as Alexander Moore has suggested (Moore 1980: 216), but have become 'normal' tourist destinations. Theming is not any longer something extraordinary, it has become an integral aspect of both tourism, leisure and, most importantly, of ordinary, everyday life. City-centers, shops, restaurants, and housing developments are often themed to varying degrees, so a considerable part of peoples' lives all over the world already takes place in themed environments. More precisely: theming intrudes into the life-worlds of the urban cosmopolitan middle-classes.

Consequently, there are a growing number of people who celebrate their marriages, practice their respective forms of worship, or even dwell permanently in theme parks. Important parts of life have intruded into the themed space which can in many situations no longer be designated as liminal – certainly not in the classical sense which has previously alluded to anti-structural and transformative qualities.[4] Consuming and appropriating a well-defined, unambiguous past in themed environments now appears to guarantee continuity and adds to the comfort of enjoying a structured, safe present.

Theming environments and their inhabitants at least on a surface level refers to displays of 'real' lives and their conditions, to *Lebensweltlichkeit* – that which existed before and outside the extraordinary world of adventure. Experiencing the pastness of these ordinary lives inside the themed space, however, turns the relations between normality and adventure inside out in an ironic reversal: the ordinary is seen, viewed, or experienced hands-on as the extraordinary. Yet, this extraordinarity is not so much challenging as entertaining,[5] and it is not taken too seriously by visitors – which also adds a great deal to its attraction.

This is the point where open-air historical museums with living history programmes deviate from theme parks, (where the aim is what the Disney imagineers call "heightened reality"), or where they *should* deviate, or at least *have* deviated in the past. Originally the theme park was characterised as an amusement park with rides and booths centered around a particular theme. Recently, while joyride-based amusement parks have been experiencing hard times (List

---

4   Erika Fischer–Lichte explained recently that Victor Turner's concepts of the "liminal" and the "liminoid" can be applied to leisure activities and all kinds of cultural performances as long as they bear the aspect of transformation (Fischer–Lichte 2009, cf. also Oesterle in this volume). We would argue that theming is normalized and naturalized to such an extent that there are hardly any transformative experiences to be discerned in the consumption of themed environments.

5   This holds even true for the so-called "dark theming" to which Lukas (in this volume) refers: the shocking elements are just entertaining.

2009), theme parks with historical topicalities appear to have increased in attractiveness, an example of which, the Europa-Park in Rust close to Freiburg with its mixture of spectacular rides and regionally grouped pan-European[6] historical vistas, has seen continuously increasing visitor figures in spite of economic pressures.

Given the pull-factor of entertainment-oriented theming with its "artistic license to play more directly to [...] emotional attachments" (Imagineers 2005: 23), one should probably not be overly surprised that historical museums, however consciously or unconsciously, have begun modelling the concessions and paraphernalia of their presentations partially according to theme park models. Additionally, museums have started inviting living history presenters and interpreters to enliven their traditional programmes – with mixed results. Concurrently, there is a tendency in Asian theme parks to integrate museum-like elements, thereby blurring the boundaries between themed entertainment spaces and serious educational institutions (cf. Hendry 2000).

All themed environments have the same capacities critics now credit to the more sophisticated cartoon narratives or the middlebrow novel – to challenge the reader into an intellectual game of intertextualities, while entertaining everybody. Also, both museums and theme parks rely on scientific research for their constructions of visitor-oriented spectaculum. Difference becomes apparent, however, in that while the task of the museum is to educate its visitors by introducing them to new and hitherto unknown/unseen documents, objects, and scenes, the historical theme park will content itself with rearranging those things the visitors knew before into forms that appear simultaneously new and familiar. The difference is visible when comparing such visits as those to the Hohenlohisches Freilandmuseum Wackershofen, where attempts at romanticising the life of small tenant farmers are undercut by spelling out the gruelling work conditions, lack of education and general squalor of their circumstances, to the arrangements of 'historical' sights at the Europa-Park in Rust, Germany, or Huis Ten Bosch near Nagasaki, Japan. In Rust, axes of vision have been designed to create vistas that contain enough familiar visual glimpses and moments to trigger the 'proper' national-historical identification. In Huis Ten Bosch, an idealized vision of European – more specifically Dutch – history is presented as a utopian model for Japanese visitors (cf. Schlehe/Uike-Bormann in this volume).

---

6   But not just European: Interestingly enough, the Europa-Park contains various elements staging stereotyped vistas of non-European places. Supposedly showing Africa, as well as Dutch Batavia, they represent colonial history in an orientalist form.

This is not to say that museums always live up to the expectations set for them. As Mike Wallace noted already in 1981, American museums had, at least until then, been functional preserving and incorporating "selections and silences of such an order that they falsified reality and became instruments of class hegemony" (Wallace 1981: 88). Wallace's critique focused mainly on the content level, complaining that at the time museums were not interested in securing social change, even though changing attitudes had made it possible to depict more problematic and confrontational issues.

In sharp relief, newer museums like Wackershofen with its socio-critical approach provide insights that are clearly more acceptable within the framework of a pluralist and democratic society, although the programme – and the programming – remain solidly in the hands of a controlling *appareil d'etat*. There is very little visitors can do or see other than follow the directions and read the explanatory material. In the Europa-Park, a change of vistas, a conscious change of visual angles, will provide the postmodernist intellectual segment of the visiting crowds (however small in percentage this segment may be) with the added pleasure of seemingly being able to look behind the scenes – a trick from the treasury of capitalist irony already well known to Disney Imagineers and gleaned from the 'grandfather', Phineas T. Barnum, who, in his *American Museum*, began mixing museum and early theme park elements with serious lectures as well as circus-like formats of entertainment in the mid-19th century (Barnum 2000 [1855], cf. Harris 1973).

Martine Teunissen in the present volume explores how, since when, and to which extent, at least the time-honored flag-ship of American living history museums, Colonial Williamsburg in Virginia, has managed to overcome the limitations Wallace saw in 1981. It can be argued that the inclusion of living history programmes adds to the levels of potential experience accessible to visitors in museums. In most North American open-air museums as well as in a number of British and some French and Dutch sites, costumed interpretation by trained staff is the rule, while German museums are still reluctant to adopt interpretation by costumed staff on a regular basis (see the discussion in Carstensen/Meiners/Mohrmann 2008).[7] This discussion is not continued in the present volume, but it needs to be noted that whereas the use of third person interpretation and scripted scenes/tableaux opens a range of possibilities for the interpretation of places, conditions, and even objects that stationary

---

7   In the Indonesian park Taman Mini, representatives of all provinces guide
     visitors through the cultural displays of their respective areas. As frequent-
     ly encountered in tourist sites, it is assumed that a local guide can provide
     authentic information on local history – although this is not at all guaran-
     teed in multiethnic and hierarchical societies.

exhibitions alone can not offer there are also drawbacks. For at least some visitors, the inclusion of themed presentations by costumed interpreters in a museum environment seems to blur the difference between museum and theme park.

"Costumed employees in the Historic Area at Colonial Williamsburg sometimes like to ridicule the 'clueless' visitor ... the one who gets off the bus at the Duke of Gloucester Street and expects to find a theme park, complete with thrilling rides. This visitor is part of the mythology of the place. Interpreters tell and retell the story about the visitor who, stooping to get a closer look at one of the nearly tame squirrels that are everywhere scurrying or begging for tidbits, asked: 'Is it mechanical?' The clueless visitor who thinks live squirrels are clever simulacra is a kind of stereotype. Such people do, however, exist – as we discovered while interviewing, at random, visitors on the streets of the reconstructed city. [...] When we explained that we wanted to know what visitors to Colonial Williamsburg thought of the way the museum reconstructed the past, the woman (a teacher of 'gifted children K through 12') exclaimed: 'Oh, this is a museum? I thought it was an attraction – a theme park!'" (Handler/Gable 1997: 28)

One obvious similarity between living history museums as staged historical spaces and 'historical' theme parks as stages for present entertainment remains intact anyway:

"The museum ha[s] some obvious appeals: many are charming places that demonstrate interesting old craft techniques and exhibit quaint old objects; there are, after all, real pleasures in antiquarianism. The museums are also safe, well promoted, and one of the few available 'family' experiences." (Wallace 1981: 89–90)

The relative safety of this kind of museal space is not only physical but extends to the experiential level: visitors are usually not irritated or challenged by encounters with unfamiliar living people, or confronted with problematic topics. It seems reasonable, therefore, to predict a further narrowing of the margins of difference between theme parks and museums in terms of their existence as themed environments for tourist consumption. It is a pincer movement, one direction being the museums' frantic attempts to attract visitors, the other the postmodern tourists' assumption (see above) that in any themed environment authenticity must of needs be staged (MacCannell 1973). This second arm of the pincer is stronger than the first, considering that authenticity as a consumer item can be had outside of museums, too: So-called cultural centers, folklife festivals, even hotel lobbies may serve as backdrops for cultural performances in which the performers "become living signs of themselves" (Kirshenblatt-Gimblett 1998: 18).[8]

---

8   For a recent discussion of fictions of authenticity cf. Pirker et al. 2010.

The pincer movement is further reinforced by the fact that theming can be superimposed on spaces especially if they are devoid of structures pre-determining interpretation. Amos S. Ron's contribution to this volume opens venues into the field of 19th and 20th century Protestant pilgrimages to the Holy Land as a form of reconstructing found environments as biblical. The pilgrims preferred the openness of seemingly natural spaces because these open ranges could be superinscribed with meaning and interpreted as unchanged since the days of the Christ – other than the existing historical and archaeological sites that mediated previous interpretations by other religious groups.

Stages for a Re-enacted Past

In a related vein, sites for reenactments are chosen if and because they are *not* the original sites which in many cases have been turned into historic parks with paved accessways and monuments on site. Instead, the reenactment site provides the supposedly original look *prior* to the engagement that led to the construction of the commemorative site, while the reenactment has to move to a site which is more 'original' in status than the original.

When discussing reenactments, it should be noted that the thrill of the lived-in experience of the modern living history museum is doubled where and when the seemingly historical life-world becomes host to that which the visitors know did happen around the time depicted in the museum as special events: the joust *[tjoste]* between mediaeval knights, Roman legionnaires pitching camp, a skirmish between Union pickets and raiding Rebel cavalry. Special living history programmes of this kind, providing a lifespace-plus experience, are used to entice return visitors to become regulars, and to lure first-time visitors into returning. As independent events, they are commonly referred to as *reenactments.*

The term *reenactment* bears two implications that are usually not reflected by the reenactors themselves, or by the audience for that matter. For one, the re-enactment turns the original event that is being conjured up into an *enactment,* implying a *mise-en-scène* quality few of the original events that have become subject to reenactments ever had. Secondly, the varying degrees to which the reenactors have attempted to come close to the real thing, subsumed under the heading of 'authenticity', have usually obscured both the insurmountable ironic distance between the events and their reenactments, and the essentially theatrical nature of the reenactment itself.

Attempts at re-enacting past events can be traced all the way to the Colosseum, but those reenactments were limited to monumental acts that were re-played in what was clearly thought of as a theatrical environment. Later reenactments such as Emperor Maximilian's famous tournaments can be interpreted as regressive attempts at reliving a nostalgically imagined past, while the contemporary proliferation of forms and formations of living histories as drama – which we call *Geschichtstheater* – has to do with the affective turn in history, as Vanessa Agnew has pointed out:

"contemporary reenactment is indicative of history's recent affective turn, i.e. of historical representation characterized by conjectural interpretations of the past, the collapsing of temporalities and an emphasis on affect, individual experience and daily life rather than historical events, structures and processes." (Agnew 2007: 299)

In the reenactment format, however, the individual experience is, other than in the living programmes in museums, often fused with the traditional 'battles-and-leaders'-topicality of pre-modern historiography: the reenactor participates in his or her own historical film while simultaneously watching it, so to speak (cf. Thompson 2004: 3). It is not history, however, which is passing before their eyes, but a (re-)constructed past for which a stage has been prepared on which the same willing suspension of disbelief is operative which already informed Samuel Taylor Coleridge's theory of the theatre, and which is largely based on the credibility of the presented past's pastness.

Still, reenactments as stages for a re-imagined past should not be waived off – as they often are – as fantastic battle-grounds for incurable adolescents and fans of military show and glamour. While there is certainly a considerable percentage of reenactment hobbyists for whom the hobby provides the same or at least a similarly familiar haven as any other hobby (see Gordon L. Jones' contribution in this volume), the theatrical and the didactic possibilities of reenactment range far beyond 'battlefield karaoke' or individual-scale identity politics. Reenactments have been tapped for their roots in ceremonial re-staging and ritual for reconciliation purposes as well as for the opposite, for keeping a sense of conflict awake, see Jeremy Deller's 2001 reenactment of the 1984 "Battle of Orgreave" (Deller 2001, cf. Kitamura 2010) between striking British miners and mounted police, in which many of the original combatants participated. Reenactment also lies at the core of the historical city games (re-)enacted every year in the town of Schwerte in North Rhine–Westphalia by Regina Loftus and Paul Röllke (cf. their contribution with Victoria Tafferner in this volume) where children learn about the history of the town as well as study and incorporate specific roles within the social and environmental fabric of mediaeval Svierte. Ultimately, the (all-too-often not realized) potential of reenactments includes that of the Brechtian *Lehrstück*, the Educational Play, in

which actors play largely for themselves, and by and through playing learn about the thoughts, the feelings, the responsibilities and
the perspectives of the roles and the functions these roles have – or
had – in the society represented. This holds true also for the initial
training and learning process of the costumed interpreter in a living
history museum.

Academic historiography still provides the research bases and
the background for museum curators as well as living history interpreters and reenactors, creating new programmes and critical re-
evaluations of older ones, but also reading some historiographical
contention in the new light of practical re-staging. At the same time,
the living history equivalent to the themed amusement park, fantasy LARP (Live Action Role Play), seems likely to do to the Brechtian
possibilities of reenactment and to the critical reception of living
history interpretation what postmodern tourism is doing to the difference between museum and theme park: obliterate it, creating a
perpetual, entertainment-focused and utterly a-political present. Likewise, the howsoever imaginary time-travel to seemingly other spaces
and periods with its considerable range of possibilities for independent and self-determined learning as well as for the history and literature classrooms, might be overdetermined by consumer-oriented
life-spacing that levels regional identity and distinction in favour of
tuscanic-looking housing developments with English lawns in the
foothills of, for instance, the Black Forest.

Cross-Cultural Theming and Performing

This volume does not only refer to theme parks and reenactments in
Euro-American but in Asian and African contexts as well. And we
emphasize that what is staged and performed is not necessarily the
imagination and construction of one's own past but quite often the
idea of the past (or of so-called 'traditional life') of an exotic Other.
When the 'Self' is staged in non-European contexts, then it has most
often to do with post-colonial processes of nation-building as exemplified by the case studies of Indonesia (Schlehe/Uike-Bormann)
and Tanzania (Salazar). Ethnically heterogenous post-colonial nations construct and display what is supposed to be a shared knowledge of the cultural backgrounds of diverse ethnic groups which are
acknowledged by the nation-state. For that reason, folkloristic aspects that seem to stand for continuity over time, mystifying both
historical fractures as well as current fragmentations and conflicts,
are carefully selected and displayed.

On the other hand, when it comes to displays of 'traditional'
foreign cultures, these can be traced back to theatricality in the

cross-cultural encounters of first contacts (Balme 2006) as well as to European 19th century "show-spaces" (Poignant 2004: 7), in which indigenous people where made objects of curiosity in "Western systems of mass entertainment and education involving display and performance" (ibid.) in circuses, fairs, exhibitions and museums. Relations of colonial power and a "vulgar evolutionism" (Stanley 1998: 17) were made visible: indigenous people had to play the role of the savage Other to the Western civilized Self. Although some historical and literary studies mention that these indigenous people were "not just passive pawns" (ibid.: 15) but discerned a certain agency, e.g. by observing the observers, they hardly refer to anthropological studies revealing how European colonisers were perceived and imitated e.g. in mimetic performances and possession cults in African cultures (Kramer 1989). Obviously, mimetic practices in dealing with the foreign have deep roots in many cultures.

For the situation at present, in a globalized world where the gazes are mutual and multi-directional, we think that it is of special interest on the one hand to reflect on how Europe is displayed and appropriated in popular cultures in Asia (as exemplified by Huis Ten Bosch and other Japanese parks), and on the other hand to consider how 'local cultures' are staged for tourists all over the world. It is remarkable that recent studies stress that – notwithstanding the asymmetrical power relations in many cross-cultural encounters in the commercialized contexts of international tourism – performances can also "provide a ground to imitate and thereby approach one another" (Balme 2006: 6). Dreschke (in this volume) calls this "playing ethnology". Furthermore, besides criticising ongoing exploitative structures and commodification of cultures, the aspect of 'native' self-representation connected to the emergence of local cultural movements in the Global South[9] comes to the fore: this means that the agency of the performers, e.g. in cultural centres, especially when they are controlled by indigenous groups, is emphasized. Joy Hendry (Hendry 2005 and in this volume) goes even further, stating that their ways of insisting on cultural ownership and reclaiming 'their' culture can be regarded as healing. Although there might be some romantic visions involved in this kind of identity politics, what can be concluded from this is the desire all over the world to identify with certain versions of the past. Which ones are selected and how they are displayed and performed can only be understood in specific local and national contexts as well as in peculiar ways of relating to the global world. Therefore, transcultural perspectives are

---

9   The notion of self-representation is usually restricted to indigenous peoples and displays which means that, apparently, there is a need to emphasize that these groups are represented by themselves and not by others.

needed even when we look at popular leisure worlds that seem to deal with nothing but entertainment.

Conclusion

History used to be passed on in tales, legends, myths, expressive genres – personified, affective, staged for consumption and identity formation by the respective interpretive community. Oral traditions were not fixed, and rituals always involved the audience as contemporary theatre sometimes does (cf. Oesterle in this volume). While it would be a clear overstatement to argue that the de-theming of history by academic historiography has failed and given way to a free-for-all of individual appropriations of historical matter, the tendency in the Western world to de-hegemonise the discourse of histories is obvious. However, it is as yet not clear which direction the new participation historiography might be taking. Even if there was no linear practice of histories being conveyed solely along and through academically informed school curricula, the contemporary proliferation and overlap of historical as well as historiographic agency seems to be a historic novelty.

An important factor in this context is of course the political economy of popular historical cultures. The difference between historical re-enactors performing for their own fun and live interpretation directed by a governmental or a private commercial institution may not be visible to audiences, but it entails a host of questions and possibly problems regarding agency, authenticity and quality management.

Wherever stagings of pasts take place, and whatever themes and values are projected onto these pasts, themed environments, reenactments and live interpretation always create positioned representations. They provide space for subjective engagement and they speak to all human senses. They are enjoyable and entertaining which makes them all the more effective. It is this effectivity which warrants a conscious and responsible use of the resources and possibilities offered by these forms of conveying historical knowledge in popular format.

References

Agnew, Vanessa. 2007. "History's Affective Turn: Historical Re-enactment and Its Work in the Present." *Rethinking History* 11.3: 299-312.

Balme, Christopher. 2006. *Pacific Performances: Theatricality and Cross-Cultural Encounter in the South Seas.* Hampshire: Palgrave Macmillan Ltd.

Barnum P.[hineas] T.[aylor]. 2000. *The Life of P.T. Barnum, Written By Himself.* Ed. Terence Whalen. Urbana: University of Illinois Press [NY 1855].

Carstensen, Jan/Uwe Meiners/Ruth-E. Mohrmann, eds. 2008. *Living History im Museum. Möglichkeiten und Grenzen einer populären Vermittlungsform.* Münster: Waxmann.

Deller, Jeremy. 2001. "The Battle of Orgreave." *Artangel* http://www.artangel.org.uk/projects/2001/the_battle_of_orgreave (accessed 15 Jan 2010).

Fischer-Lichte, Erika. 2009. "Einleitung: Zur Aktualität von Turners Studien zum Übergang vom Ritual zum Theater." *Vom Ritual zum Theater. Der Ernst des menschlichen Spiels.* Frankfurt am Main: Campus. i-xxiii.

Friedman, Jonathan. 2008. "Myth, History and Political Identity." *Modernities, Class, and the Contradictions of Globalization. The Anthropology of Global Systems.* Eds. Kajsa Ekholm Friedman/Jonathan Friedman. Lanham et al.: Rowman & Littlefield. 89-107.

Gottdiener, Mark. 2001. *The Theming of America. American Dreams, Media Fantasies, and Themed Environments.* Boulder: Westview Press.

Handler, Richard/Eric Gable. 1997. *The New History in an Old Museum. Creating the Past at Colonial Williamsburg.* Durham: Duke University Press.

Harris, Neil. 1973. *Humbug: The Art of P.T. Barnum.* Boston, MA: Little, Brown.

Hendry, Joy. 2000. *The Orient Strikes Back: A Global View of Cultural Display.* Oxford: Berg.

Hendry, Joy. 2005. *Reclaiming Culture, Indigenous People and Self-Representation.* New York: Palgrave.

Imagineers. 1996. *Walt Disney Imagineering: A Behind the Dreams Look at Making the Magic Real.* New York: Hyperion.

Imagineers. 2005. *The Imagineering Field Guide to the Magic Kingdom.* New York: Disney Editions.

Kirshenblatt-Gimblett, Barbara. 1998. *Destination Culture: Tourism, Museums, and Heritage.* Berkeley: University of California Press.

Kitamura, Katie. 2010. "Recreating Chaos: Jeremy Deller's The Battle of Orgreave." *Historical Reenactment. From Realism to the*

Affective Turn. Eds. Iain McCalman/Paul A. Pickering. Basingstoke: Palgrave Macmillan. 39-49.

Korte, Barbara/Sylvia Paletschek, eds. 2009. *History goes Pop. Zur Repräsention von Geschichte in populären Medien und Genres*. Bielefeld: transcript.

Kramer, Fritz. 1989. "The Otherness of the European." *Culture and History* 6: 107-123.

"List of Defunct Amusement Parks". http://en.wikipedia.org/wiki/ List_of _defunct_amusement_parks (accessed 31 Aug 2009).

MacCannell, Dean. 1973. "Staged Authenticity: Arrangements of Social Space in Tourist Settings." *American Journal of Sociology* 79.3: 589-603.

Moore, Alexander. 1980. "Walt Disney World: Bounded Ritual Space and the Playful Pilgrimage Center." *Anthropological Quarterly* 53: 207-218.

Pirker, Eva Ulrike/Mark Rüdiger/Christa Klein/Thorsten Leiendecker/Carolyn Oesterle/Miriam Sénécheau/Michiko Uike-Bormann, eds. 2010. *Echte Geschichte. Authentizitätsfiktionen in populären Geschichtskulturen*. Bielefeld: transcript.

Poignant, Roslyn. 2004. *Professional Savages: Captive Lives and Western Spectacle*. New Haven/London: Yale University Press.

Rowan, Yorke. 2004. "Repacking the Pilgrimage: Visiting the Holy Land in Orlando." *Marketing Heritage. Archaeology and the Consumption of the Past*. Eds. Yorke Rowan/Uzi Baram. Walnut Creek, CA: Alta Mira Press. 249-266.

Stanley, Nick. 1998. *Being Ourselves for You: The Global Display of Cultures*. London: Middlesex University Press.

Thompson, Jenny. 2004. *Wargames. Inside the World of 20th-Century War Reenactors*. Washington: Smithsonian.

Wallace, Michael. 1981. "Visiting the Past: History Museums in the United States." *Radical History Review* 25: 63-96.

Wallace, Mike. 1996. *Mickey Mouse History and Other Essays on American Memory*. Philadelphia: Temple University Press.

Wood, Natalie T./Caroline Munoz. 2007. "No Rules, Just Right or Is It? The Role of Themed Restaurants as Cultural Ambassadors." *Tourism and Hospitality Research* 7.3/4: 242-255.

Transcultural Settings:
Theme Parks and Lifespace

The Presence of Pastness:
Themed Environments and Beyond

CORNELIUS HOLTORF

The past is a phenomenon of the present. I do not mean to deny that there was a past or that this past can be studied by various academic disciplines. What I mean is that irrespective of a past that once was, there also is the past as a phenomenon manifested in various ways in the here and now (Lowenthal 1985; Schörken 1995). From the perspective of archaeology it is self-evident that traces of the past can be recovered today and that much can be learned from their analysis and interpretation. This paper, however, takes its starting point in the observation of a phenomenon that after two decades as an archaeologist I still find very curious indeed – the sheer fact that today anybody cares about the past at all. There are, for instance, millions of visitors each year who enjoy historical themeparks and other themed environments with historical and archaeological themes, whether in Las Vegas or elsewhere (Fig. 1; Holtorf 2009a).

I find it extraordinary that so many of my contemporaries appreciate environments themed with historical and archaeological topics, take their children to historical museums, visit archaeological monuments in their vacations, buy books about the past, play historical computer games or watch archaeological documentaries on TV. The past I am talking about may be 300, 3,000 or indeed 30,000 years before the present. In my experience, although many people are of course aware of a good number of historical and archaeological facts and insights about the past, their fascination with the past tends to come before any felt urge to acquire firm knowledge about that past. This is not the place to discuss the reasons of that interest (cf. Lowenthal 1985; Schörken 1995; Holtorf 2009b). But what is obvious is that the dream of wanting 'to become an archaeologist' tends to take priority over the desire to gain answers to specific questions about the past.

As a matter of fact, the 'archaeologist' as a character is by itself an intriguing phenomenon of contemporary society. As I discussed in more detail elsewhere (Holtorf 2007, 2009a), this branded and highly popular figure that appears widely in popular culture – from Hollywood blockbusters to computer games and from best selling literary fiction to TV advertising – corresponds to the popular interest in the past which I have just described. In popular culture, archaeology is a verb. The archaeologist is widely portrayed as a dreamhero whom we accompany on a journey of exploring, digging, revealing, analysing, interpreting, preserving and rescuing. Even among those who later became professional archaeologists it was not usually a curiosity to learn about certain questions about the past that motivated them to their studies but much more likely a childhood fascination with digging up ancient civilizations and travelling the world in the footsteps of whatever archaeological media hero they first encountered.

Fig. 1: Caesar after two thousand years.
Why are people interested in the past at all?

Photograph: Cornelius Holtorf 2001

This paper is going to take the analysis one step beyond my previous research on archaeology as a contemporary phenomenon. In gradually closing in on the question why anybody might be interested in the past at all, I would here like to pose the question *how* the past as such acquires meaning and becomes perceptible and indeed accessible in present life-worlds in the first place.

Seeing a Past That is Not There

In his contribution to the present volume on reenactment groups staging the American Civil War, Gordon L. Jones suggests that "reenacting is about making a past visible. It is about seeing something that isn't there [...] It is about the human desire to transform imagined images of the intangible past into a tangible present, not unlike the way a painter paints or a sculptor sculpts" (in this volume: 219). I would like to suggest that this is not only true for reenactments. The same can be said more generally, whenever the past becomes visible as a phenomenon of the present.

Historical museums, archaeological monuments, fiction or non-fiction literature about the past, historical story-telling, computer games, and TV documentaries all make you see something that isn't actually there. They make the past visible, if not tangibly then at least virtually. Such representations of the past can be academically evaluated as to their accuracy and the degree to which they evoke something that may or may not resemble an actual past reality that once was. What I find more interesting is to investigate how these media actually operate in successfully evoking present-day representations of the past in the first place. For there can be no doubt that they are very successful in making the past visible although it isn't really there. In this paper I am, however, restricting myself to discussing ruins and other archaeological sites and artefacts that evoke the past.

Fig. 2: A ruin makes you see a past that isn't there

Photograph: Cornelius Holtorf 2007

Looking at a ruin, you almost literally see the past (Fig. 2). How peculiar this really is can be illustrated by the imagined first response to this site from a visitor from Mars: "Oh look, half the building is missing! How strange!" A visitor from Earth will almost certainly never ask that same question but concede that the building has seen better days. In other words, although the extraterrestrial describes exactly what both visitors are *looking at,* this is very different from what the Earthling would actually *see.* What we see is something that isn't there, a historical narrative. It is nevertheless clearly visible to us because we have learned how to interpret our surroundings in correspondence with our understanding of the past. That knowledge (or historical consciousness) is not arbitrary and selected by individual preference, but a social construct and achievement of society. What we know about the past is the result of social events and processes ranging from attending formal lessons and conversing with relatives, colleagues and friends, to reading fiction or non-fiction literature and engaging with mass media content.

Strictly speaking, what we see when we are looking at a ruin is never a depiction of the past as it once was. It is not even a depiction of the past as we think it was, because we do not need to have a firm picture of a past reality in our minds in order for the ruin to make the past 'visible'. Our picture may in some cases oscillate between various versions of how we picture the past or it may be rather blurred and unspecific. What is more, we may lack a clear conception of which particular past we actually see when we look at the ruin: the time when the building was new? or when it was last used? or some time in between those events? In this respect, ruins differ from other manifestations of the past in the present. Themed environments, historical museums, fiction or non-fiction literature about the past, computer games and TV documentaries often depict a specific episode of the past in rather explicit terms, whether through words or pictures. But in the case of a ruin, chronological specificity does not seem to matter very much. If it is not the past we see when looking at ruins what then do we see?

I would like to argue that in the world in which we live (and a Martian does not) a ruin makes us see the ruin's *pastness.* According to the dictionary, pastness in this context can be defined as "the quality or condition of being past" (The Free Dictionary 2009).[1] The question thus emerges how the ruin makes a given contemporary audience see in it a quality or condition of being past. This is a very different question from asking whether a given site is old in the sense that it was built a long time ago, and indeed from enquiring how old it may be. If pastness is the present quality or condition of

---

1   A second meaning given is the "emotion or feeling evoked by memory".

being past, then its presence is not dependent on a specific age (Holtorf 2005: 127-129). Indeed, as heritage analyst David Lowenthal (2002: 17) has emphasized, pastness tends to be generalizing all past periods into one. What matters most is a particular appearance corresponding to the past in your imagination (Crang 1996). In other words, whether or not a ruin possesses pastness has little or nothing to do with the past it represents, i.e. when it was built or originally in use. The term pastness thus corresponds to what American writer Phillip R. Burger (2000: 285) identified as a sense of "prehistoricness" in the Pellucidar novels of Edgar Rice Burroughs about an imaginary world populated by dinosaurs and primitive humans.

A study of ruins and other phenomena in our life-world that make pastness visible must start with the question how the perception of pastness is generated.

The Material Construction of Pastness

Pastness is an idea that can be applied to the quality or condition of physical objects. These objects may be buildings but they could also be portable artefacts. In neither case do they need to be particularly old in the sense that they originated in the past – although they must be old in the sense that they possess pastness. In some cases it is perfectly obvious that an object possessing pastness is very new indeed. The ruin shown in Fig. 2, for example, was built in its present state as recently as the mid 1990s. This building is 'of the past' because its designer wanted it to be of the past. Pastness is thus an idea that can be built into physical objects. The technique through which this is achieved has been termed "narrative placemaking" by Joe Rohde, a creative executive of Walt Disney Imagineering (Rohde 2007). Rohde had the overall responsibility for the design of Disney's Animal Kingdom in Florida, of which the building depicted in Fig. 2 forms a part. Within the park, the building is part of the generic 'African' village of Harambe, and it was deemed best if that village was not brand new but of the past (Wright 2007: 66). Hence it got one.

If we are interested in understanding how pastness comes about, it is instructive to look in more detail at buildings that were designed in order to possess pastness. In doing so I am suggesting a provisional theory of pastness. That theory, if viable, should be able to explain pastness in other contexts and even outside of themed environments. We should be able to learn something about the conditions under which even archaeological monuments and historical sites possess pastness and indeed what happens when they do not meet these conditions.

A Theory of Pastness

What follows is an attempt, in three steps, at provisionally formulating a general theory of pastness in our present. Future work will need to refine that theory and assess its validity.

1. PASTNESS REQUIRES MATERIAL CLUES

An object's materiality speaks to its age through obvious traces of wear and tear, decay and disintegration. Patina, cracks and missing bits are the clues of an object being past, the clues that evoke a fragile heritage and that seem to beg for the attention of a conservator. At the same time, such material manifestations of pastness have also long attracted a particular appreciation and the Austrian art historian Alois Riegl (1857-1905) identified in them what he famously called "age value" (Schmidt 2008: 46-48).

Some commentators may think that Disney theme parks provide superficial stimulation without much value. In fact they provide enormous depth, and the imagineers give great attention to detail. The 'Harambe' building in Fig. 2 is obviously in a state of decay, with an upper floor no longer existing, the walls gradually dilapidating and grass growing on the exposed bricks, the plaster on the façade in places missing, and cracks in the asphalt in front of the building. It appears that nature has again begun to take over the site from human civilization. But none of that is the result of thousands of visitors passing by outside the building on one of the busiest pathways in a major Disney theme park urgently calling out for maintenance. It is instead the result of a design that intended this place to appear just like that.

Some footprints of the walls of the fortress perimeter which once surrounded fictional Harambe are still visible for the attentive visitor on the ground (barely noticeable at the bottom right of Fig. 2). An engraving on the surface of a bench ("Uhuru 1961") commemorates the year when an unspecified political change brought freedom (*Uhuru* in Swahili) to Harambe (Wright 2007: 72). Numerous other details create a history of the town. Not surprisingly, Joe Rohde (2007a) states: "I believe in depth." Elsewhere he explained how this depth is achieved: "There are details within details within details to anchor you in the fact that we are talking about the real world, not an illustrated children's book fantasy world" (Rohde 2007b).

The level of attention given to material clues and other details ensures that guests in the theme park do not admire the verisimilitude of what is ultimately complete artifice but that they are made to put the very distinction between real and fake behind them. Narrative placemaking well done results in surroundings that are to the same extent genuine and artificial, where both categories melt into built stories and ideas that actually transcend the distinction between them.

Fig. 3: Michelangelo's frescoes on the ceiling of the Sistine Chapel in Rome, before and after restoration.

Juxtaposition by Calliopejen 2007. Source: http://en.wikipedia.org/wiki/File:Gardenbeforeandafter.jpg

When appropriate material clues are missing, an object lacks pastness and may subsequently not be perceived as of the past. A prominent example for this effect was the restoration of Michelangelo's frescoes on the ceiling of the Sistine Chapel in Rome. When it reopened in various stages during the 1990s, after a decade of diligent restoration, the familiar scenes lacked their familiar cracks and patina and appeared in some very bright colours. Subsequently a controversy erupted whether the conservators had gone too far and removed some layers of Michelangelo's original art work (Wikipedia 2009). The public debate also focused on whether the paintings should have been restored to their original impression at all. To some, with the removal of the material clues of the painting's age, the restored works of Michelangelo looked too new. The Irish artist William Crozier, for example, stated in an interview (Fallon 1993: 183): "What they have taken away is the age of the paint." In other words, the paintings are now lacking in pastness. Disney Imagineering, on the other hand, proceeds exactly the other way around. They use character paint to create the impression of "states of ageing whenever we need to make something new look old" (Wright 2007: 10).

2. Pastness Requires Correspondence With the Expectations of the Audience

Material clues and sophistication in detail are not, however, sufficient for achieving a perception of pastness. A second criterion to be fulfilled is the matching of the appearance of a given object and its audiences' pre-understandings. Intended audiences of themed environments need to recognize and understand the stories and ideas that narrative placemaking materializes. In other words, how guests in themed environments *expect* a certain historic object might look should correspond to how it *actually* looks. "To be credible historical witnesses", David Lowenthal (1985: 354) suggested, "antiquities must to some extent conform with modern stereotypes."

For example, a theme park will struggle to create a place that successfully evokes ancient Greek civilization if its architecture does not correspond to how we are picturing it in our minds with the columns in white marble and all. Europa-Park Rust thus created its Poseidon temple in the way a Greek temple is supposed to look, although some concessions were made for the rollercoaster that goes right through it (Fig. 4a). The fact that the temples were originally painted in bright colours must not get in the way of providing a plausible and meaningful impression to guests (Holtorf 2009b: 48). Colourful depictions of Greek temples, as in the temporary arrangement at Agrigento's Concordia temple, do not make them look old but new (Fig. 4b).

Fig. 4a (left): Greek temple in white at Europa-Park Rust, Germany. Photograph: Cornelius Holtorf 2009

Fig. 4b (right): Colour reconstruction of the Concordia Temple at Agrigento, Italy. Photograph: Clemens Franz 2006. Reproduced with GNU Free Documentation License. Source: http://en.wikipedia. org/wiki/File:Agrigento_Concordia_Tempel_mit_Geruest.jpg

By the same token, Main Street U.S.A. which forms part of several Magic Kingdom-style Disney theme parks, needed to reflect the guests' expectations of the early 20th century American town which it is meant to represent. Fred Beckenstein, a senior Disneyland Paris manager, once stated in an interview (cited in Dickson 1993: 34) that "we're not trying to design what really existed in 1900, we're trying to design what people think they remember about what existed." Edgar Rice Burrough's early 20th century outlandish science fiction about the prehistoric land of Pellucidar inside the hollow Earth likewise gains a basic credibility from matching the – in significant parts inaccurate – science of his readers, thus lending his story "a patina of truth" and as a result creating a sense of "prehistoricness" (Burger 2000: 281, 285). This accomplishment of successfully being able to create pastness is mirrored in the realm of much other science fiction where a correspondence with the future that people expect creates a flair of futureness.

As a consequence, neither Disney theme parks nor science fiction literature can be deemed to be in the business of selling escapism to other worlds, due to the fact that they only confirm what audiences already know from their own world. John Hench (1908-2004), then a senior manager at WED Enterprises (now Walt Disney Imagineering), expressed precisely this when he once emphasized the extent to which Walt Disney and his Company through the architecture and design of Disneyland first and foremost wanted to reassure their audience (Haas 1978).

Historical representations based on stereotypes and people's own expectations and desires are inevitably anathema for educators (e.g. Carson 1995; Schlehe/Uike-Bormann in this volume). It is true that you are unable in this way to learn what a mid-Western American town around the turn of the last century actually looked like. Such places will not challenge visitors with elements of history that do not seem to fit their expectations; visitors will not be prompted to rethink their own assumptions and indeed confront their prejudices. At the same time, Disney's placemaking allows visitors to encounter and experience a rendition of this very time period for themselves in the sense that it presences the past – which is what the German historian Rolf Schörken (1995: 13-14) called "Vergegenwärtigung" of the past. Main street U.S.A. may not give an accurate image of a past reality as it once might have been but it does provide a plausible and meaningful time travel experience (however restricted) to turn of the 19th century America (Crang 1996; Holtorf 2010). That, too, provides learning opportunities, not only by allowing a degree of emotional engagement with the past – thus also making the past accessible to a broader audience – but also by inviting reflections about history and how we live today (Hjemdahl 2002; Lukas 2008:

163-167). According to designer John Hench, Main Street U.S.A. also "reminds you of some things about *yourself* that you've forgotten about" (Haas 1978: 18).

It has occasionally been said, perhaps most notoriously by the American public historian Mike Wallace (1985: 33), that Walt Disney taught people more history, in a more memorable way, through his theme parks than they ever learned in school. American historical geographer Richard Francaviglia added that Disney's fascination with historical architecture and design may lie at the roots of two trends in society that have become popular since the 1970s: neotraditional architecture, and historic preservation programmes to revive the country's Main Streets. As a result, towns like Medina, Ohio, are now more Victorian in appearance than they were during the Victorian period. Therefore, he argued that "those who think of Disney's version of history as unreal need to redefine reality in order to understand what is occurring" (Francaviglia 1995: 73). This should make us think not only about the misconceptions that may have resulted but also about the opportunities such learning about the past provides.

This discussion is closely connected to a changing understanding of authenticity that is fast gaining ground throughout the heritage sector although it is hardly new (Holtorf/Schadla-Hall 1999; Schmidt 2008). Indeed, curators have long been observing that most visitors do not distinguish between reconstructed and original buildings though they are very concerned about authenticity (Lowenthal 1985: 355). The shift I mean is best expressed in the following anecdote reported by David Lowenthal (2002: 20, citing Cary Carson) about Disney's one-time plan to build a theme park on American history near the historic site of Colonial Williamsburg, Virginia:

"Staff [at Colonial Williamsburg] take pride in purveying real history, as opposed to the fictions of Disneyland. Worried about Disney's prospective history theme park in their backyard in northern Virginia, Colonial Williamsburg staff were shocked to find that most people saw little difference and were not bothered if they did. Asked if they thought Williamsburg 'authentic,' ten discussants drawn from the general public all agreed that it was: "'And Disneyland?' and without a pause, every one of them said, 'Oh yes, yes, Disneyland is authentic too.'[The moderator] asked, 'How can this be? We all know that Disney's America ... is going to be totally made up. It isn't even a real historical site. Everything will be artificial. And you all know that Colonial Williamsburg is a real place, even if much restored.' 'Sure,' they said, but ... 'Disney always does things first-class, and if they set out to do American history, they'll hire the best historians money can buy ... to create a completely plausible, completely believable appearance of American history.'"

Authenticity here has shifted its meaning away from the conventional understanding as something historically accurate and consisting of genuine fabric as opposed to what is imaginary and a modern addition. Instead, authenticity has come to refer to a state of credibility and trustworthiness, based on extrinsic appearances that surround sites and objects. And when is something most credible? When it corresponds to people's preconceptions and looks as they imagine it might, thus confirming what they already know. It can therefore be said that audiences create their own authenticities, and that these are changing over time. People's understandings of the past and their expectations of its appearance vary from one context to another, to the same extent that they vary among professional historians and archaeologists from one academic school and from one generation of scholars to another.

American anthropologist Scott Lukas (2007: 81-82) introduced the concept of "consumer authenticity", which he defined as what is "immediately knowable" to various consumer groups by affecting all their senses or, semiotically speaking, as what has been achieved "when signs no longer draw attention to themselves". Consumer authenticity, which occurs not only in themed environments but throughout the realm of tourism, can be created through design and placemaking. This reinforces my earlier observation that placemaking evokes a specific kind of authenticity that transcends any strict opposition between real and artificial.

3. Pastness Requires a Plausible and Meaningful Narrative Relating Then and Now

A minimum of material clues and correspondence with the audience's expectations is required for a site or artefact to possess the quality or condition of being past. A final criterion of pastness is the story an object tells about its history, i.e. the narrative that links past origin and contemporary presence. The story must be plausible and meaningful to its audience if the pastness of the object is not to be cast into doubt.

The building of Harambe, the paintings in the Sistine Chapel, Greek temples, Main Street U.S.A. and Colonial Williamsburg all have in common that they are firmly located on various locations of a well-known historical storyline that connects the Stone Age with the 21st century. The historical distance may in some cases be greater than in others but we have acquired the competence to fill in the gaps. From ancient Greece to Michelangelo, from historical African towns and Colonial America to early 20th century Main Streets in the US runs a continuum of historical change and development that we are very familiar with from education and countless references in the media and popular culture. In fact, we are so familiar with it that we notice this self-evident historical narrative only when something does not appear to fit. For example, claims that some Homo sapiens finds date millions of years before the earliest accepted evidence, that extraterrestrials played a role in erecting some of the most prominent prehistoric monuments, or that there were major human civilizations well before the age of the known civilizations, cannot easily be aligned with current models of human evolution and cultural development. Whatever material clues there may be and however the evidence (skulls, tools, monuments, etc.) conforms to people's expectations of what it ought to look like, their inconsistency with the overall storyline of history as we know it makes people doubt their pastness.

Fig. 5: A Bosnian pyramid?

Photograph: Mhare 2007. Source:
http://en.wikipedia.org/wiki/File:Bosnian_Pyramid.jpg

A case in point are the so-called Bosnian pyramids at Visoko in Bosnia-Herzegovina. These huge, mountain-like structures are claimed to be previously unknown pyramids of a lost civilization dating to as early as 12,000 BC. Although these structures were not formally designed to be of the past they were certainly not simply 'discovered' either, so perhaps we should say that they were recently first conceived as ancient sites. Irrespective of different interpretations of the material clues presented and different expectations of what the remains of an ancient pyramid might actually look like, the dispute carried out in the media has been very much about the plausibility and thus meaningfulness of the story attached to them, linking their past with the present. Whereas most academics found the idea of such pyramids at the given time and place extremely unlikely because it does not conform to the historical narrative they are familiar with, some Bosnians appreciated the evidence of a newly discovered, glorious Bosnian past reinforcing national pride in a war-torn country (Pruitt 2009). As a result of the varying appeal of these different stories linking then and now, the pyramids are either considered remains of the past or a hoax of the present.

An example as heated and controversial as the Bosnian pyramids inevitably raises the issue of a politics of plausibility. Who (or what) controls what is or is not plausible, and for whom? As people are being socialized together and their standards of judgment are continuously shaped by the social groups to which they belong, plausibility cannot be reduced to a matter of personal evaluation or subjective preference. It is rather a matter of "social sense" and the outcome of everyday discourses of what to believe and whom to trust (Fine 2007). At the same time, what some of us find plausible may disadvantage others' legitimate interests in society. One might ask, for example, whether we should trust a discourse that denies the Bosnians ancient pyramids as a major heritage site due to a lack of academic plausibility when that same discourse grants plausibility and thereby heritage sites of world significance to Egypt or Mexico. One might also ask, of course, whether we should believe in the elaborate invention of imaginary pyramids by a small group of activists when it takes precious attention and extremely scarce resources away from the investigation, management and protection of Bosnia's undisputed archaeological heritage. Such questions play a role – not always explicitly, or even consciously – in evaluating the plausibility and meaningfulness of historical narratives and thus of the presence of pastness.

Rethinking Temporality and Materiality

Earlier I expressed the hope that a theory of pastness, if correct, should be able to explain pastness also in other present contexts and beyond themed environments. Indeed, I would like to argue that the three criteria I have discussed are relevant to an understanding of the conditions under which archaeological monuments and historical sites generally acquire pastness. The significance in heritage of material clues such as patina is well illustrated by the wide appreciation of "age value", as first laid out by Alois Riegl in his analysis of heritage values (cf. Lowenthal 1985: 148-182). That heritage can possess more pastness when its appearance confirms our preconceptions, even if that means that it becomes historically less accurate, I showed at the example of classical Greek temples that we 'recognize' in white but that originally were brightly coloured.

Finally, the importance of plausible and meaningful narratives relating then with now became obvious when considering claims to human heritage, like pyramids in Bosnia, that lack sufficiently persuasive stories to silence sceptical academics and fail to generate pastness for them.

Pertinent to the similarities between themed environments and cultural heritage is also an anecdote reported by the American architectural historian Edward Harwood (2002: 49). He recalled a scene in which he stood with a group of students in the 18th century landscape garden at Stourhead in southern England looking towards the Pantheon, a folly inspired by its historic counterpart in Rome:

"None of them had seen anything quite like it before, and they tried to explain what was before them by connecting it with other places they knew. The first student to voice her reaction said, 'It's like Disneyland,' and there was general agreement with that parallel."

The question we need to consider in the future is thus neither whether a given object is part of real heritage or a copy or fake in a themed environment, i.e. whether it is old or new, nor whether all historic landscapes are really theme parks. Given the reaction of the student and my approach in this paper, these are futile questions. All such sites have in common that they make us see something that isn't there – the past. Both a successful themed environment evoking the past and a famous archaeological site or artefact will need to be staged appropriately in order to possess the property of being past. Instead, we have to ask under which exact conditions, if any, people consider a given object to be plausibly of the past and what that means for its role in society and the ideas it communicates to specific audiences. From determining age through various dating techniques we need to move on to investigating the conditions under which pastness occurs in the present, the inherent properties of pastness and how it functions in society. To me, the heritage sector needs ready answers to questions like these in order to be able to make sense of the wide range of phenomena in which the past is manifested in the present and for which archaeological sites are only one example.

The wider theoretical challenges which emerge from this shift of approach are profound. They call into question the two axes of temporality and materiality around which the disciplines of archaeology and to some extent also history are revolving.[2] Indeed, this shift of perspective effectively sidelines traditional archaeological and historical research agendas and makes them appear, rightly or wrong-

---

2   I have been inspired in this section by Shannon Lee Dawdy forthcoming.

ly, like fairly esoteric occupations that lack much contemporary currency.

When all historical periods appear to condense into a single state of pastness they all 'happen' at the same time which is the present. Although all periods consequently collapse into one single state of pastness seen from the vantage point of the present, this state can nevertheless manifest itself in a number of very different ways in specific examples (just look at the diversity of my illustrations!). The point is not to question, or even deny, that there *was* a past but to acknowledge that what matters today are all the various pasts that coexist in the present.

Replacing our familiar focus on age with a new emphasis on the presence of pastness points first of all to a failure of conventional understandings of temporality. The central significance of pastness means that some conventional notions of the historical disciplines as we know them cease to be relevant. Linear chronographies of past presents following on from each other in historical sequences mutate into chaotic chronologies of present pasts in which the ages are whirled together and new histories are being formed. As I discussed in this paper, the resulting temporal whirlpool of heritage follows certain patterns and principles and is not a random mix.

Also failing is, secondly, a conventional understanding of materiality in archaeology. When artifice and reality merge and when designers can build ideas about the past into the material world through techniques of narrative placemaking, material culture can quite obviously to exactly the same extent form a record of more than one period simultaneously. Reducing a site or object that evidently possesses the quality or condition of being past (as in Fig. 2) to a creation of the present misses its entire point. Authenticity does not rest in the fabric but in the credibility of its appearance.

Conclusion: From Age as Artefact to Pastness as Medium

I argued a decade ago in a paper I co-authored with the English public archaeology specialist Tim Schadla-Hall that age and authenticity are artefacts in the sense that they can be constructed in the present (Holtorf/Schadla-Hall 1999). At the end of the current paper proposing a theory of pastness I wish to take this argument one step further. For when age has mutated into pastness, it is an artefact also in the sense that it communicates ideas, inviting – and indeed requiring – interpretation by the human observer.

Seen in the light of narrative placemaking, pastness is an aesthetic medium through which material culture communicates, whether the history of a site or its own specific biography. Pastness thus affects the ways in which we engage with material and social realities in our lifeworlds. This is very much intended when pastness occurs in themed environments as they are precisely about meeting their customers' parallel needs of stimulation and reassurance. But it occurs no less in other contexts in the contemporary world when we encounter pastness in museums or at heritage sites that seek to entertain and educate their visitors.

My theory of pastness has implications for the practice of managing heritage. The heritage sector needs to recognize that the significance of heritage does not exclusively lie in its character as evidence and witness of the past so that histories can be told and memories preserved. The quality or condition of being past always needs to be established first but even in heritage it is earned, not given. In this paper I discussed how pastness is acquired and received. It emerged that conventional understandings in the heritage sector of temporality and materiality need to be rethought in a profound way. The boundary between what is genuinely old and what is artificially new loses its meaning. How can anybody today understand Disneyland without an appreciation of its various historic references? By the same token, how can anybody today understand ancient Rome without an appreciation of Las Vegas which manifests so well (as in Fig. 1) the significance of this ancient civilization as a major cultural reference point in the present? In themed environments the realms of history and cultural meaning merge into one.

Pastness is a vibrant medium that lets large audiences see something that is not there: the past. Next time you visit a heritage site you will be forgiven for thinking that it's like Disneyland.

Acknowledgements

I would like to thank the Freiburg based DFG project for inviting me to their workshop during which an earlier version of this paper was presented, and all participants and presenters for stimulating discussions. Another version was presented and discussed at a seminar of the "Places as Stories" project in Kalmar, supported by Riksbanken Jubileumsfond. I am grateful to Gary A. Fine for sending me promptly his paper, and to Shannon Dawdy for inspiring some of my conclusions. Valuable comments on earlier drafts of this paper were made by Peter Aronsson, Wolfgang Hochbruck, David Lowenthal, Scott Lukas, Carolyn Oesterle, Bodil Petersson, and Angela Piccini. Many thanks to you all!

References

Burger, Phillip R. 2000. "Afterword." *At the Earth's Core* [1914]. E. Rice Burroughs. Lincoln/London: University of Nebraska Press (Bison Books). 279-290.

Carson, Cary. 1995. "Mirror, Mirror, on the Wall, Whose History Is the Fairest of Them All?" *The Public Historian* 17.4: 61-67.

Crang, Mike. 1996. "Magic Kingdom or a Quixotic Quest for Authenticity?" *Annals of Tourism Research* 23.2: 415-431.

Dawdy, Shannon Lee. Forthcoming. "Clockpunk Anthropology and the Ruins of Modernity." *Current Anthropology.*

Dickson, Jane. 1993. "Who's Afraid of the Big Bad Mouse?" *The Sunday Times Magazine* 28 March: 30-34.

Fallon, Brian. 1993. "William Crozier." *Irish Arts Review Yearbook* 9: 183-186.

Fine, Gary A. 2007. "Rumor, Trust and Civil Society: Collective Memory and Cultures of Judgment." *Diogenes* 54.1: 5-18.

Francaviglia, Richard. 1995. "History After Disney: The Significance of 'Imagineered' Historical Places." *The Public Historian* 17.4: 69-74.

Haas, Charlie. 1978. "Disneyland Is Good For You." *New West* 4 Dec 1978: 13-19. Available at http://www.scribd.com/doc/176648 05/Disneyland-Is-Good-For-You (accessed 3 Jan 2010).

Harwood, Edward. 2002. "Rhetoric, Authenticity and Reception. The Eighteenth-Century Landscape Garden, the Modern Theme Park, and Their Audiences." *Theme Park Landscapes: Antecedents and Variations.* Eds. Terence Young/Robert Riley. Washington, DC: Dumbarton Oaks Research Library and Collection. 49-68. Available at http://www.doaks.org/publications/doaks_on line_publications/TParks/TPch3.pdf (accessed 30 Dec 2009).

Hjemdahl, Kirsti M. 2002. "History as a Cultural Playground." *Ethnologia Europaea* 32.2: 105-124.

Holtorf, Cornelius. 2005. *From Stonehenge to Las Vegas. Archaeology as Popular Culture.* Lanham: Altamira Press.

Holtorf, Cornelius. 2007. *Archaeology Is a Brand! The Meaning of Archaeology in Contemporary Popular Culture.* Oxford: Archaeopress.

Holtorf, Cornelius. 2009a. "Imagine This: Archaeology in the Experience Society." *Contemporary Archaeologies: Excavating Now.* Eds. Cornelius Holtorf/Angela Piccini. Frankfurt am Main: Peter Lang. 47-64.

Holtorf, Cornelius. 2009b. "Heritage Values in Contemporary Popular Culture." *Heritage Values in Contemporary Society.* Eds. George Smith/Phyllis Mauch Messenger/Hilary Soderland. Walnut Creek: Left Coast Press. 43-54.

Holtorf, Cornelius. 2010. "On the Possibility of Time-Travel." *Lund Archaeological Review* 15-16: 31-41.

Holtorf, Cornelius/Tim Schadla-Hall. 1999. "Age as Artefact. On Archaeological Authenticity." *European Journal of Archaeology* 2: 229-247.

Lowenthal, David. 1985. *The Past Is a Foreign Country*. Cambridge: Cambridge University Press.

Lowenthal, David. 2002. "The Past as a Theme Park." *Theme Park Landscapes: Antecedents and Variations*. Eds. Terence Young/ Robert Riley. Washington, DC: Dumbarton Oaks Research Library and Collection. 11-23. Available at http://www.doaks. org/publications/doaks_online_publications/TParks/TPch1.pdf (accessed 30 Dec 2009).

Lukas, Scott A. 2007. "Theming as a Sensory Phenomenon: Discovering the Senses on the Las Vegas Strip." *The Themed Space. Locating Culture, Nation, and Self*. Ed. Scott A. Lukas. Lanham: Lexington. 75-95.

Lukas, Scott A. 2008. *Theme Park*. London: Reaktion.

Pruitt, Tera C. 2009. "Contextualising Alternative Archaeology. Socio-Politics and Approaches." *Archaeological Review from Cambridge* 24.1: 55-75.

Rohde, Joe. 2007a. "From Myth to Mountain: Insights into Virtual Placemaking." *Computer Graphics 41.3*. Available at http://www. siggraph.org/publications/newsletter/volume/from-myth-to-mo untain-insights-into-virtual-placemaking (accessed 20 Dec 2009).

Rohde, Joe. 2007b. http://www.joerohde.com/english/citations.php (accessed 7 Dec 2007)

Schmidt, Leo. 2008. *Einführung in die Denkmalpflege*. Stuttgart: Theiss.

Schörken, Rolf. 1995. *Begegnungen mit Geschichte. Vom außerwissenschaftlichen Umgang mit der Historie in Literatur und Medien*. Stuttgart: Klett-Cotta.

The Free Dictionary. "Pastness." http://www.thefreedictionary.com/ pastness (accessed 23 Dec 2009).

Wallace, Mike. 1985. "Mickey Mouse History: Portraying the Past at Disney World." *Radical History Review* 32: 33-57.

Wikipedia. 2009. "The Restoration of the Sistine Chapel." http://en. wikipedia.org/wiki/Restoration_of_the_Sistine_Chapel_frescoes (accessed 30 Dec 2009).

Wright, Alex. 2007. *The Imagineering Field Guide to Disney's Animal Kingdom. An Imagineer's-Eye Tour*. New York: Disney Editions.

"The Past, Foreign Countries and Fantasy ...
They All Make for a Good Outing":
Staging the Past in Japan and Some Other Locations

JOY HENDRY

In the 1980s, when there was plenty of money around in Japan, and the newly introduced world of Tōkyō Disneyland was drawing large numbers of visitors, the theme park phenomenon reached a new level of sophistication. Recreating worlds, whether they were of the past or of contemporary foreign locations, almost became an art form. A huge variety of places were built, with considerable capital investment although no single pattern of financial backing, and visitors could travel all over this world and several past and fantasy worlds without ever leaving the shores of Japan. Taken together, the contents of the parks, as well as the events they staged, could be compared with almost anything found elsewhere in the 'real' world of other themed environments, then or since. Given the resources, Japanese park builders seemed to have no limits to the ingenuity of their park design. In the last twenty years, the resources have dwindled, but so, it seems, has the interest of the Japanese public... except in a few cases.

This paper will examine some examples of this themed[1] park phenomenon to illustrate its breadth and depth, and it will seek to situate the Japanese case within three broader theoretical frameworks. The first will simply set out to demonstrate that, during the period when these places were most popular, visitors made little distinction in their choices between past and present; indeed, they didn't seem to make much distinction between 'true' representa-

---

1   I use the expression 'themed' park, rather than 'theme' park, as the latter has taken on connotations in the English language which are often rather inappropriate in Japan, despite the use of a direct transcription into Japanese of the words *tēma pāku*. In Japanese another term, *yūenji,* literally a playing place, would more accurately describe a theme park, as used at least in the UK.

41

tions (or copies of other places) and fantasy. The theory developed here reflects a theme that underpins another collection of papers about travel, or *tabi* in Japanese, based on a research panel of the Japan Anthropology Workshop where "the collapsing of time and space in contemporary Japanese experience of travel was one of the common themes explored by the participants" (Guichard-Anguis 2009: 3). The link with notions of *tabi*, or Japanese forms of travel, leads into the second theoretical framework, which argues that Japanese parks represent Japanese ideas of history and heritage that may or may not coincide with those found elsewhere, and a few examples will be presented on characteristics I have chosen as particularly Japanese.

Thirdly, an attempt will be made to draw this paper into the context of the conference at which it was presented, by offering a possible framework to explain some of the apparently global interest in the kind of themed environments representing the past that we were discussing, in a wide variety of countries. My own initial study of the Japanese parks did draw on a variety of influences from around the world (cf. Hendry 2000), and the Japanese parks may also have been influencing others, but a decade has passed since that research was completed, and I have since been working on several other examples of cultural display. I will briefly discuss a couple of these, especially as they also seem to be part of a similarly global phenomenon, and I shall suggest how they may offer a possible explanation of the popularity for visitors of visiting representations of their own past in whatever form they may be created and displayed.

The Theme Park Phenomenon in Japan: Some Examples

The time of greatest excitement about building themed environments in Japan was during the height of the so-called economic miracle, when resources seemed unlimited, and a new-found appetite for leisure, known as a *rejā būmu* (leisure boom), brought people out in large numbers, looking for new things to do with their time, and unusual events to attend. There was still nervousness about travelling abroad, and for many, that leisure time was also limited to two or three consecutive days at most, so the opportunity to see the highlights of a foreign country within just such a period, was for a while a very appropriate attraction. Visiting such parks also answered a kind of yearning shared for generations by many Japanese about being able to travel to new places, to experience something unusual, to undergo a *tabi*, a word that means journey, but also indicates something possibly life-changing, thought provoking, and stimulating (Guichard-Anguis 2009: 3-6). The idea is also a recurring literary theme in Japan (ibid.: 6-8), which probably explains why many of the parks make reference to characters that appear in literature of one form or another, as we shall see.

My own research on the subject actually began through a project looking at gardens in Japan, which in itself followed a dimension of an interest in "wrapping culture", in this case the wrapping of space (Hendry 1993). Gardens in Japan often represent other worlds, sometimes miniature reproductions of famous views, sometimes making reference to particular periods in the past, and sometimes – perhaps in a shrine or temple – a representation of an afterlife. Gardens are enclosed, as the character for their depiction makes clear, and so they, too, might qualify to be 'themed environments', and in my view, they could be seen as having paved the way for the more complex constructions that followed them, and became known as theme parks, or in the Japanese transcription, *tēma pāku*. Some such parks even started with gardens, and they are all set in gardens of one sort or another, some featuring the garden aspect more than others, but all using 'wrapped' aspects of the natural environment to appeal to the senses, and make a pleasant context for the buildings that were used to represent foreign countries in the parks.

An early park to be built was said to be inspired by the scenery of Hokkaidō, which is often described as more like Europe than the rest of Japan, but in this case to have represented a kind of vast nature (*daishizen*), which characterises Canada. Canadian World was commissioned by the local council to provide employment for people who were made redundant when the coal mines were closed down in the area. In this case, Prince Edward Island was chosen as a closer focus within Canada, largely because it is the site of a story, popular in Japan, of a feisty young adopted girl known as Anne of Green Gables, whose adventures formed a literary focus for the park. The eponymous house, Green Gables itself, was constructed there, a copy of an original to be found in Prince Edward Island, and containing a museum about the author, Lucy Maud Montgomery. The neighbourhood of Avonlea, which housed the fictive adopted parents of Anne, is also built around it, containing many of the scenes from the novels about her, which were carefully recreated there. In the height of its success, the park employed actors from Canada to play the parts of Anne, her school teacher, and her friends, Gilbert and Diana.

Interestingly, rides played only a small part in this park, where ponies and a horse and cart offered the speediest excitement, the cart roof displaying the 'theme' in the shape of Anne's straw hat!

Fig. 1: A 'low-tech' ride at Canadian World, Hokkaidō, Japan. The roof of the cart illustrates the literary theme of Anne of Green Gables

Photograph: Joy Hendry

Instead, the fantasy world of Anne and her home, Green Gables, were set among cultural features chosen to represent Canada, such as St. John's Clock Tower, copy of the original in Prince Edward Island, a series of totem poles to remind of the Indigenous inhabitants, and an area of shops, cafés and restaurants apparently built on the model of a street in Quebec, so as not to forget the importance of the French in Canada. In a 'craft zone', visitors could, at the height of the park's success, learn how to make patchwork quilts, cut stained glass, and grow a variety of herbs from people who travelled from Canada to demonstrate the requisite skills. In the schoolhouse, constructed along the lines of the one Anne attended in the stories, they could have a 'mini English conversation lesson' with Anne herself. And in the afternoon, they could take tea with her as well.

Tōkyō Disneyland is of course different to this low key themed environment. It is much more centrally located, within easy reach of the enormous city of Tōkyō, it has big, thrilling rides, and it has many of the architectural features of the original Disney dream lands in the United States. It was built with economic aims in mind, and its success in that respect cannot fail to have influenced and inspired the other themed park builders in Japan, but its role was also to create a fun experience for its predominantly *Japanese* punters. The year of its construction, 1983, became known as *rejā gannen* (the first year of leisure) in Japan (Notoji 1990: 226), but a driving force for its choice was a pervading curiosity about the United States, just as other parks assumed a curiosity about a series of other countries.

For American visitors, the first park may have been built as Disney's dream of his childhood, an earlier positive image of a life his compatriots would recognise (cf. Bryman 1995: 11-12); for Japan, it was a huge and happy representation of a foreign land that knew how to make theme parks. When it was being planned, the Disney advisers suggested that the Japanese company might want to draw on Japanese history, and recreate stories of their own past, with a 'samurai land', for example, but the local team wanted none of this. They were building a piece of America in Japan, and for some, this was the best that America had to offer (cf. Brannen 1992: 216)! Several studies have been made of Tōkyō Disneyland, each of them identifying subtle differences from the American versions. Raz (1986) makes comparisons with other forms of entertainment in Japan, for example, Awata and Takanarita (1987) with festivals, and van Maanen (1992) has an interesting suggestion about Japanese seeking freedom from constraints in the park, whilst the so-called 'free' Americans seem to enjoy being constrained.

The biggest and most famous of Japan's themed foreign villages is called Huis Ten Bosch (see Schlehe/Uike-Bormann in this volume for more detail of this park), after the Queen's Palace in Holland, which is actually reproduced within the park, surrounded by the same spacious gardens as may be found in The Hague. The park covers a huge area in excess of 152 hectares, it has some six kilometres of canals, and it quite successfully recreates an atmosphere of actually being in the Netherlands. It is located near the island of Dejima, where the Dutch were granted a concessionary territory during Japan's 250 years of otherwise virtual isolation, so it has a real historical connection, and some of the displays in the park tell the stories of people who lived there at the time. It started out as quite a small 'Holland village', but has grown into a very well-equipped resort, with hotels, second homes in a variety of Dutch period styles, and a design for community life in the new millennium, as well as reconstructions of many Dutch street scenes. One of the hotels is a copy of the Hotel Amsterdam, with facilities so luxurious that they have attracted the same high status, so the fantasy of spending time in Europe can quite well be recreated for visitors who know no better.

Another park which has been successful, and remained in business in 2009 when this paper was written, is known as Parque España, again a biggish park, located in the south of the Ise peninsula, for long a destination for Japanese travellers who try at least once in their lifetime to visit the important Ise Shrine there. This park does not boast many copies of actual Spanish buildings, instead going for an attempt to create an Iberian 'atmosphere' *(funiki)*, but it has plenty of entertainment, again a literary theme in the person of Don Quixote, accompanied of course by Sancho Panza, and a range of franchised stores selling goods from Latin America as well as Spain. It is divided into four sections, depicting in turn the city *(la ciudad)*, the country *(el campo)*, the seaside *(el mar)* and *la fiesta*, where various rides are located in a style reminiscent of the Gaudí architecture of Barcelona. At least in the early days, it employed a large number of Spanish performers, who would sing and dance in the street, as well as offering high quality flamenco for those who would stump up for an expensive meal within the already quite pricey park.

A museum built in the style of the castle origins of Francisco Xavier, who was the first European missionary to arrive in Japan, offered exhibitions of the Roman and Moorish influences in Spain, as well as a display of the techniques of guitar production, when I did my research there. Another section of the park is built as a Roman coliseum, where shows are performed every hour or so, notably again featuring Cervantes' characters, among others things, and a large space that was visible, but not actually accessible to visitors, seemed to depict a site of the kinds of ruins that might be excavated on Spanish terrain.

Some Japanese Characteristics of the Parks

During the period when these places were most popular, interpreters argued that the presentations drew in a similar fashion on representations of the (Japanese) past and the geographically distant present, and it was proposed that travelling back into Japanese history was an experience as "exotic" *(ekizochikku)* as travelling abroad (Creighton 1997: 246; Ivy 1995: 50; cf. Lowenthal 1985). Neither did the park builders make much distinction between true representations and fantasy. Generally, these themed parks offered a chance for a fun day out, or even a few days holiday, and many of them offered the journey *(tabi)* as part of the package, perhaps to add to the sense of making a trip to another world. The ones we have described demonstrate an interest at the time in foreign countries, but there are also parks in Japan that recreate aspects of Japanese history, and in all cases, the displays include quite accurate representations of other periods of time, as well as other ways of doing things. Ironically, perhaps, they also very often draw on literary themes, and the entertainment available may include plays (for the Japanese historical parks) as well as the dancing and musical shows more commonly found in the 'foreign' ones.

Two pairs of comparisons will illustrate this apparent overlap between the past, the foreign, and the sense of fantasy that underpins the whole themed park phenomenon, and therefore, as mentioned above, fits into existing Japanese patterns.[2] The first is a pair of establishments that set out to represent life in the British Isles, though actually predominantly England. One of these was a local venture, fired by the passion of a gentleman who loved the works and times of William Shakespeare; the other, a kind of campus of a national educational institution, dedicated to the teaching of English for contemporary Japanese. The first builds copies of real buildings so well researched that the claim of the place is to have a more authentic version of the birthplace of the Bard than that found in Stratford on Avon (because it has copied the 16th century style "unsullied by the passage of time and unchanged by subsequent inhabitants"). The other focuses on creating an atmosphere again, this time of a London club, but also a pub, where students of the school can practice the appropriate English they have learned.

Fig. 2: The New Place, later (now non-existent) home of William Shakespeare, reproduced in Maruyama, Japan

Photograph: Joy Hendry

The Maruyama Shakespeare Park, despite being focused on the fictional works of an English writer, takes some trouble to present the historical period in which he lived, including more information about 16th century London than I have ever seen on public display in one single location in London itself; the creation and main-

2   Several scholars have argued for a postmodern interpretation of the phenomenon, linked to a kind of nostalgia for a simpler, more attractive life (e.g. Creighton 1997; Graburn 1995, Ivy 1995, cf. Urry 1990); but links to a prior existence of Japanese forms of display seems to me to be a more compelling argument (cf. Hendry 2000: 17; cf. Moon 1997: 178).

tenance of gardens in the knot and physic styles; and the complete reconstruction of a residence known as The New Place, the later home of William Shakespeare that was subsequently burnt down, so leaves no actual remains. The whole place was designed and built by English craftsmen, using English materials, and English models were employed for the creation of the life-size figures of the family of Shakespeare who people the birthplace, also furnished in 16th century English style. A Disney-style audioanimatronic version of William is seated in the New Place, and the tap of a button has him turn around and speak to a friend.

At British Hills, the educational establishment originally set up for the practice in English surroundings of the language of that country, the buildings were also sent out from England, and they represent a variety of English styles, from a central castle to a series of dormitories, each built to show off the style of a historical period, and named after a writer of the time. Crafts, such as cake-baking and lace-making may be studied here, and to learn table manners is a compulsory part of the proceedings. I am not sure whether the climate was also planned, but the location is quite high in the mountains, and the day I arrived, we drove through fine sunshine until just before we passed the entrance gates, whereupon we entered a cloud, and mist and drizzle descended on this little fantasy piece of England for the rest of the afternoon! Despite its educational standing, the place supplements its income by offering golf in the summer and skiing in the winter as recreational activities entirely separate from the English tuition, so the 'fun' has not been abandoned.

A couple of Japanese historical parks located in a fairly central part of the main island illustrate similar contrasts. On the one hand, there is Meiji *mura* (village), a collection of houses brought, or reconstructed, to illustrate the architecture of the first period of Westernisation in Japan, known as the Meiji period, after the Emperor of the time. It is designated as an open-air museum, and academically well regarded, as a clear depiction of an aspect of the momentous history of those years. Several of the houses on display there were those apparently actually occupied by famous characters of the time, others show the way that technology was introduced, and generally the story is well documented with references to scholarly texts. On the other hand, the *Sengokujidai mura* (village of the Warring Period), is unashamedly a *tēma pāku* (theme park), with much fantasy in the way that the story of the time is depicted, including technological wonders such as shuddering floors, and big, alarming film footage of a battle, alongside life-size suits of armour, all to simulate the experience for the visitor of being on the battlefield. Local youths grew their hair and shaped their eyebrows to work convincingly as young soldiers of the time, and there are no fewer than three theatres to add glitz to the time travel experience.

Yet, the buildings of the Warring Period park are also carefully constructed from models of the time, one of them a complete copy of Azuchi castle, a location that played an important role in the events. The theatres are also made to look as they might have at the time, and one of the actors is detailed to open the proceedings by instructing the audience in the way they would have behaved, had they lived then – down to giving out scraps of paper for them to wrap around the coins they should throw at the stage to mark their appreciation. At the Meiji village, where academic authenticity is the order of the day, one of the curators explained to me how the creation of an appropriate atmosphere includes a mixture of contemporary and reproduction furniture, facsimiles of documents, such as newspapers and letters, and "a spot of imaginative fun" in the choice of classical music to play, and the Western style flower arrangements in the alcove (see Hendry 2000: 145 for a photograph).

It seems, then, that striving towards accuracy has been a characteristic of most of these Japanese parks, albeit in Japanese style, whether they are designated as museums, which would set them apart in a European view, or themed amusement parks, which offer a surprising degree of authenticity by that same outside standard. One further pair of examples will perhaps serve to clinch the case, although the first park has apparently now succumbed to the poorer economic climate and closed down. It was one of several German parks, known as *Glückskönigreich* (the Happy Kingdom), and it was located in Hokkaidō again, like Canadian World, but this time within access of Obihiro airport so visitors could fly in to the make-believe Germany, even getting picked up in a special bus at the airport. Happy marching music played cheerily out of loud speakers as visitors made their way among the copies of actual German buildings again, this time constructed by a German workforce, flown in for the purpose, accompanied by tons of 400-year old granite paving stones, conveniently being removed from Berlin and Dresden just in time for the construction of the cobble-stoned square.

A copy of a German castle was also constructed in this park, in fact the extant home of Count Ernst Philipp von Schaumburg-Lippe whose words in the passports that served as entrance tickets greeted and welcomed Japanese visitors to the reproduction of his home in Japan. Hotel rooms were available within, and three times a day, a concert of German music was rendered by German musicians in the Great Hall. Elsewhere 'real' German beer could be purchased and consumed, or ordered for future delivery, and a demonstration of the production of German sausages added a special charm to the outlet for this ethnic foodstuff. The literary theme here was built around the stories of the Brothers Grimm, and some of the buildings were copies of those associated with the lives of the pair, whose characters had been transformed into statues, soft toys and a variety of other souvenir products. Much further south, in an establishment known as Little World: Museum of Man, southern Germany had become the focus, and prettily painted Bavarian houses are featured, again constructed by craftspeople from the area, but this time persuaded into their task by Japanese anthropologists. When I visited that park, it was autumn, and a veritable Oktoberfest was in full swing, again with musicians from Bavaria providing much of the atmosphere.

Fig. 3: Concert of German music at Glückskönigreich, near Obihiro, Japan, in a reconstruction of a 'real' German castle

Photograph: Joy Hendry

Little World boasts the same authenticity as the National Museum of Ethnology, built at the grounds remaining from the Universal Exhibition held in Osaka in 1970, each having been headed by an anthropologist who was in charge of acquiring their 'collections'. In both cases, these are often items commissioned from the peoples whose worlds are on display, neither drew the line at making copies of things that were unavailable, or that they liked in other museums, and they employed designers to set them off in an attractive style. Nor was a little fun to be excluded, especially at Little World, where visitors may try on for photographs some of the garments that have been acquired, collect passport stamps as they visit the different cultural zones, and try out a variety of exotic foods at the on-site restaurant. Museums, yes, but a little different in style and content from the European models that first inspired and influenced them, just as the themed amusement parks have drawn away from the American model that Disneyland provided.

Japanese Parks in a Global Context

How then do these Japanese parks fit into what has clearly now become a global phenomenon? This paper has identified certain peculiarly Japanese characteristics of the contemporary parks, whatever Western-derived name may be given to them, but actually Japan has also been contributing to a world interest in cultural display for more than a century and a half. The focus here has so far been largely on the entertainment value of such parks, examining in particular those associated with a period of economic prosperity and a new found leisure boom. However, there have been many other reasons for constructing fantasy cultural worlds, past and present, and in the book I wrote about them, several were examined (Hendry 2000). The oldest were those sent to the world fairs and exhibitions that kicked off in Europe in the middle of the 19th century, but soon spread widely around the world as a way for a nation to exhibit its standing, and enter the capitalistic trading circus. Japan built up quite a formidable reputation for the construction of these small worlds by investing heavily in the delegations they sent to these events, at first clearly for political and diplomatic reasons, but soon building up a presence in the world of global trade.

Another reason for building parks to represent the past was to conserve the forms of architecture that were rapidly becoming displaced by the oceans of reinforced concrete washing around the world. This fashion began in Sweden when Hazelius managed to acquire a piece of land at Skansen where, in the face of considerable opposition, he began to have old houses transported and reconstructed, so that there is now a representation of most parts of the country. These 'skansens' took off in several parts of Europe, and a similar phenomenon developed in Japan, where whole villages have been conserved and protected for visitors to see for themselves what life used to be like in them. Again, the theme of "nostalgia" has been used to interpret these places (see Hendry 2000: 146 for references), and there was sometimes a link between historical incidents and the choice of a foreign country to represent. We have already seen the case of the Holland village, which preceded the construction of

Huis Ten Bosch, and a German village was built in Miyako Island, Okinawa, at the site where a German merchant ship was wrecked in 1893. In this case, much is made of the philanthropy of the island dwellers who rescued the seamen, and elements of the park are designated as "symbols of peace" (Hendry 2000: 45), these forming two other themes found in the reconstructed worlds we have seen.

The new kind of cultural display that I have been examining in the last few years links the past, and very often looks to the future, but a theme that would seem to go beyond the idea of nostalgia is that of healing, also a concept recently associated with the islands of Okinawa. Again the busy urban life is the bugbear, and just as people have been looking at their more peaceful-seeming past existences with nostalgia, they visit the quieter, 'slower' life of these islands to get some respite from city stress. Okinawa is also one of the areas of Japan that claims indigenous origins different from those of the mainland, and the notion of healing is also quite commonly associated with the construction of culture centres found in various parts of the 'indigenous world'. I have interpreted these centres as an element of a global movement of cultural reclamation now taking place in several former colonies such as Canada and New Zealand (Aotearoa), where peoples who lost much of their language and former culture in the assimilation process administered during the nation-building efforts of the colonial powers, can at last represent themselves in the ways that they see fit,[3] and which thereby offer a source of healing for them (see Hendry 2005 for more detail of this movement).

In Japan, despite the Okinawan references, the main example of this kind of cultural reclamation is to be found among the Ainu people, many of whom live in the northern island of Hokkaidō, which we have already seen as a site of theme park construction. Back in the early seventies, when I first visited Hokkaidō, there was an early example of the phenomenon in the shape of an Ainu 'village' located in the north east, near the beautiful Akan lake. Like many of the parks we have described, it consisted of a collection of houses, and like the 'historical' parks, these were houses that were no longer in use – they were the 'traditional' Ainu houses, out of which the Ainu people had been persuaded to move, in order to 'modernise', and, in this case, Japanise. The people working in the park were wearing distinctive Ainu clothes, but when I asked them about their language and their Ainu way of life, they revealed that that they were students from Tōkyō and declared that the language

---

3   In practice, on the ground, the people involved in self-representation usually belong to heterogeneous groups so the representation may well be contested.

(and people) had pretty much died out. There was one old man there who was said still to know the language, but for the most part this park was telling the story – mainly for tourists – of the past of a people who had been subjected to a heavy assimilation programme.

*Fig. 4: The Ainu 'village' at Akan-ko, Japan, in 1971 (left),
and the same site in 2004 (right)*

Photograph: Joy Hendry

Happily, when I returned in 2004, this place had been transformed. It was still quite touristy; indeed, there were many more shops offering goods to visitors, but the place was populated by people who were proud to declare themselves Ainu. It still had a traditional house on display, with an Ainu interpreter to explain how it was used, and there was an Ainu theatre, with Ainu actors, dancers and musicians ready to interpret Ainu stories, and play Ainu traditional instruments. An Ainu museum held more objects, and some re-constructions of Ainu scenes, and some of the shops had Ainu craftspeople making goods for sale. To understand how this trans-formation had come about took me several years of research, and almost a year in Canada, for the Ainu people had almost given up their cultural heritage when I first visited that site. To cut a long story short (see Hendry 2005 for an extended version), it was the global movement of indigenous revival, which reached a high point in 1993 in the Year of Indigenous People, which helped the Ainu to regroup and gather strength, a process that is now quite success-fully underway.

Hokkaidō has several Ainu parks now, and there is an Ainu culture centre in a prime location in Tōkyō. In Canada, where I did a longer and more serious study of the First Nations culture centres, there is evidence of exchanges with Ainu people, along with several others, and I know at least two Ainu researchers who have travelled to Canada for supervision of their PhD work. The Canadian government has been supporting the First Nations' endeavour to reclaim their own representations since 1967, when they facilitated the construction of a beautiful Native Canadian pavilion for EXPO 67 in the city of Montreal. One of the people involved in that project was Tom Hill, head of the museum at the Woodland Cultural Centre in Brantford, Ontario, when I did an in-depth study of its foundation and continuing work in 2003. During that time, I stayed in the home of Keith Lickers, another of its founding members, who wrote the rationale for the budget they needed to set up the centre. Interviews and longer conversations with both of these men, as well as many other members of the Haudenosaunee people whose culture it represents, made clear the sense of healing that such a centre offers to those who are able to visit it, or to work there.

The museum that tells the story of their past is the largest, and most popular attraction, and it was built along the lines of the 1967 pavilion. It shows first the land that was theirs and how they lived in it, then how they welcomed and helped the explorers, missionaries and traders who arrived from Europe, and then how relations developed and disintegrated between them, as the nation of Canada was set up and they were subjected to a policy of assimilation. It doesn't stop there, however, for all kinds of things have happened since, and it eventually places the fate of the Haudenosaunee and other First Nations in the context of the modern nation. Alongside the museum, there is an exhibition hall, where shows change regularly, allowing local artists and visiting people to display their work and demonstrate the continuity of the people deemed, like the Ainu, to have been 'dying out'. There is a library, language revival classes, and live performances of dancing and theatre, as well as other activities such as fashion shows and sporting events renewed from their 'traditional' past. Finally, there is a shop, where books, art, and souvenirs can be purchased, and people can carry home material evidence of their own history and identity, told by those who share their ancestral past, and for these people, even more importantly, their continuity. There may be some fantasy here, too, but it is fantasy with a strong real purpose!

In Canada, it is made clear that culture centres such as these, of which there are quite a number, serve an important role of healing the sense of hurt and humiliation which remains within the living memory of the older people who were punished at school for using their native tongues and made to feel inferior to the 'modern' world.[4] There are many other roles that the centres play, and other agents of the revitalisation of their past, such as language immersion schools, and my argument here is not that healing is the only value of parks and other institutions and activities that 'stage' the past. However, I think it worth considering whether this may be an aspect of the interest in parks in other parts of the world, too. Globalisation (however defined) and rapid social change have often severed the sense of identity that people growing up in a more stable, anchored community would share, and seeking ancestral links, even perhaps selecting links (cf. Mathews 2000) is an activity that could serve a healing purpose in many more ways that the one briefly presented here

From politics to healing, then, from play to serious endeavour, a range of possibilities exist for 'staging the past', and the economic resources available to Japan at the time when they were first flowering offered creative opportunities that have also built a fantastic framework for their subsequent interpretation.

References

Awata Fusaha/Tōru Takanarita. 1987. *Dizuniirando no Keizaigaku* [The Economics of Disneyland]. Tōkyō: Asahi Bunko.

Brannen, Mary Yoko. 1992. "'Bwana Mickey': Constructing Cultural Consumption at Tōkyō Disneyland." *Remade in Japan*. Ed. Joseph Tobin. New Haven/London: Yale University Press. 216-34.

Bryman, Alan. 1995. *Disney and his Worlds*. London: Routledge.

Creighton, Millie. 1997. "Consuming Rural Japan: The Marketing of Tradition and Nostalgia in the Japanese Travel Industry." *Ethnology* 36.3: 239-54.

Graburn, Nelson. 1995. "Tourism, Modernity and Nostalgia." *The Future of Anthropology and its Relevance to the Contemporary World*. Eds. Akbar Ahmed/Cris Shore. London: Athlone Press.

Guichard-Anguis, Sylvie. 2009. "Introduction: The Culture of Travel (*tabi no bunka*) and Japanese Tourism." *Japanese Tourism and Travel Culture*. Eds. Sylvie Guichard-Anguis/Okpyo Moon. London/New York: Routledge. 1-17.

Hendry, Joy. 1993. *Wrapping Culture: Politeness, Presentation and Power in Japan and Other Societies*. Oxford: Clarendon Press.

---

4   The Aboriginal Healing Foundation of Canada has, for example, taken on the task of administering a part of the funding allocated in 2007 to compensate the victims of this school system for loss of language and family life.

Hendry, Joy. 2000. *The Orient Strikes Back: A Global View of Cultural Display*. Oxford/New York: Berg.

Hendry, Joy. 2005. *Reclaiming Culture: Indigenous People and Self-Representation*. New York: Palgrave.

Ivy, Marilyn. 1995. *Discourses of the Vanishing: Modernity, Phantasm, Japan*. Chicago: University of Chicago Press.

Lowenthal, David. 1985. *The Past Is a Foreign Country*. Cambridge: Cambridge University Press.

Mathews, Gordon. 2000. *Global Culture, Individual Identity: Searching for Home in the Cultural Supermarket*. London/New York: Routledge.

Moon, Okpyo. 1997. "Tourism and Cultural Development: Japanese and Korean Contexts." *Tourism and Cultural Development in Asia and Oceania*. Eds. Shinji Yamashita/Kadir H. Din/J.S. Eades. Bangi: Penerbit Universiti Kebangsaan Malaysia. 178-93.

Notoji Masako. 1990. *Dizuniirando to iu Seichi* [The Sacred Place Called Disneyland]. Tōkyō: Iwanami Shinsho.

Raz, Aviad. 1999. *Riding the Black Ship: Japan and Tōkyō Disneyland*. Cambridge, MA/London: Harvard University Press.

Urry, John. 1990. *The Tourist Gaze*. London: Sage.

Van Maanen, John. 1992. "Displacing Disney: Some Notes on the Flow of Culture." *Qualitative Sociology* 15.1: 5-35.

Staging the Past in Cultural Theme Parks:

Representations of Self and Other

in Asia and Europe

JUDITH SCHLEHE / MICHIKO UIKE-BORMANN

Introduction

The new global conception of leisure for the affluent involves the consumption of products that generate experience and emotions (cf. Clavé 2007: 158). Simulated environments and performances play a crucial role in global popular culture, not just for leisure and entertainment, but also for political ends: as a creation of images and identities connected to historical heritage, as invented traditions, imagined communities, ongoing negotiations of Self, Other and positions in the world and, last but not least, as sites of contemporary social life and practice.

This paper explores the different meanings underlying national, local and commercial cultural politics in Europe and Asia from an anthropological angle. Our research sites are cultural theme parks[1] which we regard as cultural products, systems of representation and symbolic microcosms closely linked to media images and, at times, to museums and classrooms. By examining the staging of culture and history in these parks we are working on two levels: We investigate the politics of representation revealed by producers and workers (employees/representatives), and we explore the appropriations by and agency of visitors.

Our case studies from Europa-Park, a German family-run business, Huis Ten Bosch, a Japanese park run by a company (with shareholders like banks and transport companies), and Taman Mini, an Indonesian park controlled by the government,[2] illustrate different

---

1   Cultural theme parks are parks which use cultures as their themes. Themes are seen as structured narratives.

2   The empirical material used here was collected during fieldwork in Germany, Japan and Indonesia in 2007 and 2008. Michiko Uike-Bormann conducted three months of fieldwork in Japan, Judith Schlehe three months in

ways of staging the Self and the Other. Whereas Europa-Park focuses on the Other within the Self by depicting European countries as part of a united Europe and non-European cultures as appropriations of European colonialism, Huis Ten Bosch refers to the ultimate Other of Holland as imagined by the Japanese. With its focus on diverse Indonesian ethnic cultures, Taman Mini exclusively concentrates on the Self and on the construction of a postcolonial national identity.

A description of the settings of these parks as well as the respective producers' and visitors' perspectives will be followed by interpretations of the parks within their particular socio-cultural contexts. We would suggest that cultural theme parks do not only aim at pure entertainment but function as models for specific social orders.

Germany: Europa-Park

In contrast to our examples from Indonesia and Japan, which have a more educative tone and emphasize cultural display, theme parks in Germany tend to focus on the fun aspects and on the attractions and rides for which 'culture' serves as a nice wrapping.[3]

Germany's biggest and most successful theme park, Europa-Park, is located in the village of Rust in Southwest Germany, close to France and Switzerland. More than four million people visited Europa-Park in 2008.[4] The park opened in 1975 and is owned and run by the Mack family who have a long tradition in the amusement park industry as manufacturers of fun rides. The park consists of 13 European themed zones in an area of 85 hectares, every zone representing another European country or region.[5] Most of the at-

---

Indonesia. In each of these countries, several parks have been visited with a focus on Huis Ten Bosch and Taman Mini. Another week-long stay in Japan and several visits to Europa-Park in Rust completed the fieldstudies. Fieldwork languages were Japanese, Indonesian and German. The project is part of the DFG-research group *History in Popular Cultures (Historische Lebenswelten in populären Wissenskulturen der Gegenwart)*.

3   This is the case not only in theme parks in the strictest sense, but also in other themed environments like the Tropical Islands Resort, a themed indoor adventure pool and water park in Brand (Niederlausitz), near Berlin. Here we can find a 'tropical village' with a Samoan *fale*, a Thai house, a Borneo longhouse etc. For a more detailed account of Tropical Islands Resort see Engels-Schwarzpaul (2007a); (2007b).

4   50 % of Europa-Park's visitors come from Germany and 19 % from France and Switzerland respectively (cf. Europa-Park 2010a).

5   These areas are: Germany, England, France, Greece, Holland, Italy, Austria, Portugal, Russia, Switzerland, Scandinavia, Spain, and Iceland.

tractions, shows and rides are integrated into the architecture of the themed areas.

Staging Europe – Staging Colonialism

Drawing on clichéd architecture the park showcases different European cultures: a Greek village with whitewashed houses and an ancient temple housing the water roller coaster Poseidon, a downsized replica of Shakespeare's Globe, Tudor style houses, Dutch windmills, a Russian village with gold-plated onion towers, a Valais village etc. On Europa-Park's homepage, the first sentence that comes up when searching for an overview of the various zones is: "At Europa-Park, the vision of a united continent has taken shape a long time ago. Discover the most beautiful European countries first hand. Here, Europe is not just a spot on the map, it comes alive in the hearts of the guests" (Europa-Park 2010b). The Europe staged in the park is an ideal place, beautiful and harmonious – a place far beyond actual political contention and conflict where a united Europe is alive in peoples' hearts. This is central to the park's construction of its corporate image and is continuously stressed by the Mack family who cultivate their social and political commitment promoting the European ideal.

In representing the European neighbors by means of positively connoted stereotypes, the Europe at display is a colorful, picturesque mosaic of discrete and bounded national/cultural entities, the 'essence' of which is represented by cultural icons and symbols such as windmills or onion towers. Complexity, the dynamics and hybridity of culture(s), the entanglement of cultural processes and actual social and political conflicts and inequalities as well as any hints of poverty or less beautiful aspects of life are lacking (cf. Schlehe 2004: 301). Encounters with 'real' people from the represented countries seem to be very limited and not intended so that encounters with the Other take place mainly in the form of (visual) consumption of dioramic townscapes and material culture: Multiculturality turns into a mere backdrop (*Kulisse*) (ibid.).

For the producers of the park it is essential to generate atmosphere and emotion. They did not set out to create a French zone which looks like France but which resembles what people *think* France looks like. Thus the park's producers do not intend to reproduce 'reality' but *concepts* of reality (cf. Dawid 2005: 28). They meet the visitors' expectations and conform to popular images and perceptions generated by mass media and tourist experiences. This aspect is crucial in developing new areas of the park. But the main interest is the implementation of new rides and roller coasters as one member of the Visioneering department explained to us.[6] When planning a new attraction, e.g. a water ride, the park's producers consider which kind of theme or European country would work best as a backdrop for this new attraction within a coherent themed space. In the development process the Visioneers draw on images, experiences and associations in the visitors' minds that may evoke positive feelings and memories of previous holidays and which now may be used to generate consumption – the primary purpose of the park.

Surprisingly enough, non-European cultures are also represented in Europa-Park. Integrated into the Dutch area, the attraction "Pirates in Batavia" is a boat trip where visitors can witness a fictional attack by pirates as well as life in the port town of Batavia in the former Dutch colony known as Indonesia, today. Here colonial conquest is staged as heroic adventure and exotic spectacle.[7] Visitors can experience a plethora of exotic sights and sounds – colorful scenery, animated puppets, and reconstructions as well as some originals allow them to immerse themselves in an adventurous and mysterious world. In the waiting area they are put in the right mood for the ride with dioramas showing white colonial masters bending over maps and discovering and conquering the foreign lands. When one of the authors did the ride together with a Balinese guest, the visitor was pleased and impressed to see that in Europa-Park, Batavia (today's Jakarta, capital of Indonesia) is staged primarily with reminiscences to Bali, although it is located on the island of Java: Balinese motives and ornaments, Hindu deities and Indian cultural elements are part of the décor as if Islam had not spread on Java from the 16th century on. Furthermore, the guest criticized many details for being inappropriate: a wall hanging from Thailand, mock traditional costumes, the mechanized puppet of a female dancer wearing clothes from Kalimantan together with moccasin shoes which are not used in Indonesia at all, and a feather headdress which looks like that of Native Americans. What he found most remarkable was that the puppet moved her hips in such a way a traditional Indonesian dancer never would. The Balinese visitor's comments hint at the relationship and hierarchies between different Indonesian ethnic groups on the one hand and at a claim of authenticity in their representation and display on the other hand. The German manage-

---

6   Europa-Park's Visioneering Department is responsible for creative development, design and planning of new areas, comparable with Disney's Imagineers (imagination and engineering).

7   Other examples are the "Colonial Food Station", an African themed restaurant and a jungle cruise in the "Adventure Land" passing by exotic markets with black 'cannibals'.

ment of the park, however, primarily aims at creating the 'feel' of a specific country.

Besides this thematization and idealization of colonialism in "Pirates of Batavia" there are several other references to the past in Europa-Park. Numerous genuine historical objects can be located throughout the park. The German zone contains an original part of the Berlin Wall and a half-timbered house built in 1474 *(Gotisches Vogtshaus)*. A sign emphasizes that it had been built "almost two decades before Columbus discovered America". Balthasar Castle adds some romance and a link to local history: The park is built on the grounds of this moated castle from 1442, which is still located in its original site and listed as an historical monument. In the Russian zone, visitors can enter an original training module of the MIR space station which includes an exhibition that provides insights into technical facts and the life of astronauts.

These few examples illustrate how – with the integration of historical objects – theme parks have entered the realm of open-air museums which have traditionally been associated with the task of preserving and presenting historical objects and monuments. By strengthening its museum-like aspects the theme park seems to converge its historical roots it shares with the open-air museum: the great international exhibitions and world's fairs of the 19th century (cf. Heck 1997: 52-53).

However, unlike exhibits in an open-air museum the historical objects presented in Europa-Park are lacking in context. As decontextualized bits and pieces they are deprived of their socio-cultural and historical framework and serve instead as markers of authenticity adding to the atmosphere. According to one of the park managers, originals fascinate and inspire people: "For us, they are great *mise en scène* elements – authentic and genuine historical objects perfect the illusion and intensify the feeling that one really *is* in this kind of world" (translation).

In Europa-Park, reference to the past is thus more about creating an ambiance of bygone times through an amalgam of originals, reconstructions, reproductions and 'ancient' or 'historical' looking buildings and objects. As in many theme parks, the past depicted in Europa-Park is quite unspecific, a mixture of different styles and periods:[8]

---

8   The represented historical periods range from Bronze Age to Roman Age, the Middle Ages, Renaissance, and Industrial Age to the more recent past and offer a quintessence of European cultural history (cf. Dawid 2005: 27). There is even an attraction that offers time–travel, a multimedia–show called "Wonders of the World". In a laboratory, the audience pretends to be testing a professor's time machine: A laser show with sound effects pre-

"Conflation, a habitual jumbling of various times, is another common feature of the theme park past. Both the architects and the audiences lump it all together, commingling epochs, disregarding calendars and contexts. Indifferent to linear chronology, they assign events to generalized 'good old days' (or bad old days) or to the storyteller's 'once upon a time'." (Lowenthal 2002: 16)

RIDES, THRILLS AND 'REAL LIFE'

For most visitors, the main attraction of Europa-Park is the rides. They visit the park for fun, thrill and excitement; the cultural and historical representations mainly function as a setting that adds to the park's atmosphere and attraction. Families make up 70% of all visitors, the majority of whom are repeaters. Most of the people we spoke to stated that they came to the park "because of the kids". For older children and teenagers the primary goal seems to be to ride every single roller coaster – not an easy task given the size of the park and the number of attractions; they obviously want to make the most of the scarce time and the high entrance fee.[9]

We found that the visitors very much appreciated the enormous attention to detail and the effort put into the creation and design of the European themed areas. Many of them had already visited one or more of the countries depicted in the park and for them, it was part of the fun to assess the display and relate it to their own memories and experiences which, in turn, intensified their involvement. Several people thought that Europa-Park's Greece was more beautiful than the real one.

The ubiquitous stereotyping does not seem to diminish the pleasure and fun. Even though being completely aware of the simplifications and essentializations, few visitors criticized the employment of clichés or stereotypes in the staging of cultures and histories, since after all, "it is fun and one wants to be entertained".

But it is not fun only – 'real life' pervades the theme park world in ways one would not necessarily expect: In 2005, a catholic and a protestant deacon have been delegated to the Europa-Park to hold services and to be present as pastoral contact persons mainly for visitors, but also for employees and artists.[10] There are four chapels in the park, the biggest of which, the Norwegian stave church in the

---

sents – from a Western angle – the highlights of human history from Stone Age to the present.

9   Admission prices are 35 Euro for adults and 31 Euro for children.

10   This cooperation with the Catholic Archdiocese Freiburg and the Evangelical Church in Baden plays an important role in the park's construction of a corporate identity and is due to the Mack family's active promotion of their Christian faith.

Scandinavian area, is also used for real weddings.[11] The deacons explained to us that 2/3 of the park's visitors officially belong to a religious denomination and that most of them, however, do not practice their faith (see Ron in this volume for a more detailed account of religion and theme parks).

The two clergymen see nothing exceptional in holding services or weddings and christenings in a theme park as a place of consumption and amusement since for them it is self-evident to "go where the people are". Besides approaching and addressing people and offering them advice and conversation they also welcome groups – often youth or church groups – for brief devotionals and services. Judging by the numerous entries in the Norwegian stave church's intercessions book,[12] one understands that many visitors really seem to make use of this place in a spiritual sense; some using the church for prayer, others for a quiet rest, contemplation and regeneration from the excitement and thrill of the attractions outside. For the Protestant deacon places like this open up space for deceleration (*Entschleunigung*) and enable people who would not enter a church under normal circumstances "to flirt with their church again". It becomes clear then, that the church makes use of the park to reach people they would otherwise not relate to.

The examples above show quite diverse usages and appropriations of the park. For some visitors it is more than a consumerist place of excitement and entertainment, which illustrates how leisure and tourism can become spaces not just for distraction and escapism but for dealing with all kinds of needs, in this case even the experience of tranquility, contemplation, or spirituality.

Japan: Huis Ten Bosch

Themed leisure spaces are not a Western phenomenon. In Asia, too, we find examples of themed environments created for leisure and consumption, but also for education and information. In Japan, there was a boom in the late 1980s and early 1990s when several theme parks were built all over the country in connection with tourism development and internationalization politics (*kokusaika*). Unlike *yūenchi*, which can be described as amusement parks, many of the Japanese *tēma pāku*, or theme parks, do not center on roller coasters and rides, but on the display of culture(s). Whereas there are also parks about Japanese culture and history, specific types of

---

11   In the park, the two deacons hold about 30 weddings a year.
12   The entries amount to eight to ten pages every day (cf. Langer 2007).

Japanese theme parks are so-called foreign villages, *gaikoku mura*. These parks stage foreign, 'exotic', and mostly European cultures within in Japan.[13] With utmost attention to detail they offer themed environments from architecture, attractions and merchandise to restaurants and hotels (see Hendry in this volume for another account of Japanese theme parks).

Huis Ten Bosch,[14] a park recreating the Netherlands near Nagasaki on Japan's southernmost island Kyūshū, is a puzzling example of cultural display and the biggest of Japan's *gaikoku mura*. Not only a theme park in the strictest sense, it is a 152 hectare recreation of an imagined historical Dutch town, which includes a gated community named Wassenaar.[15] Huis Ten Bosch's ambitious vision is to create a new living environment and a model city for the future; it claims to be a resort town rather than a theme park.[16] As such it stands out from the rest of the *gaikoku mura* and has been the subject of considerable academic interest so far (e.g. Gleiter 1999; Treib 2002; Appelgren 2007).

Huis Ten Bosch opened in 1992 after the enormous success of its predecessor Nagasaki Holland Village which started business in 1983, the year Tōkyō Disneyland opened.[17] Huis Ten Bosch attract-

---

13 *Gaikoku mura* and their representations of European culture(s) fit into a pattern of general fascination with the West and appropriation, recontextualization and resemantization of Western products and cultural artifacts in Japanese popular culture and consumerism (cf. e.g. Tobin 1992; for Japanese fascination with the West in *manga* and *anime* cf. van Staden 2009).

14 Huis Ten Bosch literally means "house in the woods/forest" and is also the name of the residence of the Dutch royal family in Den Haag. The theme park Huis Ten Bosch also includes a full size reproduction of this palace housing a museum.

15 Wassenaar is a town in the Netherlands north of Den Haag, known as an expensive residential neighborhood.

16 Initial investment amounted to an enormous 2.5 billion Dollar (240 billion yen). As Huis Ten Bosch was initially planned as a 'regular' town, the idea was to build a theme park subject to an entrance fee for refinancing the project. After a certain period of time – this was the plan – Huis Ten Bosch would gradually turn into a proper town and one could do without entrance fees and a theme park fenced off from public access. Eventually, this plan did not work out; in 2003 Huis Ten Bosch went bankrupt and was acquired by Nomura Principal Finance Co., Ltd. that set up a rehabilitation plan.

17 The founding myth of Huis Ten Bosch, which is the brainchild of Kamichika Yoshikuni, states that he went on a business trip to the Mediterranean with Dutch business partners and was impressed by the beautiful landscape and European culture. This trip inspired him to build a Dutch themed town in Ōmura Bay, which he thought to be at least as beautiful as the Mediterranean Sea. Similar founding myths and official narratives can be found in many *gaikoku mura*.

ed more than two million visitors in 2007. It consists of ten zones named after Dutch cities and includes hotels, restaurants, shops, attractions and several museums.

STAGING THE PAST – STAGING THE FOREIGN

Looking at the staged topics in Japanese theme parks it is striking that the majority of them recreate the past, or the foreign – or a combination of the two, foreign pasts. Thus, most of the above mentioned *gaikoku mura* refer to a premodern, historicized Europe.

This is also the case in Huis Ten Bosch's thematization of the Netherlands. According to a marketing brochure, Huis Ten Bosch offers travel in history, culture and nature. Other than Europa-Park, Huis Ten Bosch has no rides and roller coasters and its main attraction is its town- and landscapes. The park's layout has been designed in accordance with the development of Dutch cities from the 11th century fishing villages to the 20th century urban cities. Following this pattern of development of the cities which gradually expanded from the center outwards, the park's producers were able to construct an imagined history for their newly developed town and make Huis Ten Bosch appear as though it had developed organically.

Located on Ōmura Bay it has a port with a marina and canals connecting the different zones. Huis Ten Bosch's townscape is a combination of houses that are modeled after actual Dutch buildings, mostly from the 17th century, and reproductions of historical landmarks such as the Domtoren, Holland's tallest church tower in Utrecht, the town hall of Gouda, or Huis Ten Bosch palace.[18] Of course, the park also has windmills and tulip fields.

But why Holland? Huis Ten Bosch's homepage has an answer on-hand:

"During the Edo period when Japan was closed to the outside world, Nagasaki was the only port open for international trade. The arrival of a ship named De Liefde[19] from Holland in 1600 on Kyūshū Island was the start of exchange between Japan and Holland." (Huis Ten Bosch n.d.)

---

18 In an interview with Matsuda Yūji, an architect involved in the planning and construction of Huis Ten Bosch, he presented several thick photo albums replete with numerous pictures of architectural details of houses and historical buildings in Dutch cities. These were taken during a trip to the Netherlands made especially for purposes of research in Dutch town-planning and architecture in order to make Huis Ten Bosch as authentic as possible.

19 A reproduction of De Liefde is located in the port of Huis Ten Bosch. A show in the Grand Voyage Theater also stages the story of De Liefde's journey from the Netherlands to Japanese shores. Visitors watch a film

In telling "the story behind the creation of Huis Ten Bosch" the park refers to the history of Japan's encounter with the West in the Nagasaki region: The introduction of Western culture, science and technology to Japan began in Nagasaki with the arrival of the Portuguese in 1571. The Dutch followed in 1600 and the Dutch East India Company established a trading post in Hirado (Nagasaki prefecture). During Japan's seclusion from the world imposed by the Tokugawa shogunate from the early 17th to the 19th century *(sakoku)*, the Dutch, willing to trade without engaging in missionary activities, were the only Westerners allowed to stay in the country. They were ordered to move their trading post to Dejima, a small artificial island in the port of Nagasaki. During *sakoku*, Dejima remained the only window to the West, becoming an important gateway for trade and exchange. Thus Nagasaki's heritage includes Portuguese, Dutch and Chinese influences still evident in architectural styles, festivals and cuisine. Local identity in the Nagasaki area relies on this historic connection with the Dutch. Thus anchored in local history, it made sense for Huis Ten Bosch to be created as a Dutch instead of an Italian, French or Spanish village. The historically and culturally meaningful identity and the branding as an international and multicultural European resort town further worked as an authenticating strategy for Huis Ten Bosch.

Huis Ten Bosch is continuously referred to as a present day Dejima, a place introducing the Netherlands to Japan and fostering Dutch-Japanese friendship and intercultural exchange (cf. Appelgren 2007: 107). Here again, we have an idealist tone as described above in the case of Europa-Park. As a tourist destination, Huis Ten Bosch capitalizes on this local past and is often included in tours of the island of Kyūshū alongside 'real' historical sights referring to the historical connection with the West like Dejima or the city of Nagasaki.[20]

Compared to Europa-Park, however, Huis Ten Bosch puts a stronger emphasis on educational aspects. The park boasts a range of museums, like a glass and a porcelain museum,[21] and the Von

---

while being jolted and shaken in their moving seats as to create the illusion of being on board the De Liefde.

20 The small artificial island of Dejima has vanished and merged into Nagasaki due to land reclamation in the port area. In 1996 the City of Nagasaki started a restoration project to create authentic replicas of former structures and buildings. It is still underway but completed parts are already open to the public. With museum displays and recreated scenes from daily life on the island, Dejima today can also be called a themed and simulated environment.

21 The region around Nagasaki is famous throughout Japan for its tradition of porcelain production, greatly influenced by traditions and techniques from

Siebold Museum depicts the lives of the Dutch in Dejima, named after Philipp Franz von Siebold, a German physician who lived and worked in Dejima and introduced Western medicine to Japan.[22]

Huis Ten Bosch conflates both traveling to a foreign country and traveling to the past. Theme parks are "the ultimate providers of distance (other peoples, other times, other places) in the here-and-now" (Dicks 2003: 3) and thus Huis Ten Bosch's staging of a foreign – that is Dutch – past brings close an Other distant in place and time.

The contemporary proliferation of sites that display culture in a visitable form also includes stagings of the past as a visitable experience (Dicks 2003), and theme parks and heritage sites have become central modes of cultural display. In *The Past is a Foreign Country*, David Lowenthal explores the benefits and burdens of the past and the way we construct and produce, use and appropriate the past (Lowenthal 1985); for him, the past and foreign countries share an inherent alterity, a difference. At Huis Ten Bosch, they are both the Other to the Japanese visitors, offering exoticism and diversion. But it seems that only an amalgamation of the two makes for the ultimate experience. According to the informants, representations of a modern, present or urban Europe would not be very interesting or desirable to them as "London and Paris don't look very different from Tōkyō or Ōsaka!" In a globalized world, recognizable differences between different countries seem not to be significant for the Japanese consumers of Europe – or, to say it with David Lowenthal: "The *past* is a foreign country."

YEARNING FOR THE OTHER

And what do visitors make of the place? 70 % of Huis Ten Bosch's visitors are female and as there are not many attractions catering to children, the average age of the visitors being considerably higher

---

Korea and China. Porcelain from the region was brought to Europe by the Dutch East India Company and attracted European royalty and had a great impact on porcelain production worldwide. The museum explains the history of porcelain production in terms of East–West exchange and transnational linkages and houses a recreation of the Porcelain Cabinet of Charlottenburg Castle in Berlin.

22 Siebold is well-known in Japan; his name is closely associated with Western influence to Japan and with the locality of Dejima/Nagasaki. After returning to Europe he also played a crucial role in introducing Japanese culture to the West.

than in Tōkyō Disneyland.[23] Visitors are mostly Japanese, but there are also many Koreans, Taiwanese and Chinese – the percentage of Chinese guests is expected to increase considerably in the future.

Consumption of the foreign is the visitors' foremost activity: the visual consumption of the thoroughly-themed Dutch scenery and beautiful flowers, the picture-taking in designated photo spots and the consumption in shops and restaurants that sell goods and foods with a Dutch or general European touch (e.g. cheese, wine); sometimes, Japanized versions of European foods that blend the foreign and the domestic are offered. An encounter with the foreign through contact with actual people from Holland, however, seems to be very limited. In 2008, one Dutch man and six Dutch women worked at the Horseland where visitors can try horseback riding on Friesian horses, another Dutch man was in charge of the Bicycle Shop where bikes may be rent for cruising the streets of the park.[24] In its better times, Huis Ten Bosch had employed more Dutch people as performers, artists, or demonstrators of traditional crafts such as cheese making.[25] The number of Dutch employees has been reduced for financial reasons, which, in turn, accounts for a shift in the marketing of Huis Ten Bosch as a European resort town rather than as an exclusively Dutch place.

For most of the Japanese and Asian visitors it seemed not to be a specific interest in the Netherlands which made them visit Huis Ten Bosch. Those interviewed also stated that nobody visited the park explicitly to learn something about Dutch culture. Rather, it is seen as a form of educating oneself casually, a mixture of education and entertainment.

---

23 There are also some seasonal variations; in the winter season, when the park is illuminated at night, it attracts many couples, during spring and summer holidays mainly families, and off season more elderly people.

24 These Dutch informants thought of Huis Ten Bosch as very beautiful and assessed the representation of the Netherlands as very positive. One girl stated "Huis Ten Bosch is Holland over the top!" and more Dutch than the Netherlands itself.

25 There even used to be Dutch students from Leiden University's Japanese Studies department working and learning in the park. The university had an official branch in Huis Ten Bosch, adding some academic authority and credibility to the Huis Ten Bosch project. Students usually stayed one year, studying Japanese and working in the park. This cooperation ended in 2000, though it still emerges in literature about theme parks as in Clavé (2007: 44–45).

Fig. 1: A Japanese visitor at Huis Ten Bosch, dressing up Dutch

Photograph: Michiko Uike-Bormann

In terms of Orientalism – the stereotypical construction of an oriental Other versus a European Self as described by Said (1978) – Japanese visitors at foreign country theme parks reverse the gaze. Accordingly, the title of Joy Hendry's book on Japanese theme parks that deal with European cultures reads "The Orient strikes back" (Hendry 2000). Whether these types of cultural display can be interpreted as a form of "reverse Orientalism" (ibid.: 94) cannot be easily answered. The concept of reverse Orientalism might be misleading because it suggests an historical and structural symmetry between Orient and Occident, or Japan and 'the West'; it is the question of appropriation of the foreign, however, which is essential in interpreting foreign country theme parks in Japan. A central concept in this context is the notion of *akogare* (desire, yearning): a fascination with and a sense of yearning or longing towards things European play an important role in *gaikoku mura*'s negotiating of the Self and the Other.

Shoppers at Huis Ten Bosch buying souvenirs (*omiyage*) will receive them in *oranje* plastic bags; and the text printed on them reads:

"Huis Ten Bosch has crossed the border of Holland. Leading to a place nobody has seen yet. To a place of dreams carrying the torch of Europe. Joy, happiness, healing and relaxation. Huis Ten Bosch is your own utopia. The sacred crest of lions facing the crown is the symbol of our dedication of [sic] the utopia."

These catchphrases show how Japanese *akogare* for European culture draws on romanticization and idealization. But this desire is directed towards a place that does not exist in reality, it is a utopian vision for the Japanese visitor in search of the foreign experience. Huis Ten Bosch is marketed as a place nobody has seen yet, a place of dreams – still it is Europe, European culture and European architecture in an idealized and essentialized form – which is the source of these Japanese dreams.

Jörg Gleiter (1999) reads Huis Ten Bosch and its combination of premodern Dutch architecture on the surface and Japanese high tech behind the scenes as an example for his interpretive approach in which he views Japanese foreign country theme parks as machines separating technical modernity from its Western aesthetic equivalent. This renders an aestheticized and premodern Europe in opposition to a highly technologized and modern Japan. Europe loses its referential power as a role model for Japan's modernity and is staged in terms of musealization and miniaturization as the premodern Other to Japan (ibid.). Whereas one may agree with Gleiter's arguments, another perspective should be added: Central to the philosophy of Huis Ten Bosch is its eco concept, which is claimed to be based on the Dutch approach to environmental preservation and aims at the construction of an ecocity in harmony with nature.

According to Ikeda Takekuni, leading architect of the project, a committee of 15 persons was set up to conduct all the planning work. It consisted of Japanese and Dutch experts, divided into those in charge of the "hardware" and those responsible for the "software". The former included professionals in architecture, city planning, landscape gardening etc., the latter experts on art, history, culture and literature.[26] Ikeda explains how modern rationalism and the ideology and sense of values which supported the development of science and technology of 20th century's civilization have led to a weakened sensitivity towards nature and the development of a throw-away culture damaging the harmony between man and nature. Using the Netherlands as a role model for further development, one could restore this harmony (Ikeda 1994: 9-10).[27] At Huis Ten Bosch this is realized through state-of-the-art Japanese technology in recycling, waste water reprocessing and other ecological measures to reduce pollution and the destructive effects of modern urban

---

26 The committee included only one woman.
27 Since Huis Ten Bosch is built on barren reclaimed land, the Netherlands with their century-long experience in land reclamation served as a good role model. Judging by his several visits to the Netherlands, Ikeda believes that the Dutch pay tribute to their cultural heritage and preserve old buildings and structures and protect their environment (Ikeda 1994: 10).

life. All this technology is concealed from the visitors' gaze and banned to the park's backstage areas underground.

Huis Ten Bosch's living environment with its aesthetic environs in harmony with nature, picturesque European alleys and its vast landscape carefully designed for visual consumption contrast with the densely populated Japanese cities; their crowded living conditions and ubiquitous signs, wires and advertisements. Our informants all stressed the importance of sensing a European atmosphere (*yoroppa no funiki wo ajiwau*) as the main reason to visit Huis Ten Bosch. According to them, a day out in this Dutch themed environment offers relaxation and relief from a stressful urban life. As *ikūkan* (space of difference), a place opposed to everyday life,[28] Huis Ten Bosch brings a both temporally and spatially distant place into the here and now and provides the Japanese visitors with alternatives to their daily lives. This suggests that, in the eyes of theme park visitors, Holland – and Europe, in general – can indeed serve as a role model for Japan in terms of lifestyle, attitudes towards leisure and work-life-balance as well as aesthetic townscape and ecological consciousness. The park producers' and visitors' perspectives should also be taken into account, as they shed another light on Hendry's interpretation of a reversion of orientalist discourse and especially on Gleiter's approach of a reversion of established hegemonies and role models which tends to regard only the outer form and appearance of the Dutch theming in the park.

The ambiguity regarding the relationship between the West and Japan becomes clear in the following statement by Ikeda: "Although we basically used Dutch architecture as a model, we tried to build a town based on the manners and concepts of the city of Edo" (Ikeda 1994: 10).[29] Huis Ten Bosch's philosophy thus appears to be an amalgamation of Dutch and Japanese elements which re-examines the historic connection with the Dutch and allows the Japanese to recognize anew traditional Japanese values as represented by the Edo period.

Theming at Huis Ten Bosch, however, has long since transgressed the limited space of the theme park:

"Thus, its [Huis Ten Bosch's] (curious) message is that in another country, at another time, one can find the means to develop a feasible community center for Japan today and in the future. Behind this assumption lies the notion that the experience of the theme park can provide the basis for themed living – by eradicating the borders around the theme park, the theme park is rendered

---

28　As such it shows parallels to Foucault's concept of other space (Foucault 1986).

29　Edo is the former name of today's Tōkyō and was residence of the Tokugawa shogunate from 1603–1868.

coincident with the contemporary landscape and viable as a setting for contemporary communal and individual living." (Treib 2002: 216-217)

TRANSGRESSIONS AND THEMED LIVING

The boundaries of theme parks are permeable and we find processes of transgression between themed areas and daily life. Huis
Ten Bosch is a case in point.

Directly adjacent to the park area lies Wassenaar, an upper
class gated community. It consists of villas modeled after Dutch
houses from the 17th to the 19th century, with no two houses looking the same. Wassenaar was built during the bubble economy
when real estate prices were high and catered to wealthy people
from metropolitan regions who would enjoy the green scenery and
exclusive lifestyle. Condominiums were included for the less affluent.[30] Wassenaar goes even further than the rest of Huis Ten Bosch
in transgressing the boundaries between simulated and 'real' life
and it "blurs the distinction between development as a theatrical
background against which to be seen and development as an actual
stage upon which to live" (Treib 2002: 227).

But why should one want to live in a Dutch town in Japan? In
everyday life, there are many inconveniences for the inhabitants of
Wassenaar: there are no grocery stores, no schools and only sparse
employment possibilities in the vicinity. Residents stated that they
chose Wassenaar as a home because of the green scenery, beautiful
environment and quiet location; one even said that it was somehow
'unreal' and like a dream (yume mitai) to live in a place like Wassenaar, given the usual cramped and bad housing conditions in Japan. None of those interviewed had moved to Wassenaar because
they wanted to live in a Dutch style house or in a Dutch themed environment; they would not have cared if the houses had been
French or Italian style. For them, Wassenaar represents an upscale
European lifestyle; living in an exclusive neighborhood like this
seems to be a reaffirmation of the upper middle class identity of
most of the inhabitants. Many of them are seniors who enjoy Wassenaar's tranquility and a leisurely lifestyle which they conceptual-
ize as European and rather non-Japanese, considering the long
working hours of a typical middle class Japanese salaryman (sararī-
man/employee).

Whereas Huis Ten Bosch provides an anti-structure, a place opposed to normal life for visitors, there are also inhabitants of Was-

---

30 According to an inhabitant, there are 120 villas, only 20 of which are permanently occupied. The rest of them are used as holiday homes or owned
   by companies as time-share units, a few are vacant. 70% of the condominiums are permanently occupied.

senaar whose normal life takes place primarily in this themed environment as Huis Ten Bosch is also their workplace. For people such as a shop-keeper in Huis Ten Bosch's shopping arcade Passage, the director of Huis Ten Bosch's hotel division, or the dentist who has his office in Huis Ten Bosch Hills,[31] Huis Ten Bosch is more than 'just' a theme park – it is a place of everyday social life and practice.[32]

This also applies to the members of Huis Ten Bosch's volunteer association Huis Ten Bosch Supporters who offer information and assistance and act as contact persons for visitors and facilitators between the company and patrons. For the volunteers the park is an essential part of their life and becomes meaningful as a place for educating themselves, and for meeting people. It also functions as a source of identity as many volunteers take pride in being a part of Huis Ten Bosch the philosophy of which they identify with. The way in which the volunteers relate to the park shows how the sense of community and attachment to this themed environment transgresses and shifts the boundaries between utopian spaces of difference and 'real life' communities.

Indonesia: Taman Mini Indonesia Indah

In the 20th century young nation states in Southeast Asia strove to create and legitimize their particular national narratives and to foster social cohesion[33] and national unity by various means (Houben 2008), including history teaching, museums, memorials, the mass media – and cultural and ethnic theme parks.

---

31 Huis Ten Bosch Hills is a housing complex with high-rise apartments not directly adjacent but close-by the park area. It looks quite like other apartment buildings in urban areas in Japan, but facades are in a brick-red tone and the overall style seems neo-classical to match the rest of Huis Ten Bosch.

32 In public, though, Huis Ten Bosch is conceptualized as a theme park rather than a 'real' or ordinary town. As a place it has a blurred and ambiguous identity ranging from tourist destination and recreational site to ambitious town planning project (cf. Appelgren 2007: 138).

33 Southeast Asia is subject to a large number of cultural conflicts – conflicts which thematize culture. The main issues of those – primarily domestic, often violent – conflicts are historicity and cultural identity (including language and religion) (Croissant/Trinn 2009). Therefore, the public understanding of history, the management of cultural pluralism, and the construction of collective identities is of utmost importance.

In Indonesia, with its large variety of ethnic groups,[34] where the Dutch colonial rule ended in 1945, one of the most important popular sites for staging history, tradition and ethnicity is its central culture park, Taman Mini Indonesia Indah (Beautiful Indonesia-in-Miniature).[35] This state-sponsored park, which can be designated as something between open-air museum, ethnic theme park and edutainment site opened in Jakarta in 1975. 'Typical' traditional houses *(rumah adat)* from all administrative provinces,[36] depictions of ethnic groups and so-called indigenous customs,[37] monuments, places of worship for all officially recognized religions, recreational and entertainment facilities, and 16 museums (including one of modern science and technology)[38] are arranged together in an area of 150 hectare around an artificial lake which displays the islands of Indonesia.

STAGING SUHARTO'S CULTURAL POLICY

The national identity is constructed and shaped in Taman Mini which was the ultimate icon of President Suharto's authoritarian New Order Regime (1966-1998).[39] Culture politics was and still is based on the motto "Unity in Diversity" (*Bhinneka tunggal ika*), and Taman Mini perfectly illustrates the New Order's hegemonic ideology and the management and integration of ethnic diversity and cultural heritage. The President's wife, Ibu Tien Suharto, had the idea for Taman Mini, inspired by Disneyland in the United States[40] and Timland in Thailand. She said: "In this park both national and

---

34   There are about 300 ethnolinguistic groups, but about 45% of the population is Javanese.

35   Literally: garden of beautiful Indonesia-in-Miniature, which refers to the symbol of a garden with many flowers - or in this case ethnic groups.

36   This part of the park could also be designated as heritage park or as living museum. Few people in Indonesia still live in the manner suggested by the reconstructed displays. So-called traditional architectural forms can nowadays mostly be found in government buildings, hotels etc.

37   There are popular entertainment, classical and folk cultural performances as well as religious ceremonies.

38   The museums range from Museum Indonesia which displays regional cultures and an Asmat museum focussing on artefacts from this particular ethnic group to a war museum, dedicated to the war of independence, and modern and didactically sophisticated museums for science and technology.

39   We can refer to prolific research on this aspect: Anderson 1990; Pemberton 1994; Hitchcock 1997; Errington 1997; Schefold 1998. These are excellent studies on the role played by nationalism. But they are based on the displays themselves, without considering the visitors' actual reception of them.

40   Disneyland's influence is most obvious in a cinderella-like children's palace which looks quite alien amongst the traditional houses.

regional cultures and arts can be further developed, so we not only know our past and beautiful heritage, but also revive and develop the cultures and arts of the various regions, adding more beautiful color to our national culture" (Tien Suharto 1978: 13). Strengthening the union and unity of Indonesia and providing recreation, education and information for both domestic and international visitors was the explicit purpose for building this park, but even so, it caters primarily to a market of domestic rather than foreign tourists. Yet, only the 'indigenous' *suku* (ethnic groups) were recognized and displayed as components of the Indonesian nation. Material representations of the immigrant Chinese, Indian, Arab, or European cultures were lacking. And there were no plural visions, no traces of migration or any other flows, mixes and hybridization of cultures. Each province was represented by an exhibition area (*anjungan*) with traditional houses of the dominant or most famous ethnic group(s), typical items like ethnic costumes and artifacts, cultural performances, art exhibitions, souvenir shops, stalls selling regional food and, last but not least, human representatives: to date province government employees (at present between five and 30 persons per province) act as guides for the visitors. They provide explanations on the culture, traditions and resources of their respective home areas.[41]

Although the official narrative and founding myth complies with Ibu Tien's original idea and invention of the park stimulated by Disneyland, the colonial legacy should not be overlooked. The colonial exhibitions in Batavia in 1893, in Surabaya in 1911, and in Semarang in 1914, themselves derivations of the great international exhibitions and world's fairs of Europe, provided models for a fusion of visual displays of tradition with modernity, progress and technological development (Coté 2000). The exhibition in Semarang presented the world in miniature as well as a "native section" in which "all major regions of the archipelago were represented in architectural and craft displays organized by the colonial administration" (ibid.: 360). Hence, the basic concept of Taman Mini can be traced back to Dutch colonial constructions and classificatory systems: the colonial mapping of *adat* communities, culturally discrete areas, each with their own defined cultural norms (Antlöv 2005: 44; cf. also Hefner 2001:

---

41 Many of these guides or 'cultural ambassadors' do not know much of their culture of origin either because they have been living in Jakarta for a long time or because they are just civil servants without any special cultural knowledge. An interesting example is served by an old Papua guide who had left his home village at the age of seven and had gone to a missionary school in the province capital. When asked about his cultural knowledge, he said that he had read many books by Dutch missionaries and early anthropologists. Some of the things he explained to visitors were thus extracts from old Western writings.

42).[42] Decontextualized, essentialized and simplified regional cultures serve for the celebration of romanticized and exoticized traditions. As Bruner formulates: "Cultural heterogeneity is put in its place – fixed, aligned, domesticated – and turned into recreational exhibition" (Bruner 2005: 121). Orientalization and self-orientalization appear to be two sides of the same coin.

Thus, the staging of the past does not intend to broaden knowledge about or to raise a consciousness for history in the Western sense of the term. With the exception of the war museum, colonialism is almost completely excluded, as are all other external influences. As appears to be common at Europa-Park, Huis Ten Bosch or any theme park, conflicts, social criticism, violence and anything which could disturb a harmonious atmosphere and the illusion of continuity between the past and the present are by and large omitted.[43] Rather, the project of traditionalization (cf. Schlehe 2008) refers to a bygone age of timeless tradition and the creation of nostalgic markers of identity in the process of nation building.

The fact that colonialism and other foreign influences are not often thematized in Taman Mini may be interpreted in a similar vein to Hoffstaedter's (2008) suggested interpretation of Malaysia's culture parks when he writes:

"The parks leaning to the display of a traditional Malay past in the present may be seen as a negation of the colonial impetus in modernization. The aim, then, seems to be not so much to erase the colonial past from history as to take Malay culture out of its context, so that modernization can stand as an indigenous Malay achievement." (Hoffstaedter 2008: 145)

If we apply this interpretation to the Indonesian park, it is supported not only by the focus on traditional houses but also by most of the displays at the museums in Taman Mini which stress Indonesian achievements and the role of Indonesians in history.[44] The issue is the Self rather than the Other.

Another crucial and closely related aspect pertains to cultural identity which is strongly focused on display and performance. Anthropology regards the house in Southeast Asia as a model for social organization, not separable from kinship, gender and the economic domain, and as a manifestation of beliefs (Sparkes/Howell

---

42 Indonesia's earliest nationalist thinkers were highly influenced by Dutch scholars in the early 1920s. They saw in the country's traditional system *(adat)* something that gave it a natural coherence (cf. Bourchier 2007: 114).

43 There are remarkable exceptions, for instance, in the Aceh pavilion where many old photographs of resistance against the Dutch are to be found. This can be explained by the long lasting war against Dutch colonialism in Aceh.

44 Sartono Kartodirdjo (2001: 14) designates this as 'history from within'.

2003). But as one visitor explained in respect to the traditional hous-es *(rumah adat)* in Taman Mini: "The houses are empty and mean-ingless if there is no dance performance taking place, no gamelan music played."[45] This can be understood in several ways: Visitors do not miss written explanations in order to relate to the historical ob-jects displayed. Nobody complains about the scarce information provided. Although in some houses there are historical dioramas or glass display cases, most often filled with traditional wedding clothes, there is hardly any ethnographic or historical background knowledge provided.[46] Yet, the informants did not expect historical everyday life-worlds to be staged, contextualized, explained, or ana-lyzed. In general there is a tendency for many Indonesians to relate to the past not primarily through history or historiography for the sake of knowledge but by strengthening themselves through im-agined participation (in felt co-presence) in the power and glory of former heroes or powerful kingdoms. Accordingly, with many houses or replicas of aristocratic origin,[47] the visitors demand art perform-ances rather than explanations of social organization. The traditional arts – not daily life – are seen as the core of traditional culture. Since colonial times, and enforced by Suharto's New Order, there is a strong tendency that neither practices nor beliefs are considered *adat*: "Only that which can be displayed and performed is *adat*" (Ac-ciaioli 1985: 158). Further stimulated by tourism, for many ethnic groups "culture has become art, ritual has become theatre, and prac-tice has become performance" (ibid.: 153). Culture *(kebudayaan)* re-fers to houses, clothing, ornamentation, and folklore, music, songs, dances, theatre. Therefore Schrauwers speaks of "showcase culture" (Schrauwers 1998).

RE–NEGOTIATION IN THE POST–SUHARTO *REFORMASI* ERA

In a recent book published by Taman Mini (Jaya 2008), its editors do not mention any changes in the park's concept as if everything had stayed the same since its formation. Nevertheless, the crucial question remains: What happened to Taman Mini after the fall of Suharto in 1998, and what is going on in the present period follow-ing the reforms (post-*reformasi*) of democratization, decentralization, regional autonomy, and the related establishment of new provinces?

---

45 All citations from interviews are translated from Indonesian by the author.

46 Contrary to what the literature of the 1990s claims, there are indeed dif-ferences between the displays in the pavilions. For instance the Batak house has a diorama with an old kitchen, whereas in the Moluccas the sea and its products are in the centre.

47 The houses are often larger than any traditional houses in the respective regions of origin.

What does this cultural arena that is so closely connected to the overthrown New Order regime mean to producers and visitors today in an Indonesia that has now become a model for reconciling Islam with modernization and liberal democracy?

Due to recent democratization processes, local cultural politics are on the rise and increasingly influential with regard to the cultural and political constitution of the nation-state in Indonesia. Consequently, one would have expected the park to lose all significance and face closure in the context of this new emphasis on regional cultural identities instead of the former centralized one.

But surprisingly the contrary is evident: numerous new buildings are under construction and the park has been extended, arguably due to the new provinces' striving for representation in Taman Mini with the construction of huge and impressive new houses. But even in the areas of old provinces,[48] many notable new houses are erected because the regional governments are being urged to represent more ethnic groups than just the dominant one.[49] Interestingly enough, this has begun to change the public display of power relations and hierarchies: whereas before, Java, as the site of state power, hegemonic over the other ethnic groups of Indonesia, had clearly been the center of attention in the park, there is considerable symbolic competition, now. Provinces with oil supply and other valuable natural resources (e.g. Riau, East-Kalimantan) have benefited from the economic decentralization and they demonstrate their wealth with impressive pavilions and cultural performances in Taman Mini. For instance, Lampung, a province which never attracted much attention, looks far more impressive now than Central Java – what a revolution!

PERFORMING CULTURE, CULTURAL PROPERTY AND NEO-NATIONALISM

There are remarkable differences between the presentations of material and performed culture at Taman Mini. Performances tend to be far more vivid and open to changes, and there are also differences between traditional and modern ones. Since 1987 the park has organized a performance program (consisting of song contests, dance, music, and theater) with the explicit aim of preserving local cultural practices, especially by means of *adat* ceremonies. Traditional performances in popularized short versions are put on stage,

---

48 At present, the park houses 26 old regional pavilions and six pavilions of new provinces.

49 The guides/representatives often belittle other ethnic groups within their own provinces. A Bugis guide, for instance, described the Toraja as "primitive" while a Minangkabau guide did the same with regard to the Mentawai.

but they are not necessarily superficial and shallow. In the Central Java and Yogyakarta areas of Taman Mini, for instance, *ruwatan massal* (purification) ceremonies may be attended: in the three-hour-shadow plays performed by famous and highly respected *dalang* (puppeteers/masters), many offerings are dedicated to the gods and spirits of Java. The people to be purified – all dressed in white clothes without any personal accessories – pray, receive blessings and are ritually washed by their parents and the *dalang*. By taking part in the ceremony they feel strengthened against all evil. Everybody born in a special constellation who can afford to pay the price of 1.5 million rupiah (ca. 120 Euro) should participate in the ceremony at least once before marriage.

On the other hand, there are performances which stress openness to modernization and to the global world culture. The park's manager for art and culture says after *reformasi* a door has now been opened and there is a "window to the world": music from India, American theatre and the Chinese *barongsay* (dragon dance) are being performed. According to his future vision of the park, there will be an original Indonesian area and further areas displaying Chinese, Indian, Arab, and European influences.

One of the biggest events organized in Taman Mini is New Year's Eve. The Selamatan Agung ceremony for the celebration of the Islamic and Javanese New Year in 2008 was a very colorful mixture of cultural performances, interreligious dialogue, and political statements. Representatives of all religions sat and prayed publicly side by side in a hall packed with numerous invited guests from Jakarta's high society. At the same time there was a national meeting of *orang paranormal* (people with extraordinary power, traditional healers) and the sultans and rajas from 104 traditional kingdoms and sultanates across the archipelago were present. They themselves in royal gowns and their families in traditional garb and glittering jewelry, they took part in the obligatory national hymn, a combination of rituals and prayers, a short and modernized version of a royal *bedoyo* dance, a parade *(kirab agung)* with offerings from different areas of Indonesia and a joint meal *(selamatan)*. Participants explained that the purpose of the rituals was to pray for the country's prosperity and to protect the country against future disasters (cf. Schlehe 2010a). A royal procession through the whole park was supposed to transfer (by proxy) new strength to the various parts of the country. On the following day an English language newspaper cited the Cultural and Tourism Ministry's director general of cultural values, art and film, Mukhlis Paeni, who stressed the importance of reviving traditional cultural events, not only as part of the newly launched Visit Indonesia Year 2008 program to lure tourists but also to safeguard the country's cultural heritage: "These kings and sultanates are guardians of our roots. We must encourage them to take active roles otherwise we will see more of our heritage claimed by other countries" (Fitri 2008).

This refers to several unintended effects of democratization in Indonesia. One is that through decentralization – by which the government attempted to achieve an increase in local democracy – the traditional elite regained symbolic power and status (cf. van Klinken 2007). For them, Taman Mini proves to be the perfect place to demonstrate this. Another point is an increasing neo-nationalism which is expressed in nationalist rhetoric.[50] A revival of *adat* goes hand in hand with claims for heritage and culture as national property, especially with regard to the country's neighbor, Malaysia. Recently, there had been much public discussion and excitement about a certain mask dance *(reog)* which was said to have been 'stolen' by Malaysia although it had originated in East-Java (Ponorogo). In the last few years, this dance has therefore been performed in Taman Mini more frequently than before. Nationalist and anti-Malaysian sentiments strengthen cultural identity, especially as there are – besides economic competition and various other conflicts[51] – considerable disguised and denied cultural resemblances between Indonesia and Malaysia (cf. Harrison 2006).

In an interview Mukhlis Paeni explained that at present, the goal of pluralism being already achieved and people knowing about their ethnic differences, the new leading concept for Indonesia is multiculturalism and a stress on similarities. Hence, there are also efforts to prevent the return of hierarchical structures.

In a similar manner and probably as an effort for reconciliation there has been a strong emphasis on cultural similarities between Indonesia and its neighboring countries during an opening of an exhibition of traditional spinning tops (*gasing*) in Taman Mini in December 2007. These toys were explicitly introduced as icons of the unity of Southeast Asia. Thus, the park can be seen as an arena for the negotiation of local, national and regional identities. Only the

---

50 "Neo-Nation" was also the title of an exhibition in Yogyakarta in early 2008 where in his opening speech the Sultan stressed the necessity of protecting Indonesia's cultural property and heritage. But at the same time he stated: "This new nationalism can only be achieved by cultural dynamics in the form of cultural transformations (Nasionalisme baru itu hanya bisa dicapai melalui dinamika budaya dalam wujud transformasi budaya)" (Hamengku Buwono X).

51 Indonesia and Malaysia compete for tourists, and there are conflicts as e.g. a territory dispute over a maritime region in the Sulawesi Sea, an area presumed to be rich in oil and gas; seeming complicity of Malaysian firms in illegal logging; reports about the maltreatment of Indonesian migrant workers in Malaysia (Rüland 2009).

global world and the ultimate Other is – with the exception of some performances – excluded. This is in accordance with the fact that Indonesia has actively resisted at least some aspects of cultural globalization (cf. Kluver/Wayne Fu 2008: 336).

THE VISITORS' PERCEPTIONS AND AGENCY

The management's claim of four million visitors per year is difficult to verify,[52] but in any case, there are considerable numbers of visitors on Sundays and on public holidays. Due to the cheap entrance fee (Rp. 9,000; ca. 70 European Cents), company outings and picnics often take place there. People make use of the park as a recreational site, and it seems that the vast majority of them are not as much interested in the displays as they are in the green space, the cleanliness, and the relaxing atmosphere. A striking example is the Timor house which has been designated as a museum after Timor Leste's independence in 2002. The visitors do not expect to learn about the history of the violent events leading to East Timor's separation from Indonesia, but they do enjoy sitting in the shade of the next pavilion or taking photos of each other with the exotic background of puppets in East Timorese costumes (Schlehe 2004).

Migrants, however, usually visit the pavilions of their region of origin. Children (and at times adults, too) come to learn traditional dances – notably not necessarily from their own region of origin (Choesin 2000) –, students (mostly school children) have the task of collecting information on traditional ethnic cultures, and many visitors come to see the traditional or modern performances or attend private or public ceremonies taking place in the park. Some come for religious purposes as in the above described *ruwatan* ceremony or they go to the Mosque or to a Church. In these cases, there is a transgression between the visitors' playful liminality and everyday life in a themed environment. In any of these cases, people perform their contemporary culture at Taman Mini.

These findings correspond to Hoffstaedter's results from Malaysia that "Domestic tourists actually thought themselves well represented by the exhibits" (Hoffstaedter 2008: 147). Although some people criticize certain details of the houses as not being authentic, the vast majority of the interviewed visitors liked the houses, and were often proud of the ones representing their homelands. Bruner recognizes a reaffirmation of Toba Batak migrants' identity at Taman Mini: "What the Toba Batak see there is what they know they are. They do not discover the Other but rather witness a perform-

---

52 Before 1998, the number of visitors per year is said to have ranged between seven and eight million.

ance of themselves in a different context" (Bruner 2005: 227). According to him, the displayed items evoke memories of a total cultural heritage and a vital ethnic identity, thereby going far beyond the Indonesian government's official reading of Taman Mini (ibid.: 229); in this sense, the contemporary social life and practice of the audience supersedes the producers' intention.

Although there is definitely a potential for the audience to reinterpret the intended meaning in order to strengthen ethnic identities, there is little evidence for Bruner's idealistic interpretation. The houses might be used as community centers for migrants, where they have informal meetings or celebrate marriages, Idul Fitri or Christmas, watch performances, use their language, and share feelings of homesickness. The houses are also significant for children of migrants who have been born in Jakarta.[53] Nevertheless, the production of a 'vital ethnic identity' does not seem to concur with the actual reactions of the visitors, who remain largely unmoved by the parks' cultural fashionings. Many know traditional houses from school lessons and pictures and are not really interested in the details. The majority of Jakartans are more attracted to entertainment orientated parks (e.g. the commercial Ancol Park) and to other themed spaces, including the very popular life-style oriented, fully air-conditioned shopping malls, which are predominantly decorated in a modern Western style but increasingly so in an Islamic fashion.

Interestingly enough, Taman Mini's manager for public relations, an anthropologist, took one of the authors to another site which he thought was typical for the display not of Indonesian but of foreign cultures at present: a luxurious housing complex on the outskirts of Jakarta (Cibubur). Gated communities are places where we find the Other to Indonesian culture and architecture: Neo-Victorian, Classic European and Mediterranean houses and even a little theme park staging not only an Indonesian 'village' but also a Chinese, a Japanese, and an American one.[54]

It seems that the people of Jakarta are less impressed by the cultural and national elements reproduced within Taman Mini than the government would hope, and that the foreign-themed living space, on the other hand, is regarded as highly prestigious.

---

53 An old Papua who had been working in Taman Mini since 1975 said that his own children knew Papua houses only from Taman Mini because they never had the opportunity to visit their father's homeland.

54 Whereas a newly opened Buddha Bar in Jakarta does not seem to be successful because it is not regarded as exotic by Jakartans (Kleine-Brockhoff 2009), a huge project is currently being planned in Bali: An original Bavarian village (Desa Bavaria) with full infrastructure will be erected there (Desa Bavaria n.d.).

A Novelty: The Chinese Park

The most striking novelty in Taman Mini in recent times has been the construction of a Chinese Indonesian Cultural Park (Taman Budaya Tionghoa Indonesia) within the park. This is of enormous symbolic significance as the Chinese in Indonesia (3% of the population) had suffered from severe discrimination for a long time, particularly under Suharto's rule. Public expression of Chinese culture had been suppressed for more than three decades, and there were many outbursts of violence against Chinese, including a particularly severe one in 1998.[55] Only after the introduction of *reformasi* and the abolition of the legalized discrimination against the Chinese from the year 2000 on a public revival of their culture and traditions took place (Knörr 2009).

The significance of the building of a Chinese Indonesian Cultural Park within Taman Mini can only be understood within this context. It is a powerful symbol for the new recognition and self confidence of the *suku* Cina (ethnic Chinese) as an integral part of the Indonesian nation. Reference to history plays an important role here as it is especially the integration of the Chinese into the idea of Indonesian heritage and their contribution to the struggle for independence which is stressed as reason and legitimation for their incorporation in Taman Mini.[56] Concurrently, however, the investment of Chinese business in Indonesia is contingent on a feeling of safety in light of past unrest, and one could also read the inclusion of Chinese culture in the park as a calculated attempt to allay such fears.[57]

The Chinese Indonesian Cultural Park, which is still under construction, consists already of a huge entrance gate, several houses, and a museum. A library, souvenir shops, and food stalls will follow. Contrary to the other areas of Taman Mini which are financed by the provinces, everything will be paid by private donors.[58]

---

55 The Chinese Indonesians were scapegoated for the economic misery of the financial crisis. During the riots, women of Chinese origin were systematically raped. As Robinson formulates: "The public facade of the normative paternalism of the New Order was stripped away to reveal the violent militarized masculinity at its core" (Robinson 2009: 3).

56 Obviously, anti-colonial resistance is still the "yardstick of legitimacy" as van Klinken puts it (2001: 339), what is new is the inclusion of the Chinese in the nationalist myth.

57 It is said that the Chinese Indonesians control approximately 80% of the national economy.

58 Once more we can see an interesting parallel to the colonial exhibition in Semarang in 1914. Here the Chinese pavilion was quite exceptional as it was not under the supervision of the colonial administration. The wealthy

*Fig. 2: The Chinese Park in Taman Mini during
Lunar New Year's celebrations in 2010*

Photograph: Judith Schlehe

A business woman in charge of construction explained in an interview in late 2007 that the park would focus on Chinese culture. Religion, she explained, was not yet deemed appropriate in the park setting, although since 2005 Confucianism (*konghuchu*) has been officially recognized as one of the six government-sanctioned religions.[59] However, this acceptance had not yet filtered down to the lower levels of bureaucracy and the general consciousness of the majority of Indonesians, a feeling which was confirmed several times in interviews and conversations. Many people stressed that only Chinese 'culture' would be acceptable for public display, and not religion. Despite a strongly delineated sense of cultural and religious culture which seemed to be circulating in general discourse, within a year (by the end of 2008) concrete plans were being made to build a Chinese Confucian-Buddhist temple (*klenteng*) next to the other houses of worship in Taman Mini. This Klenteng Kong Miao is presently under construction and has a projected date of completion for the end of 2010. As the majority of Indonesians still see Chinese as 'foreign' in relation to the 'local' culture and population (cf. Knörr 2009: 87), it remains to be seen how the public will comment on the new buildings: Will they welcome them as a proof of a new multicul-

---

Chinese community of Semarang had provided the land for the exhibition and was a major financial guarantor (cf. Coté 2000: 357).

59 88% of the Indonesian population are Muslims, 9% Christians (Catholics and Protestants), 3% Hindus and Buddhists.

turalism or inclusive citizenship – or will they criticize them for being alien to Indonesia or as further evidence of Chinese affluence?[60]

Although at first glance, there seems to be nothing new about the concept and staging of culture in post-*reformasi* Indonesia as reflected in Taman Mini, a second glance reveals shifting power relations and a new emphasis on multiculturality which run parallel to a revival and re-invention of tradition (*adat*). This is closely related to both neo-nationalism and commercialization of culture. It seems to be unclear at the moment how these trends will be negotiated with two other strong tendencies: contemporary Islamic revival and the cosmopolitanism of the upper class. Further observation and analysis would need to include not only other themed spaces, but the wider cultural discourses in Indonesia.

Conclusion: Contested Practices and Meanings

Although we do not claim a systematic comparison between Germany, Japan and Indonesia here, some striking issues emerge in a reading of these spaces. Perhaps most importantly is that due to cultural transfers the parks are based on similar principles (order, cleanliness, security, and control as it was introduced by world fairs, colonial exhibitions, and Disney-parks) and appear alike but bear highly unstable and varied meanings in their respective contexts. The intersecting influences of politics, economy and culture – the contested meanings of 'culture' – come to the fore.

It is obvious that all three parks are showcases of invented traditional cultures. A stereotypical past represents continuity, belonging, nostalgia, romanticism and, last but not least, a 'light' version of the Other. When cultural parks depict the past, they do not relate it to historic validity, actual memory, or present experiences and subjectivities; they are sites of timelessness, instead.

To consume something different and detached from the everyday world is entertaining and relaxing as long as it does not make any further demands. Differences in time, space, and culture would be potentially irritating and disturbing since they might raise questions. Therefore, in all three cultural theme parks, differences are codified and (re)produced in a way that reduces them to static essences and simple markers of identity and identification. The image of Self and Other, the discourse of cultural alterity, is carefully orchestrated: in Europa-Park cultural diversity comprises of decora-

---

60 The celebration of Chinese New Year (Imlek) in February 2010 in Taman Mini indicates a tendency to incorporate Chinese–Indonesian cultural elements in the popular culture of Indonesia (Schlehe 2010b) (see figure 2).

tion and background to the rides which provide the main attraction; in Huis Ten Bosch the remaking of a Dutch city in Japanese terms changes an actual place to an imaginary territory created as a utopian counter-image for Japanese consumers; whereas Taman Mini represents an image of Self (Indonesia) rather than Other. More precisely: it locates the Other (ethnic diversity) within the Self (national culture) by inclusion or exclusion as was illustrated by the example of the new Chinese park.

Hence, the display of differences and their functions vary with the structural setting: In the family-run business in Germany, difference serves to attract and entertain as many paying visitors as possible; in the company-owned park in Japan, business orientation is combined with edutainment goals, staging difference as romance; in the state-sponsored context in Indonesia, the conceptualization and visualization of cultures as parts of the national identity is in the foreground.

One has to keep in mind that the categories of Self and Other are not fixed and that the boundaries between them are not definite and static, but constantly shifting and blurring. In Huis Ten Bosch the 'foreign past' is appropriated by relating the local history to the Netherlands; in Taman Mini one's 'own past' is differentiated by the display of diversity and varying degrees of exoticism and by ongoing processes of inclusion and exclusion; whereas in Europa-Park, the multitude of equally valued cultural sources of a 'European self' is stressed and the incorporation of a colonial Other is made to appear natural. Thus, ambiguities are not completely excluded but the parks make them appear manageable – which adds immensely to their attractiveness.

Finally, there are notable transgressions between the ludic and liminal spaces of theme parks and present-day life-worlds (cf. Lukas 2007 and Lukas in this volume). Themed environments are naturalized in that they provide contexts for more and more aspects of modern urban life. Shopping malls, restaurants, city centers, private houses, internet-based cyberworlds are themed as well. Theming is no longer restricted to bounded spaces like theme parks, but intrudes into the everyday contexts outside their boundaries and vice versa: Life takes place in themed frameworks. It is therefore only a matter of logic that religion is also increasingly thematized, both within cultural parks and in newly created religious theme parks.[61] Some visitors of Europa-Park as well as of Taman Mini make use of

---

61 Examples are the Holy Land Experience in Orlando, Florida, the Akshardham Cultural Complex in New Delhi, a Hindu temple theme park as described by Brosius (2009), or Bukit Kasih, a little inter-religious park in North Sulawesi, Indonesia (for Protestant themed environments cf. Ron in this volume).

these themed environments in a spiritual sense. And, as the Japanese case showed, some people even move permanently to a theme park, making it their normal cultural context. Thereby they ultimately blur the boundaries between cultural park, resort, and gated community, as well as the one between what has been called the anti-structure of tourism and their everyday life.

Obviously there is a remarkable class division. Presently, only the rich can afford to live permanently in themed environments and most cultural parks are not accessible for everybody due to the high entrance fees (state-sponsored Taman Mini is an exception in this regard). It needs to be mentioned that visitors pay for the exclusion of all disturbances. They can consume foreign settings without being confronted with foreign people; they can appropriate cultures and history without being faced with political, social, or ecological problems. Indeed, encounters and mutual understanding of culturally diverse peoples, life-worlds, and mental concepts, are avoided and excluded to guarantee pleasure. It is therefore our concern that most theme parks and themed environments are models for a world and for a social order as we think it should *not* be. Nevertheless, different actors make different use of these spaces, and there is definitely the potential to negotiate and overcome one-dimensional representations of Self and Other.

References

Acciaioli, Greg. 1985. "Culture as Art: From Practice to Spectacle in Indonesia." *Canberra Anthropology* 8.1/2: 148-172.

Anderson, Benedict. 1990. "Cartoons and Monuments: The Evolution of Political Communication under the New Order." *Language and Power. Exploring Political Cultures in Indonesia.* Ed. Benedict Anderson. Ithaca: Cornell University Press. 170-185.

Antlöv, Hans. 2005. "The Social Construction of Power and Authority in Java." *The Java that Never Was. Academic Theories and Political Practices.* Eds. Hans Antlöv/Jörgen Hellman. Münster: LIT Verlag. 43-66.

Appelgren, Staffan. 2007. *Huis Ten Bosch. Mimesis and Simulation in a Japanese Dutch Town.* Göteborg: Göteborg University.

Bourchier, David. 2007. "The Romance of adat in the Indonesian Political Imagination and the Current Revival." *The Revival of Tradition in Indonesian Politics. The Deployment of adat from Colonialism to Indigenism.* Eds. J.S. Davidson/D. Henley. London: Routledge. 113-129.

Brosius, Christiane. 2009. *India Shining. Cosmopolitan Pleasures of India's New Middle Classes.* New Delhi: Routledge (forthcoming).

Bruner, Edward M. 2005. *Culture on Tour. Ethnographies of Travel.* Chicago/London: University of Chicago Press.

Choesin, Ezra M. 1990. "Kebudayaan Sanggar Tari: Kerangka Struktur Interaksi dalam Sanggar Tari Padepakan D.I. Yogyakarta di TMII." *Skripsi Sarjana Universitas Indonesia, Fakultas Ilmu Sosial dan Ilmu Politik.* (unpublished).

Clavé, Salvador Anton. 2007. *The Global Theme Park Industry.* Oxfordshire: CABI.

Coté, Joost. 2000. "'To See Is to Know': The Pedagogy of the Colonial Exhibition, Semarang, 1914." *Paedagogica Historica* 36.1: 340-366.

Croissant, Aurel/Christoph Trinn. 2009. "Culture, Identity and Conflict in Asia and Southeast Asia." *Asien: The German Journal of Contemporary Asia* 110.2009: 13-43.

Dawid, Anka. 2004. "Poseidon, Pommes und Piraten – zum Unterhaltungswert der Archäologie im Europa-Park Rust." *Museumsblatt* 38: 26-30.

Desa Bavaria. n.d. "Desa Bavaria Projekt." http://www.desabavaria.de/ (accessed 2 Apr 2010).

Europa-Park. 2010a. "Der Europa-Park in Stichworten." http://presse.europapark.de/lang-de/c822/m359/d7328/default.html (accessed 15 Jan 2010).

Europa-Park 2010b. "Themepark-Overview." http://www.europapark.de/lang-en/c244/default.html (accessed 2 Apr 2010).

Dicks, Bella. 2003. *Culture on Display. The Production of Contemporary Visitability.* Maidenhead: Open University Press.

Engels-Schwarzpaul, Christina. 2007a. "'A Warm Grey Fabric Lined on the Inside with the Most Lustrous and Colourful of Silks': Dreams of Airships and Tropical Islands." *The Journal of Architecture* 12.5: 525-542.

Engels-Schwarzpaul, Christina. 2007b. "Travel in Tropical Islands: Enemies Coexisting in Peace." *Interstices. Journal of Architecture and Related Arts* 8: 21-30.

Errington, Sherry. 1997. "The Cosmic Theme Park of the Javanese." *Rima* 31.1: 7-36.

Fitri, Emmy. 2008. "Kings, Sultans, Royal Families Mark Islamic New Year in Style." *Jakarta Post* 11 Jan.

Foucault, Michel. 1986. "Of Other Spaces." *Diacritics* 16: 22-27.

Gleiter, Jörg H. 1999. "Exotisierung des Trivialen – Japanische Themenparks." *Voyage. Jahrbuch für Reise- und Tourismusforschung 3: Künstliche Ferienwelten – Leben und Erleben im Freizeitreservat.* Köln: DuMont. 48-66.

Harrison, Simon. 2006. *Fracturing Resemblances. Identity and Mimetic Conflict in Melanesia and the West.* New York/Oxford: Berghahn.

Heck, Brigitte. 1997. "Freizeitpark und Museum – Der Europapark Rust als Fallbeispiel." *Beiträge zur Volkskunde in Baden-Württemberg* 7: 39-57.

Hefner, Robert W. 2001. "Introduction: Multiculturalism and Citizenship in Malaysia, Singapore, and Indonesia." *The Politics of Multiculturalism. Pluralism and Citizenship in Malaysia, Singapore, and Indonesia*. Ed. Robert W. Hefner. Honolulu: University of Hawaii Press. 1-58.

Hendry, Joy. 2000. *The Orient Strikes Back: A Global View of Cultural Display*. Oxford: Berg.

Hitchcock, Michael. 1997. "Indonesia in Miniature." *Images of Malay-Indonesian Identity*. Eds. M. Hitchcock/V.T. King. Kuala Lumpur: Oxford University Press. 227-235.

Hoffstaedter, Gerhard. 2008. "Representing Culture in Malaysian Cultural Theme Parks: Tensions and Contradictions." *Anthropological Forum* 18.2: 139-160.

Houben, Vincent. 2008. "Historische Repräsentationen des Eigenen und Nationenbildungsprozesse in Südostasien." *Selbstbilder und Fremdbilder. Repräsentationen sozialer Ordnung im Wandel*. Eds. Jörg Baberowski et al. Frankfurt/New York: Campus. 209-234.

Huis Ten Bosch. n.d. "About Huis Ten Bosch." http://english.huis tenbosch.co.jp/about_htb/index.html (accessed 2 Apr 2010).

Ikeda Takekuni. 1994. "Hausutenbosu keikaku no kokoro [The Spirit of the Huis Ten Bosch Project]." *Hausutenbosu: sekkeishisō to sono tenkai* [Huis Ten Bosch: Design Concept and its Development]. Ed. Nihonsekkei. Tōkyō: Kōdansha. 8-11.

Jaya Purnowijaya, ed. 2008. *tmii, pesona indonesia*. Jakarta: TMII.

Kleine-Brockhoff, Moritz. 2009. "Wer braucht eine asiatische Traumwelt mitten in Asien?" *Stuttgarter Zeitung*, 2 Mar.

Klinken, Gerry van. 2001. "The Battle for History after Suharto. Beyond Sacred Days, Great Men, and Legal Milestones." *Critical Asian Studies* 33.3: 323-350.

Klinken, Gerry van. 2007. "Return of the Sultans. The Communitarian Turn in Local Politics." *The Revival of Tradition in Indonesian Politics*. Eds. J. Davidson/D. Henley. London: Routledge. 149-169.

Kluver, Randolph/Wayne Fu. 2008. "Measuring Cultural Globalization in Southeast Asia." *Globalization and Its Counter-forces in Southeast Asia*. Ed. Terence Chong. Singapore: Institute of Southeast Asian Studies. 335-358.

Knörr, Jacqueline. 2009. "'Free the Dragon' versus 'Becoming Betawi': Chinese Identity in Contemporary Jakarta." *Asian Ethnicity* 10.1: 71-90.

Langer, Stephan. 2007. "Theologie mit Seifenblasen. Die Kirchen gehen im Europa-Park neue Wege." *Konradsblatt* 36. Available

at http://www.konradsblatt.badeniaonline.de/scripts/inhalt/ar
tikel.ph?i=2187&konradsblattID=395&status=archiv&jahr=2007
& inhalt= (accessed 2 Apr 2010).

Lowenthal, David. 1985. *The Past Is a Foreign Country*. Cambridge/
New York: Cambridge University Press.

Lowenthal, David. 2002. "The Past as Theme Park." *Theme Park
Landscapes. Antecedents and Variations*. Eds. Robert Riley/Te-
rence Young. Washington: Dumbarton Oaks Research Library
and Collection. 11-23.

Lukas, Scott. 2007. *The Themed Space. Locating Culture, Nation,
and Self*. Lanham, MD: Lexington Books.

Pemberton, John. 1994. *On the Subject of 'Java'*. Ithaca: Cornell
University Press.

Robinson, Kathryn. 2009. *Gender, Islam and Democracy in Indonesia*. Oxon: Routledge.

Rüland, Jürgen. 2009. *Deepening ASEAN Cooperation through Democratization? The Indonesian Legislature and Foreign Policy-
making*. Unpublished manuscript.

Sartono Kartodirdjo. 2001. *Indonesian Historiography*. Yogyakarta:
Kanisius.

Schefold, Reimar. 1998. "The Domestication of Culture. Nation-
building and Ethnic Diversity in Indonesia." *Bijdragen tot de
Taal-, Land- en Volkenkunde* 154.2: 259-280.

Schlehe, Judith. 2004. "Themenparks: Globale Kulturrepräsentati-
on, nation building oder Freizeitvergnügen?" *Blick nach vorn.
Festgabe für Gerd Spittler*. Eds. Kurt Beck/Till Förster/Hans Peter Hahn. Köln: Rüdiger Koppe. 298-310.

Schlehe, Judith. 2010. "Anthropology of Religion: Disasters and the
Representations of Tradition and Modernity." *Religion. Special
Issue on Religions, Natural Hazards, and Disasters* 40.2 (forth-
coming).

Schlehe, Judith/Boike Rehbein. 2008. "Einleitung: Religionskon-
zepte und Modernitätsprojekte." *Religion und die Modernität von
Traditionen in Asien. Neukonfigurationen von Götter-, Geister-
und Menschenwelten*. Eds. Judith Schlehe/Boike Rehbein.
Münster: LIT Verlag. 7-17.

Schrauwers, Albert. 1998. "Returning to the 'Origin'. Church and
the State in the Ethnographies of the 'To Pamona'." *Southeast
Asian Identities. Culture and the Politics of Representations in Indonesia, Malaysia, Singapore, and Thailand*. Ed. Joel S. Kahn.
Singapore/London: Institute of Southeast Asian Studies. 203-
226.

Suharto, Tien. 1978. "Preface." *What and Who in Beautiful Indonesia. I. A Contribution to the Motherland*. Jakarta. (Indonesian
original 1975).

Sparkes, Stephen/Signe Howell, eds. 2003. *The House in Southeast Asia: A Changing Social, Economic and Political Domain.* London: RoutledgeCurzon.

Tobin, Joseph J., ed. 1992. *Remade in Japan – Everyday Life and Consumer Taste in a Changing Society.* Birmingham/New York: Vail Ballou Press.

Treib, Marc. 2002. "Theme Park, Themed Living: The Case of Huis Ten Bosch." *Theme Park Landscapes. Antecedents and Variations.* Eds. Robert Riley/Terence Young. Washington: Dumbarton Oaks Research Library and Collection. 213-234.

Van Staden, Cobus. 2009. "Heidi in Japan. What Do anime Dreams of Europe Mean for Non-Europeans?" *IIAS Newsletter* 50.2: 24.

Imagineering Tailor-Made Pasts
for Nation-Building and Tourism:
A Comparative Perspective

Noel B. Salazar

Imagineering, a concept originally developed by the Walt Disney Company, denotes the combination of creative imagination and technological engineering in the 'theming' of goods, services and places, so that visitors develop memorable experiences of their visit (cf. Imagineers 1996). The principal goal of imagineers is to create a successful balance between illusion and reality, and this by engaging all senses and moving peoples' emotions within a fantasy environment in which, paradoxically, the fantasy feels completely real. Disney's innovative methods have been successfully copied across the globe to create attractive (and predominantly leisurely) landscapes. Depending on the theme, the images, imaginaries and representations that are manipulated to construct and enact peoples and places differ. Interestingly, the myths, histories, and fantasies imagineers draw upon to appeal to people's desires and personal imaginations can be either ones associated with the locality at hand or others that are more widely circulating, from the most spectacular fantasies to the most mundane reveries (cf. Salazar 2010).

In the context of developing countries, these imaginaries – unspoken representational systems that are culturally shared and socially transmitted – draw upon colonial and postcolonial visions of Self and Other that circulate through popular culture media, (travel) literature, and academic writings in disciplines such as anthropology, archaeology, and history (cf. Salazar 2008). Since such imaginaries are multi-scalar, themed environment developers can use any number of cultural representations at any scale to present a seemingly cogent image, no matter how inaccurate, that appeals to visitors. In this chapter, I critically analyze the imaginaries at play in culturally themed environments. What happens when historical imaginaries of culture(s) are institutionalized, standardized or commoditized? Across the globe, sanitized versions of historical cultures are replicated and converted into sellable products. Such imagineering tends to be conservative, a flattening and faking that continues to serve the status quo. I illustrate some of the issues at stake by way of ethnographically grounded case studies from Indonesia and Tanzania, showing how themed environments are cleverly used to (re)produce as well as contest currently dominant imaginaries of postcolonial nations and their inhabitants. The methods I relied upon during the fieldwork include participant observation, semi-structured interviews, and the collection of secondary sources (e.g. promotional brochures and local newspaper clippings). The spatial as well as temporal comparisons serve to highlight that, while the contexts might be different, the processes at work are strikingly similar (cf. Salazar 2007).

Building Modern Postcolonial Nations through Historical Culture Parks

Anderson (1991) has described in great detail how the popularization of cultural heritage plays a pivotal role in the forming of nations as imagined political communities. It is no coincidence that young countries around the world, especially postcolonial ones, have seen in national theme parks a unique vehicle to build their nations. A heritage-themed national park serves to underline the message that the nation's foundation are its people, its different customs and cultures, held together by (often invented) common traditions. As Dahles notes, "[t]hese cultural displays provide [...] nations with the opportunity to come to terms with the rapid transformations brought about by modernization" (2001: 12). By integrating minorities into a coherent visual narrative, a national theme park promotes a sense of both nationalism and modernity. However, in multi-ethnic postcolonial nations such as Indonesia and Tanzania, this process unavoidably involves decisions "as to which cultures to privilege and which to ignore" (Stanley 1998: 59). Because imagineering simplifies peoples and places for easy consumption, themed environments inevitably become sites of struggle and the production of 'unity in diversity' through multicultural displays opens up debates about whose reality (past, present and future) is being represented, promoted, narrated, and for whom. Consolidating the cohesion and the unity of the nation through theme parks clearly comes at a price. The examples below from Indonesia and Tanzania illustrate some of the dynamics at work.

Taman Mini Indonesia Indah

Taman Mini Indonesia Indah (Beautiful Indonesia in Miniature) is a 160-hectare open-air park, situated on the south-eastern edge of Indonesia's capital, Jakarta. The park was conceived by Siti Harti-nah, the spouse of General Suharto, after visits to an analogous project in Bangkok, Thailand and to Disneyland, USA in 1971 (cf. Pemberton 1994). It was established in 1972 and officially inaugu-rated in 1975. Taman Mini is centred around a vast reflecting pond containing small artificial islands that form a large natural map of Indonesia, accessible by pedal boat but best viewed from the cable car or elevated train that pass overhead. The rationale behind the national theme section of the park was to give visitors a glimpse of the diversity of the Indonesian archipelago in a single location, as a symbol of the country's motto of *Bhinekka Tunggal Ika* (Unity in Di-versity). From the air, one sees alongside the mini-archipelago 26 massive pavilions – one for each Indonesian province in existence at the time the park was built. These constructions form the heart of the national theme park. The pavilions are dominated by traditional *rumah adat* (customary houses), containing sanitized permanent ex-hibits of arts and crafts and the customs and lifestyles of the peoples from the province, typically the costumes they might wear at a wed-ding, the furniture they use in their homes, and their jewellery. Sometimes it is possible to taste local food, browse through tourism brochures, or purchase souvenirs. During the weekends, there are often free traditional dance performances, films, and cultural shows. Indonesians going to Taman Mini to learn about and take pride in the multicultural heritage of their country and in their particular regional roots, far exceed the numbers of foreign tourists.

Anthropologists have, each in their own way, tried to make sense of Taman Mini (cf. Acciaioli 1996; Bruner 2005: 211-230; Errington 1998: 188-227; Hitchcock 1998; Pemberton 1994). Many have fo-cused on how the park represents the past as an integral part of the future, through a present which is continuously rendered as cul-tural icons of regional tradition and how it serves as a tangible ex-pression of modernization (Anderson 1991: 176-177). Indonesia's New Order government (1965-1998) sought to identify one single cultural type for each province, and to play down the extent and breadth of the actual ethnic diversity they had inherited from the Dutch colonial era. The name of the park is significant too, "as in it the cultures of Indonesia's constituent provinces have been ex-tracted as objects of 'beauty'" (Yamashita 2003: 44). In the political logic of the New Order, a flattening of both time and space, the simulacrum of Taman Mini actually exceeds the real Indonesia be-cause it is less confusing, more ordered, and can be understood and experienced as a whole. Diversity is represented for the most part as differences between domesticated different-but-same administrative regions rather than between local cultures or societies. Taman Mini thus draws together ethnicity and reinvented locality so that each presupposes the other (cf. Boellstorff 2002). As Adams notes, "all of the regional exhibits display material from the same set of categories (weapons, dances, marriage garments, baskets, etc.), regardless of the relevance of these categories to the local groups in question" (1998: 85). Adherence to this uniform set of groupings conveys the message that in spite of superficial differences, there is inherent commonality between the diverse ethnic groups (cf. Acciaioli 1996). In Boellstorff's words, "after all, what is Taman Mini if not model for a human zoo where ethnolocalities are habitats – cages for culture – and the state a zookeeper?" (2002: 31).

From the very beginning, Taman Mini was envisioned as a twin project of raising national consciousness and developing tourism. Unfortunately, most scholars have focused on the former and neglected the study of the latter. Suharto himself strongly believed that tourism would increase (foreign) revenue, enhance the nation's international status and foster domestic brotherhood. As Adams points out, the fact that Indonesia did not have a Ministry of Tourism, but rather a Ministry of Tourism, Post and Telecommunications, reflected "the premise that tourism is inseparable from communications and, hence, nation-building" (1998: 85). Taman Mini's fate after Suharto's forced resignation in 1998 is symbolic of the wider crisis of the Indonesian national project. Since then, the park has faced declining attendance and general neglect. It is still promoted through school textbooks as the place to learn about all of Indonesia and to master the archipelago's cultural diversity. However, there is invariably a discrepancy between the producers' intentions and audience reception (cf. Salazar 2010). Today, Taman Mini is one of Jakarta's most popular recreational spots, crowded on weekends with families and teenagers from the metropolis' growing middle class. Despite attempts to market the park internationally, overseas visitors have declined sharply.

Bruner (2005: 211-230) looks at alternative ways of interpreting Taman Mini, at how various Indonesian ethnicities operating within an official state-sponsored site impose their own meanings and social practices, appropriate the place, and undermine the official interpretation of the site. What is presented to domestic tourists, especially to those originally from the same province, he argues, is experienced as life, not as representation. An indicative study, conducted in 2005, suggests there is a clear mismatch between what is desired and expected by contemporary visitors and what were the original intentions of the founders of the park (cf. Wulandari 2005). The main motivation to visit is recreational, although two thirds of the visitors expect to learn something about Indonesian art and culture during the course of their visit. Like elsewhere in the world, Indonesian youngsters are actually more interested in modern technology and fashionable products than outdated ethnic traditions. Rather than being worried about the cultural unity of their country, they prefer to dream about the world 'out there' – a theme that is central in Dunia Fantasi (Fantasy World), Jakarta's other major attraction park, with imagineered sections named Europe, America and Africa. Thus Taman Mini versus Dunia Fantasi, or "socialistic nationalism" versus "capitalistic internationalism" (Jones/ Shaw 2006: 134).

While the nation-building project seems more and more difficult to realize, the link between Taman Mini and tourism is becoming more pronounced. During the New Order era, inhabitants of the provinces were often notably absent in Taman Mini. After the fall of Suharto in 1998, some provinces started bringing their people in and using the permanent exhibitions and cultural events no longer for the purpose of nation-building but, rather, to promote tourism to their region. Because seven new provinces have been created since 2000, Taman Mini needs some rethinking. The park does seem to have some adaptive capacity as is exemplified by the pavilion of the breakaway former province of East Timor, which has become the Museum of East Timor, a memorial to the period of Indonesian rule. Interestingly, one of the latest projects is the development of a Chinese Museum (Taman Budaya Tionghoa Indonesia), to document the culture and history of the large Chinese diaspora (over seven million people), highlighting their lasting contribution to an ever-developing multi-ethnic nation (cf. Schlehe/Uike-Bormann in this volume).

KIJIJI CHA MAKUMBUSHO

Kijiji cha Makumbusho (Village Museum) is situated on the north-western outskirts of Tanzania's economic capital, Dar es Salaam. The idea for this open-air museum dates back to the colonial era. Shortly before independence in 1961, the then Curator of Ethnography at the National Museum, a certain Mr. Wylie, envisioned the creation of an open-air exhibition to reflect the rich and diverse traditions of architecture. As a child of his time, he realized that "the increasing popularity of modern housing spelled doom for traditional styles and techniques, of which he hoped to preserve selected examples for both display and research purposes, including in each sample relevant household paraphernalia" (Masao 1993: 57). Mr. Wylie also planned for traditional handicraft activities, to breathe life into such a themed environment. It took time to convince the postcolonial Museum Board of the value of the salvage proposal, but in 1965 a modest budget was set aside to buy a small plot of land (two hectares) and create the museum (which, certainly when compared to the Indonesian example, looks more like a tiny hamlet than a full-sized village). Like other national theme parks, the Village Museum wants to be a place, as the official website indicates, "where you can see all Tanzania in one day" (Village Museum n.d.).

Similar to the core section of Taman Mini, but much smaller in scale, the centrepiece of the Village Museum is a collection of authentically constructed dwellings, meant to show traditional life in various parts of Tanzania. Thirteen 'traditional' units were built, representing the major varieties of vernacular architecture of mainland Tanzania (a modern, urban unit was added later for the sake of representativeness). As in the Indonesian case, there is an assumed equivalence between peoples and places, although in Tanzania the selection happened not along administrative regions but ethnic groups. The idea is one of a linear relation between ethnicity and architectural style: "Tanzania has more than 123 tribes, each of which builds its own type of house" (Mbughuni 1974: 35). However, due to shortage of funding and space, only the following groups are represented: Zaramo, Rundi, Chagga, Maasai, Haya, Hehe, Fipa, Nyakyusa, Nyamwezi, Gogo, and Ngoni. Each group has a house typical of those found in the home area, and all houses are equipped with typical items and utensils normally used by the respective people – but the museum is devoid of those same people.

Since its inception, the Village Museum has been state-funded and the Tanzania Tourist Corporation (now Tanzania Tourist Board) greatly aided in its establishment. As in Taman Mini, the Village Museum often hosts traditional music – especially *ngoma* (drumming) – and dance performances. Some of the country's most famous wood-workers, coming from the Makonde and Zaramo ethnic groups, have worked under the museum's patronage and displayed their wares on its premises. Occasionally, there have been special festivals centred on live presentations of one particular ethnic group (e.g. the Ethnic Days Festival). During these festivities, there are not only performances, but visitors can also enjoy traditional cuisine. In an attempt to promote Tanzanian cultures and traditions, over 20 ethnic groups have presented their cultures at the Village Museum.

On days without special activities, the absence of people around the houses is striking and gives the place a rather desolate and very artificial feel. In fact, it was always the explicit aim not to exhibit 'exotic' ethnicities. This goes back to President Nyerere, who was of the opinion that "human beings could not be preserved like animals in a zoo" (quoted in Schneider 2006: 114). At the same time, the first period of independent Tanzania was marked by "a general move to banish and segregate from lived experience 'traditions' that did not fit into an image of modernity" and move them to museums, places "where things rest outside the current of time and life" (Schneider 2006: 114). In the Village Museum one finds, physically taken out of everyday life, traditional housing designs, which the Tanzanian state was actively combating as outdated and to be overcome, not least through its grand project of villagisation (cf. Scott 1998). As Schneider points out, "the 'museumization' of traditions, physically and rhetorically, was an exercise in boundary creation – and a statement that such traditions had no other place in modern life" (2006: 114).

Preserving and maintaining vernacular architecture with extremely scarce resources has led to many financial and administrative challenges (cf. Masao 1993). Major and extensive repairs had to be undertaken on the house units. As concerns interpretation, signposting at, and pathways among the different house displays have been completely redone. Much of this was realized with the help of the Swedish African Museum Program, a network joining museums in Sweden and in African countries. In 1996, the program held a Conference on African Open-Air Museums in the Village Museum, and it also twinned the latter with the Skansen Open-Air Museum in Stockholm. This is a highly symbolic linkage, because Skansen was established in 1891 as the first open-air museum in the world, offering a great model for how the nation as an imagined community can be materialized in very concrete ways. Such global twinning programs reinforce the idea that the construction of national heritage follows globally diffused patterns.

Nowadays, the Village Museum attracts very few visitors. There are the occasional visits by expatriate families living in Tanzania or backpackers who landed in Dar and are waiting to travel elsewhere. International volunteers visit Makumbusho as part of their cultural immersion package. The museum administration is convinced that taking Tanzanian people in the Village Museum back to their cultural heritage enables them to see what was good or useful in their (imagined) past and which is worth incorporating in contemporary life and living (cf. Mwenesi 1998). However, there is only a very rudimentary culture of visiting museums among the Tanzanian public (and most cannot afford to do so). The decision by the managers to allow the use of their premises for traditional performances such as initiation ceremonies and wedding dances, and for organizing events to promote indigenous cuisine and traditional dances, seems to be a successful way to draw in the crowds. Among locals, Makumbusho is particularly popular in the evenings as a place where they can have *nyama choma* (roasted meat) and beer while enjoying some live music – often Congolese musicians playing Souk.

From Display to Experience, from Village Museums to Tourism Villages

While, to a certain extent, both Taman Mini and the Village Museum still fulfil their role in nation-building, through time this has become less of an urgent preoccupation of the respective governments. What is clear is that neither of the two national theme parks ever brought in the expected foreign tourist dollars. Given the precarious economic situation in both Indonesia and Tanzania, other strategies were developed to reach this second goal. This happened in a rapidly changing national and global context. In the 1990s, helped by the end of the Cold War, the world witnessed the rise of the so-called 'experience economy' (cf. Pine/Gilmore 1999). Imaginaries became a key vehicle in what is now called experience tourism. Instead of promoting places to see – sightseeing – tourism stakeholders across the globe started developing experiential packages, marketed in multi-sensorial languages. Museums and museum-like parks were considered old-fashioned. Instead, otherwise lived spaces were readied for easy tourism consumption. As developing nations such as Indonesia and Tanzania are going through a process of rapid democratization and the central governments have much less grip than before, shrewd entrepreneurs have seized the opportunity to commoditize the nostalgic potential of daily rural (often read as 'primitive') life. The imagineering, i.e. the production of visions, of images and of representations of the villages and their inhabitants, was largely initialized by external actors. The focus on the power of imaginaries in the new economy is also linked to another field, that of storytelling (cf. Löfgren 2003). Not simply showcasing cultural heritage, but being able to narrate it in imaginative ways has become an important asset (cf. Salazar et al. 2009). In what follows, I describe how these general trends took shape in Indonesia and Tanzania.

DESA WISATA

"By Desa Wisata [Tourism Village] we mean a village which offers whole atmosphere of village seen from its socio cultural life, customs, which is potential to be developed into tourism components, such as: attraction, accommodation, food and beverages, and other tourist needs. The development of a tourism village does not mean to alter what already exist, but more of calling forth its potentials which already exist in the village and cannot be separated from the village itself. In general a village one which can be developed into tourism village is a village which has already good conditions in economy, social cultural, physical natural surrounding, non-urban, and possess uniqueness in tradition. [sic]" (Suherman 2001: 105)

The economic crisis of 1997 and the fall of Suharto in 1998 radically changed Indonesia in many aspects. After more than three decades under a centralized (and autocratic) national government, the country embarked on a democratization process that quickly gave rise to regional demands for decentralization of power. In response, the central government decided to implement a new policy, devolving many of its administrative authorities to local officials at the regency and city level. In order to finance their new bureaucratic duties, local administrations needed money. Not surprisingly, many turned to tourism as an easy way to obtain the required funds. Although many *desa wisata* (tourism village) programs were originally launched by the central government (which saw them as fundamental tools of national development), local authorities were quick to appropriate the initiative. In central Java, for example, many tourism villages were launched around the same time in which the policies of regional autonomy became effective. Various villages jumped on the wagon, seeing the concept of a tourism village as an alternative to big-scale tourism developments over which they had virtually no control and from which they benefited little.

There is certainly a growing market for village tourism, especially among international tourists and those Indonesians and expatriates living in big urban centres. Tourism villages invite visitors to see and experience the daily life of the villagers: the cycle of a rice field, the visit to home-industries who produce local food and medicine, and craftsmen who make souvenirs. By rethinking what counts as cultural heritage to include the everyday, the alternative and that which has not yet been memorialized in guidebooks and official histories, another kind of Indonesian experience becomes available to the visitor (cf. Salazar 2005). Different villages have different grades of tourism involvement, depending largely on physical and non-physical characteristics of the respective villages and their proximity to other tourism attractions. Some offer a homestay experience, others are only places to stop over and have lunch. Below, I briefly discuss some of the old and new ways in which various stakeholders have tried to implement the concept of tourism-themed villages in central Java. Although the intentions are different, the examples show that the work of cultural preservationists and the interests of government and private entrepreneurs clearly overlap in the development of tourism villages.

On World Tourism Day in 1999, the then Minister of Tourism, Arts and Culture, Marzuki Usman, inaugurated Tembi (Bantul Regency, south of Yogyakarta) as a model of *desa wisata* (cf. The Jakarta Post 1999). Over the years, this project has received many national and international awards for sustainable tourism. The man behind the top-down tourism development in Tembi was an Australian entrepreneur who had chosen the picturesque village as the base of his lucrative export business of high-end handcrafted products (cf. James 2003). His renovation of some of the village houses in Dutch colonial style had fascinated many of his visiting expatriate friends and this is how the idea developed to let (affluent) visitors stay overnight. During the day, the guests could relax around the swimming pool, enjoy the local food, visit the nearby school for dancing and gamelan, pass by the craft workshop, and buy souvenirs at the gallery. To guarantee an 'authentic' view for the guests, the businessman bought the rice paddies surrounding his houses. Word-of-mouth led to a rapid increase in visitors and, after a couple of years, the Australian eventually decided to make his model house private again, thereby halting virtually all tourism development.

Tanjung (Sleman Regency, north of Yogyakarta) is often mentioned by the Indonesian authorities as a 'best practice' tourism village (cf. Ardika 2006). Like its neighbours, Tanjung was a poor farming village, rice cultivation being the major source of income. National government officials introduced the idea of village tourism to local authorities and villagers in 1999 and, in 2001, the villagers officially declared their village as a *desa wisata*. In 2003, representatives of the village signed a Village Tourism Charter and formed an official committee to oversee tourism development. The principal target market is (school) groups from larger cities (cf. Janarto 2006). Tanjung offers almost 25 programs to learn cultural activities such as dancing, making traditional textiles, knowing more about Javanese architecture, or learning how to cultivate rice. These programs are not only recreational in nature but also facilitate the acquisition of knowledge and the experience of new skills. Young villagers are usually the ones guiding visitors around and narrating the stories of the village (often without much training to do so). Interestingly, they usually present the quickly modernizing village life as time-frozen and pre-modern (cf. Salazar 2005).

A local NGO selected Candirejo (Magelang Regency, north of Yogyakarta), near the heavily visited monument of Borobudur, as one of ten villages in which to develop so-called community-based tourism. The village was selected for its original architecture and traditional daily life, beautiful rural scenery and natural resources – all things deemed worthy to be preserved. Financially supported by the Japan International Cooperation Agency and UNDP, and with expertise provided by UNESCO, Candirejo village was prepared to receive international tourists. In 2003, it was officially inaugurated as *desa wisata* by I Gde Ardika, the then Minister of Tourism and Culture. Given its proximity to a World Heritage Site, Candirejo has attracted far more international tourists than domestic visitors. It is noteworthy that the Minister chose Sambi, another village selected by the same local NGO, to announce the start of Indonesia Heritage Year in 2003 (cf. Wahyuni 2003). In both instances, the representational emphasis is clearly more on the (imagined) pre-modern past than on the present or the future.

CULTURAL TOURISM PROGRAM

"Cultural tourism is a people tourism that enables tourists to experience authentic cultures combining nature, scenery, folklore, ceremonies, dances, rituals, tales, art, handicrafts and hospitality – giving a unique insight into the way of life of the people while offering a complementary product to wildlife and beach based tourism." (TTB 2007: 2)

The Cultural Tourism Program (CTP) in Tanzania was launched in 1995 by a Dutch aid agency. In co-operation with projects already started by German and Finnish aid agencies, CTP was set up as a network of local communities, mainly Maasai in northern Tanzania, operating independently from each other and offering individually developed tour packages. These include campsites, homestays, traditional food and beverages, trained guides, and local tours involving natural heritage (forests, waterfalls, and caves) and cultural attractions (historical sites and visits to healers, story tellers, craftsmen, and cooking mamas). The main activities on offer are hiking, learning about local culture and customs, mountain climbing, cycling, canoeing, and fishing. The name CTP refers to the involvement of local people in organizing the tours and in guiding tourists through the attractions while showing them the aspects of their daily life, culture, and history. The Dutch agency financed the various CTP modules, controlled their expenditures, and organized some minimal training for local tour guides. The Tanzania Tourist Board (TTB), on the other hand, is responsible for promoting CTP to both local and international travel agencies and tour operators (cf. De Jong 1999).

Helped by the fact that experiential 'meet the people' tourism was increasingly in vogue, CTP experienced a great boom in its first years of existence. The modules are visited by both tour operators and independent low budget tourists. Because the organizing Dutch agency published widely about the success of CTP, the project was nominated for various international awards. In 2002, the International Year of Ecotourism, CTP was heralded as Tanzania's good practice example of sustainable development by the World Tourism Organization (WTO 2002: 237-240). The modules are also widely praised in guidebooks such as the *Lonely Planet* or *The Rough Guide*. Due to its perceived economic and institutional sustainability (and because it had been conceived as a five-year project from the very start), the Dutch withdrew from the project in 2001. Since then, there has been a declining cooperation between the different communities involved (cf. van der Duim et al. 2005). Currently, CTP has 26 participating communities and many villages are waiting to join. The examples below illustrate the challenges involved in representing ethnic diversity through village tourism.

As mentioned before, the Maasai are CTP's main 'attraction'. Due to countless coffee-table books, movies and snapshots, everybody seems to know this widely dispersed group of semi-nomadic pastoralists and small-scale subsistence agriculturists (cf. Salazar 2009). To foreign tourists, the sight of a virile Maasai warrior, dressed in colourful red blankets and beaded jewellery, evokes the romantic image of a modern noble savage. Capitalizing on this, quite a number of cultural tours to Arusha villages are marketed and sold as visits to Maasai *bomas* (settlements), while the villages are, at best, ethnically mixed. In Il'kidinga, a village of Arusha people (who are influenced by Maasai ancestry but who abandoned livestock herding in favour of settled cultivation), villagers benefit from the perceived similarities with the Maasai to attract more tourists. For example, they hang out red blankets as a recognizable visual marker of 'Maasai-ness'. Some of the youngsters who guide visitors around the area will 'play' the Maasai, albeit with varying success.

Tourists visiting the CTP of Mkuru do get to see 'real' Maasai, but the local guides accompanying them are often Meru (farmers, traditionally settled around the base of Mt. Meru). Their knowledge about Maasai cultural heritage and customs can be very limited. This often creates friction because bringing foreigners to a Maasai *boma* looks like a visit to a human zoo: Maasai and tourists staring at one another, without a cultural broker to facilitate communication and exchange between the two parties (cf. Salazar 2006). The Maasai visited have no clue about how they are being represented (as primitive) by the Meru guides because they do not understand English. Because tourists do not understand Swahili, they seldom notice that their 'local' guide is not a Maasai but a Meru. Of course, they also do not know that there are growing tensions between Meru and Maasai people in the area because the land they share around Mt. Meru is becoming overcrowded and overstocked.

During CTP tours in Tengeru, the local Meru guides clearly distinguish their ethnic group from the Maasai, for example by never dressing in red but often in blue (although this colour is not particularly associated with the Meru). The guides explain to foreign tourists that only the Maasai wear blankets; the Meru wear clothes. They are proud to say that the Meru are more developed compared to other 'tribes' because they have adapted faster to modernity, and that the Maasai are certainly more primitive. Not only the Maasai have suffered from stereotyping and misrepresentation (some caused by their own people). Other CTP modules in the region illustrate how complex the politics of cultural representation in village tourism can be (cf. Salazar 2010).

Conclusion

"The so-called 'museum' or 'culture park' view of heritage as something that has only to be preserved and tended, only to be kept pristine, isolated from the alterations going on all around it, is not only utopian, it is mischievous. In trying to freeze a living tradition in the name of authenticity you produce the worst sorts of inauthenticity – decadence, not purity." (Geertz 1997: 19)

Bruner notes that themed environments "are an excellent setting for anthropological inquiry as they are sites where the ethnic diversity of the nation or the region is represented for the visitors in a single locality in one panoptic sweep" (2005: 211). In this chapter, I have described how various time periods have given rise to different tailor-made types of themed environments in Indonesia and Tanzania. Taman Mini and the Village Museum were built in the 1970s to develop a feeling of national unity and nationalism in young postcolonial states, though they were clearly inspired by earlier Western projects (as varied as Disneyland in the USA and Skansen in Sweden). To a certain extent, these hybrid open-air museums/theme parks were an attempt to make sense of the multi-ethnic reality with which colonialism had left these countries after independence. Selected aspects of diversity were exhibited, without really attempting to (re)present all ethnicities. Paradoxically, these nationally themed environments visually display difference yet promote unity. Typical house types (reconstructions) are a dominant feature, along with ethnic costumes, aspects of indigenous arts and culture, dance performances, and, in some cases, regional food. While such national theme parks are recreational, they are also seriously political. They symbolize, in a modern way, centralized power (cf. Anderson 1991). Cultural heterogeneity is put in its place – fixed, aligned, domesticated – and turned into recreational exhibition (Bruner 2005: 212). Aimed at a multiplicity of audiences, such themed environments have been mainly successful in attracting domestic crowds.

The tourismification of actual villages in Indonesia and Tanzania, on the other hand, is a more recent development, both a consequence of the recent decentralization of power and a response to the increasing international demand for experiential tourism, often based on the temporal 'Othering' of those living in rural areas (cf. Fabian 2002). The theming of otherwise lived environments strategically makes use of three recurring imaginaries in the tourism of developing countries: the myth of the unchanged, the myth of the unrestrained and the myth of the uncivilized (cf. Echtner/Prasad 2003). A visit to the countryside is told and sold (often by the villagers themselves) as an exotic journey to the past, drawing on widely distributed imaginaries of Orientalism, colonialism, and imperialism, to feed romantic and nostalgic tourist dreams (cf. Salazar 2010).

Whereas ethnography reduces living peoples to writing and museums usually reduce them to artefacts, both national theme parks and tourism villages continue the late 19th and early 20th century tradition of world fairs in that the objects on exhibit include real people. In both themed environments, peoples are presented as unique, separate, and fixed, and this, ironically, is happening at the same time that the world is moving toward mobile subjects, border crossings, and vast population movements (cf. Bruner 2005: 212). Tailor-made imagineering for tourist audiences is well worth more in-depth ethnographic study, because its practices not only create an image of places and peoples, additionally the imaginative power of shrewd imagineers is stealing people's own imaginations in and through invented experiences. The central role of imaginaries as a force of tourism production and consumption of cultural heritage calls for an urgent return to empirical studies of widely circulating dreams and popular flights of fantasy in the context of tourism and beyond.

References

Acciaioli, Gregory. 1996. "Pavilions and Posters: Showcasing Diversity and Development in Contemporary Indonesia." *Eikon* 1: 27-42.

Adams, Kathleen. 1998. "Domestic Tourism and Nation-building in South Sulawesi." *Indonesia and the Malay World* 26.75: 77-96.

Anderson, Benedict R. 1991. *Imagined Communities: Reflections on the Origin and Spread of Nationalism*. Second ed. New York: Verso.

Ardika, I Gde. 2006. *The Development of Interior Tourism and the Reduction of Poverty: The Case of Java, Indonesia*. Paper presented at the International Conference about Tourism and Reduction of Poverty: Methodology and Good Practices, Toulouse, France.

Boellstorff, Tom. 2002. "Ethnolocality." *Asia Pacific Journal of Anthropology* 3.1: 24-48.

Bruner, Edward M. 2005. *Culture on Tour: Ethnographies of Travel.* Chicago: University of Chicago Press.

Dahles, Heidi. 2001. *Tourism, Heritage and National Culture in Java: Dilemmas of a Local Community.* Richmond: Curzon Press.

De Jong, Ate. 1999. *Cultural Tourism in Tanzania: Experiences of a Tourism Development Project.* The Hague: Stichting Nederlandse Vrijwilligers.

Echtner, Charlotte M./Pushkala Prasad. 2003. "The Context of Third World Tourism Marketing." *Annals of Tourism Research* 30.3: 660-682.

Errington, Shelly. 1998. *The Death of Authentic Primitive Art and Other Tales of Progress.* Berkeley: University of California Press.

Fabian, Johannes. 2002. *Time and the Other: How Anthropology Makes Its Object.* Second ed. New York: Columbia University Press.

Geertz, Clifford. 1997. "Cultural Tourism: Tradition, Identity and Heritage Construction." *Tourism and Heritage Management.* Ed. Wiendu Nuryanti. Yogyakarta: Gadjah Mada University Press. 14-24.

Hitchcock, Michael. 1998. "Tourism, Taman Mini, and National Identity." *Indonesia and the Malay World* 26.75: 124-135.

Imagineers. 1996. *Walt Disney Imagineering: A Behind the Dreams Look at Making the Magic Real.* New York: Hyperion.

James, Jamie. 2003. "Lord of the Village: An Aussie Entrepreneur finds Utopia in the Indonesian Countryside." *Time Magazine* 14 July.

Janarto, Daru K. 2006. "Learning from Humble Villagers." *The Jakarta Post* July 16.

Jones, Roy/Brian J. Shaw. 2006. "Palimpsests of Progress: Erasing the Past and Rewriting the Future in Developing Societies." *International Journal of Heritage Studies* 12.2: 122-138.

Löfgren, Orvar. 2003. "The New Economy: A Cultural History." *Global Networks* 3.3: 239-254.

Masao, Fidelis T. 1993. "Reviving the Village Museum in Dar es Salaam." *Museum International* 45.1: 57-59.

Mbughuni, L. A. 1974. *The Cultural Policy of the United Republic of Tanzania.* Paris: UNESCO Press.

Mwenesi, Leonard C. 1998. *How Is Art and Art Education Relevant for the Construction of a Tanzanian National Cultural Identity Within the Context of a Hegemonic Globalism?* Department of Secondary Education, University of Alberta.

Pemberton, John 1994. "Recollections from 'Beautiful Indonesia' (Somewhere Beyond the Postmodern)." *Public Culture* 6.2: 241-262.

Pine, B. Joseph/James H. Gilmore. 1999. *The Experience Economy: Work is Theatre & Every Business a Stage*. Boston: Harvard Business School Press.

Salazar, Noel B. 2005. "Tourism and Glocalization: 'Local' Tour Guiding." *Annals of Tourism Research* 32.3: 628-646.

Salazar, Noel B. 2006. "Touristifying Tanzania: Global Discourse, Local Guides." *Annals of Tourism Research* 33.3: 833-852.

Salazar, Noel B. 2007. "Towards a Global Culture of Heritage Interpretation? Evidence from Indonesia and Tanzania." *Tourism Recreation Research* 32.3: 23-30.

Salazar, Noel B. 2008. "Representation in Postcolonial Analysis." *International Encyclopedia of the Social Sciences*. Second ed. Ed. William A. Darity. Detroit: Macmillan Reference USA. 172-173.

Salazar, Noel B. 2009. "Imaged or Imagined? Cultural Representations and the 'Tourismification' of Peoples and Places." *Cahiers d'Études Africaines* 193-194: 49-71.

Salazar, Noel B. 2010. *Envisioning Eden: Mobilizing Imaginaries in Tourism and Beyond*. Oxford: Berghahn.

Salazar, Noel B./Jeroen Bryon/Elvira Van Den Branden. 2009. *Cultural Tourism Storytelling in 'Flanders': The Story Behind the Stories*. Leuven: Steunpunt Toerisme.

Schneider, Leander 2006. "The Maasai's New Clothes: A Developmentalist Modernity and Its Exclusions." *Africa Today* 53.1: 101-131.

Scott, James C. 1998. "Compulsory Villagization in Tanzania: Aesthetics and Miniaturization." *Seeing Like a State: How Certain Schemes to Improve the Human Condition Have Failed*. Ed. James C. Scott. New Haven: Yale University Press. 223-261.

Stanley, Nick 1998. *Being Ourselves for You: The Global Display of Cultures*. London: Middlesex University Press.

Suherman, Ahmad. 2001. *Tourism Village: A Conceptual Approach (Case of Indonesia)*. Paper presented at the Cultural Heritage, Man and Tourism Seminar, Hanoi, Vietnam, 5-7 Nov 2001.

The Jakarta Post. 1999. "Tourism Village Inaugurated." *The Jakarta Post* 29 Sep 1999.

TTB. 2007. *Tanzania Cultural Tourism*. Dar es Salaam: Tanzania Tourist Board.

Van der Duim, René/Karen Peters/Stephen Wearing. 2005. "Planning Host and Guest Interactions: Moving Beyond the Empty Meeting Ground in African Encounters." *Current Issues in Tourism* 8.4: 286-305.

Village Museum. n.d. "The Village Museum Dar es Salaam Tanzania." http://villagemuseum.homestead.com/ (accessed 2 Apr 2010).

Wahyuni, Sri. 2003. "Sambi, a Unique Heritage Village." *The Jakarta Post* 2 June.

WTO. 2002. *Sustainable Development of Ecotourism: A Compilation of Good Practices.* Madrid: World Tourism Organization.

Wulandari, Anak Agung Ayu. 2005. *Taman Mini Indonesia Indah: Entertainment or Education?* International Institute for Culture, Tourism and Development, London Metropolitan University.

Yamashita, Shinji. 2003. *Bali and Beyond: Explorations in the Anthropology of Tourism* [Jerry S. Eades, transl.]. New York: Berghahn.

Holy Land Protestant Themed Environments and the Spiritual Experience[1]

AMOS S. RON

Introduction

Like any perspective, the Protestant viewing of the Bible Land is historically, socially, and ideologically conditioned (Feldman 2007; Urry 2002). In the course of its history, Protestantism has inscribed its own understandings on the well-marked palimpsest of the Holy Land (Halbwachs 1992), in the attempt to produce a textualized sacred landscape in its own image.

This article will briefly trace the evolution of Protestant attitudes towards the Holy Land, with an emphasis on two Protestant themed environments – Nazareth Village in Nazareth and Biblical Resources Museum in Jerusalem – showing how they reflect and confirm Protestant images of the land, and exploring what such sanctification tells us about contemporary Protestant practice.

Protestant themed environments, the article argues, materialize traditional Protestant ways of seeing, while reflecting recent changes in Protestant practice that result from the postmodern emphasis on images and multi-sensory experience. By bringing theming and religion together, the article illustrates how the media pervading postmodern culture has become an integral part of the pilgrimage discourse (cf. Coleman/Eade 2004). By combining religion and theming, this study also attempts to broaden the understanding of how these two elements shape the spiritual experience of the Christian pilgrim.

---

1 This article sums up a number of works on this topic, which I have written with Amir Shani and with Jackie Feldman (both from Ben Gurion University of the Negev, Israel). Certain parts of this paper are based on and elaborated in Ron/Feldman 2009. In addition, much of the data for this article was gathered while guiding Christian pilgrims through the Holy Land for the past twenty-seven years.

The Historical Development of Protestant Concepts of Space and Travel

In the Holy Land, sacred narratives are at the origin of sacred space (Markus 1994). In the course of the history of Christian pilgrimage, beginning with the emergence of the Holy Land in the 4th century (Cardman 1982), a wide variety of religious groups and religious sensibilities imposed their own conceptual grids on the territory of Israel/Palestine (Halbwachs 1992), including the Protestants. Thus, the historical evolution of Protestant pilgrimage to the Holy Land can be divided into three main periods.

ORIGINS – 16TH CENTURY'S OPPOSITION TO PILGRIMAGE

At its outset, in the 16th century, Protestantism opposed the Catholic notion of pilgrimage. In contrast to the phenomenon of the 'holy site', which affirms the essential heterogeneity of space (Eliade 1959), in Protestant theology, space was homogeneous, as "...the whole earth is full of His glory" (Isaiah 6: 3). According to this view no place can be more holy than another. This view is well expressed by John Milton who, in his *Paradise Lost* (iii, 476-477, in Werblowsky 1988), refers to pilgrimage as the paradise of fools: "Here Pilgrims roam, that stray'd so far to seek in Golgotha him dead, who lives in Heav'n".

Calvin dismissed the veneration of relics through pilgrimage as "vain speculation" and as a challenge to the exclusive recourse to the Bible as sole repository of truth (Moore 2003: 70). Since in the Catholic tradition pilgrimage was linked with the cult of the saints, with popular folk beliefs and with the medieval system of penance and indulgences, it conflicted with the Protestant affirmation of *sola scriptura* – i.e. that the only way to God is through the written Word, rather than through the mediation of a priesthood and ritual objects. Consequently, Protestants were relative latecomers to the pilgrimage scene and still today display ambivalence towards words like 'pilgrim' and 'Holy Land' (Todd 1984: 21).

THE 19TH CENTURY'S REDISCOVERY OF THE HOLY LAND

The second stage took place from the mid 19th century on. By then, the claims of older established churches to significant places, made official by the Ottoman edict of 1852, were firm and well monumentalized (cf. Collins-Kreiner/Kliot 2000: 17). Protestants of various denominations began to come in growing numbers to test and confirm the topographical truths of the Scriptures. The increasing ease and safety of traveling to the Holy Land, the increase in disposable income, and the greater familiarity of Protestant faithful with the accounts of returning pilgrims, led to an upsurge in Protestant pilgrimage. At the same time, the rising number of pilgrims and their accommodation were inseparable from the colonial project of dismantling the Ottoman Empire in the Middle East (Bar/Cohen-Hattab 2003; Ben-Arieh 1989; Long 2003; Monk 2002; Obenzinger 1999). This was manifested in the establishment of churches, modern hotels, hostels and hospices to serve the needs of pilgrims of colonial powers.

In addition to pilgrimage to the holy sites in Palestine, the 19th century enabled American Protestants to make visits to simulated 'Holy Lands'[2] in the USA. One of the most prominent was Palestine Park at Chautauqua, NY (Rogers 2003; Rowan 2004: 257-259), "a half-acre tract of land outfitted in 1874 with a scaled Jordan River, Galilee, and Jerusalem, [which] allowed late 19th century visitors to stroll symbolically through the land of the Bible – many decked out in 'oriental' costume" (Rogers 2003: 60). In Rogers' opinion, this was the origin of modern-day Protestant pilgrimage: "The broader Protestant public began to form opinions about Palestine in line with some of their millennial hopes and expectations, and to look eastward for the beautiful, utopian, promised land pictured in their Bible illustrations" (Rogers 2003: 78).

Unquestionably, this 'Holy Land craze' was fueled by common 19th century ideologies of millenarism (Greenberg 1994), orientalism, and colonialism no less than by the advancement of modern archeology, cartography, and scientific expeditions such as the Palestine Exploration Fund (PEF) (Ben-Arieh 1989).

CONTEMPORARY PRACTICE

Today, Evangelical groups make up an important segment of the Israeli tourist market. Furthermore, for many Evangelicals, pilgrimage has become a tool not only for furthering the solidarity of church communities and increasing faith commitments, but for expressing public 'witness' to the world (Coleman 2004). Protestant pilgrims to the Holy Land come mainly on group tours, usually seven to twelve days long. Such tours are promoted by several churches and televangelists, and are sold by travel agents who specialize in the Christian market. The traveler purchases an all-inclusive package with a fixed itinerary. Participants on such tours sacrifice part of their independence and adventurousness for the sake of fellowship and security. Even if some Protestants proclaim interest in

---

2   In retrospect, it is very likely that these 'simulated Holy Lands' were the prototypes of the late 20th century religious themed environments.

modern Israel, effectively, most Protestant visitors are enclosed in an environmental bubble (Schmidt 1979). As Protestant leaders often proclaim their desire to intensify the Christian spirit among their members, this bubble is invested with spiritual value.

Unquestionably, the itineraries of Protestant groups vary. Sizer (1999) divides Protestant pilgrims to the Holy Land into three categories: Evangelicals, fundamentalists and Living Stones: "Evangelicals focus on educational tours of sites of biblical significance, while fundamentalists travel for similar reasons but include eschatological motivations for travel. The third group focuses more on experiences with indigenous Christian [i.e. Palestinian] groups in their travels" (Olsen/Timothy 2006: 9). A study conducted by Collins-Kreiner et al. indicates that Protestant pilgrims showed an interest in the land of the Bible as a whole, rather than in churches, holy sites, and monuments only (Collins-Kreiner et al. 2006: 315-316).

Protestant Ways of Seeing the Bible Land

For Protestant pilgrims, the Holy Scriptures provide the basic repertoire of potential sites (Bowman 2000). Furthermore, what counts as a sacred place is also shaped by the available 'facts on the ground' (Abu el-Haj 2001). Such 'facts' are compiled, often by government authorities, traditional churches, and/or the tourist industry, by selectively excavating, displaying, fabricating, and signposting certain remnants of the past, often in ways that reflect and project political and ideological assumptions. Yet in order to be accepted into the pilgrim's itinerary, these displays and 'revelations' must accord with a world-view rooted in theologically-grounded and historically-transmitted Protestant ways of seeing, and in the aesthetic values that derive from them.

The Expression of *Sola Scriptura* in Pilgrimage

While Protestants took exception to 'holy sites', as objects whose sanctity was transferred to them through physical contact with the divine, they have increasingly been drawn to the land as the physical illustration of significant loci of their faith, as anchored in their understanding of the Scriptures. For Protestants, the landscape calls forth words, not as heard but as seen, as if lettered across the landscape. Their outward view should call forth in inward vision the words of remembered prayers, hymns and scriptural passages (cf. Greenberg 1994: 106).

While fostering a sense of contemporaneity with the past is a hallmark of the heritage industry at large, Protestantism, from the

Reformation onwards, saw itself as a movement seeking to restore the Church to the purity of the 'original' true Church at the time of Jesus, effacing a long intermediate past. This is particularly true in the case of conservative Protestants, who ignore the fact that their understanding of the Scriptures is mediated by a long history of interpretation, promoting instead a discourse of 'Jesus, the Bible and me'. Thus, most Protestants seek (and find) the 'original' stones that Jesus might have walked on.

COMMANDING HEIGHTS AND DIFFUSE SANCTITY

Protestant pilgrimage itineraries are replete with vistas, panoramic views and open spaces. While explicit Biblical paradigms may be invoked to justify certain outlook points – Moses on Mount Nebo, Jesus at the Sermon on the Mount – these hardly suffice to explain the Protestant love of heights. The prominence of the vista may also reflect the ambiguity of the Protestant relation towards holy sites. It is "the Jesus of the land rather than the sites" (Hummel/Hummel 1995: 26) that is essential for Protestant pilgrims. The concentration of sanctity on a specified object – a tree, stone, or relic – materializes sanctity and hence, arouses Protestant theological opposition in ways that a broad, more diffuse landscape does not.

Furthermore, while the Protestant pilgrim is attracted to the Biblical sites and landscapes, he is often repulsed by 'smells and bells' – the sensuality of Catholic and Orthodox presence and ritual. As Lock (2003: 112) illustrates, rather than bow down, touch or kiss, wood and stone – Orthodox icons or Catholic statues and relics – 19th century Protestant pilgrims remained vertical: upright in their saddles, seeking the most extensive pictorial vista, the largest possible view. The distance from the site is also a distance from immersion in the Orient. Thus, the outlook, embodying a gaze that combines diffuse sanctity with distance and control is a practice constituting the Protestant pilgrim as Western. Almost every Protestant pilgrimage to Jerusalem (in contrast, for example, to Greek Orthodox pilgrimage) begins with an outlook from the Mount of Olives, and many prayer and 'meditation' sites are mountaintop vistas.

UNCLUTTERED AND UNMEDIATED NATURE

For Catholics, holiness arises from the sense of being part of a long history during which the will of Jesus has been enacted in the world through the agency of the Church (cf. Collins-Kreiner et al. 2006: 17). For Protestants, on the other hand, a holy place 'covered over' with Orthodox or Catholic churches is, in effect, a site which commemorates institutional domination rather than the 'truth' that, in their view, the ecclesiastical institution has usurped and distorted. Protestant inspiration devolves from what is interpreted as an unimpeded relationship between the individual and Christ. Consequently, Protestants want to 'witness' Christ, rather than his agents. Unlike Orthodox or Catholic Christians (cf. Bowman 1992), the influential sites among Protestants are not determined by the magnificence of the church built upon them, the sanction of an ecclesiastical hierarchy, or the aura acquired by an object or shrine through its veneration by previous generations of pilgrims. Rather, the Holy Land acquires prestige among Protestants because it contains those landscapes in which Jesus, gazing over valleys and hills towards the distant horizon, would have experienced the sublime. In Lock's words, "The Protestant task is always to return to that first simplicity which so exactly matches the Protestant's own. The plainness of the landscape is itself held up as evidence of the truth of Protestantism" (Lock 2003: 123).

SCIENCE IN THE SERVICE OF FAITH

Protestants have historically presented themselves as progressive, and sociologists from Weber on have identified Protestant theology as a key fundament for the growth of rationalism, scientific progress, industrialization and modern capitalism in the West (Keane 2007). To construct themselves as progressive, truthful and Western, they orientalized Catholicism, presenting it as 'traditional', obscurantist and medieval. Among more conservative Protestants, scientific and historical discoveries were poached to provide 'proofs' of the veracity of faith or scripture, and natural science buzzwords peppered faith discourses.

In the case of the historical geography and archaeology of Israel/Palestine, Protestant agendas played a prominent role in formative research. Thus, the aim of 19th century historical geography, according to Robinson, one of its leading practitioners, was "to lay open the treasures of Biblical geography... [that] had become so covered with the dust and rubbish of many centuries that their very existence was forgotten" (Robinson 1841: xi-xii in Silberman 2001: 493). Biblical sites were to be 'verified' and consecrated by scientific research (i.e. history, archaeology, and geography) rather than by miracles, revelatory visions, and Catholic ecclesiastical authority.

The Israeli government's signposting of archaeological sites, with references to the appropriate Biblical passages, also corresponds to the Protestant pilgrim's view: Science and the modern state uncover the past buried under the dirt and clutter of Oriental 'tradition' (Islamic presence and Oriental churches), while the wavy line which marks the separation of the 'original' from the reconstructed masonry at the sites is a graphic display of the limits of man's achievements through science. Here, the sacred and profane views of progress embedded in Protestant periodization of history are mirrored in the archaeological display. At the same time, theologically conservative Protestant groups ignore, suppress, or selectively interpret archaeological findings which contradict their understandings of the Scripture.

From Spots to Theme Sites: Stages in the Development of the Protestant Bible Land

The history of Protestant Bible Land sites is one of increasing organization and routinization. It proceeds in tandem with the institutionalization of Protestant pilgrimage in general – for example the development of package tours as the preferred means of travel, beginning with Thomas Cook tours (cf. Hummel/Hummel 1995: 9-12). Both itineraries and the construction and display of sites reflect the basic elements of Protestant ways of looking at and organizing the world, which display a chronological development of five types of sites, from unmarked 'natural' sites to theme sites.

'SPOTS' BETWEEN THE CATHOLIC SITES

As early as the 19th century, Biblical sites comprised "favourite locations which seemed to capture the Protestant imagination" (Hummel/Hummel 1995: 14). The key sites were usually situated near well-established Catholic sites, and were marked by their natural and informal look. A large tree providing some shade, flowers or thorns (depending on the season), a bird or a lizard and a few 'comfortable' rocks to sit on were usually perceived as an 'authentic' and spiritually rewarding alternative to the formal, built-up, commercialized, and usually Catholic sacred sites. Elements of antiquity, such as olive presses, tomb stones, and ruins of homes, were also perceived as visual aids that facilitated the Biblical look. Thus, the combination of nature and archaeology provided the Protestant mind with a simple and inspiring alternative to the congested traditional sites.

PROTESTANT–DEVELOPED SITES

In the 19th century, the Protestants marked out several new, alternative Biblical sites. The most prominent and enduring of these is the Garden Tomb, an alternative site of Calvary and the Tomb of Jesus, identified by British General Charles G. Gordon, in 1883. Gordon saw the landscape of Jerusalem, and the geographic position of Golgotha in particular, as a hieroglyph, a coded sign of the divinity, hinted at in the Scriptures, and made manifest to the perceptive – and progressive – Protestant observer. While Gordon's vision is grounded in an analysis of sacred Scriptures, it is Western science (surveys, archaeology) that provided the tools for deciphering the mysteries that lay obscured by Catholic 'tradition' and under the debris of the Orient. That analogy led him to identify a small hillock described by the skull-shaped contour line, located north of the city, as the true site of Golgotha and the tomb of Jesus. Note that here the love of 'uncluttered nature' and distaste for built-up shrines conflict with the search for historical veracity. In consecrating the Garden Tomb, Protestants showed "a preference for sites of solitude and prospects of beauty over those determined by topographical and historical exactitude" and "chose the aesthetic over the truthful" (Lock 2003: 117).

Fig. 1: Praying on rocks overlooking Bethlehem

Photograph: Yael Guter (Guter 1997: 82)

The site was later made even 'more natural' – i.e. more in tune with British Romantic perceptions of nature and the sublime (Lock 2003: 123) – through excavations, the planting of flowers and aromatic bushes, the erection of benches and viewing platforms, and even the importation of a first-century rolling stone to be placed by the tomb. Moreover, Gordon's founding mystical vision was later downplayed, in favor of a more rational scientific discourse. Thus, groups are now told that the hillock was identified as Golgotha based on the shape of the caves on the rock face, rather than that of a contour on an anthropomorphised PEF (Palestine Exploration Fund) map.

Catholic Church–Sponsored Corners

The Franciscan Order is the custodian of most traditional New Testament sites. Consequently, most Christian visitors visit the Catholic sites. While the various groups often differ greatly (e.g. Polish Catholics and Pentecostal African-Americans), the degree of homogeneity within a given group is usually high. Groups prefer to congregate in secluded spaces within the holy site for shared reading, prayer, meditation, singing and testimony, for a few minutes or even hours. In order to accommodate this need, several Catholic sites have developed large gardens with secluded and well-maintained spaces that can accommodate groups of various sizes. These 'outdoor classrooms' are relatively inexpensive to construct and maintain, and share the Protestant 'ideal look' of sacred space, which encourages simplicity and nature. Hence, they are frequently used for Protestant worship, while Catholics may hold their masses inside the adjacent shrine. Some such places, like the Mount of Beatitudes, which afford a vista point and gardens, have become 'must' prayer sites for Protestant groups.

Israeli Government–Developed Biblical Spots and Sites

Many Biblical sites and vistas become more central to pilgrimage practice when they become easier for pilgrims to access and recognize. Thus, over the past two decades, the Israeli government has constructed roads, bus parking areas, small viewing amphitheaters, and erected signs quoting Biblical verses or identifying Biblical sites. Such access and signposting increases the variety of Biblical sites and thus the attractiveness of the not-marked-as-Catholic Bible Land, especially for return visitors. This is significant as Evangelical Protestants – numerous and largely pro-Israel – have been earmarked by the Israeli Ministry of Tourism as one of the prime markets for tourism growth. As these sites become more accessible and attractive, pastors and tour operators increasingly include them in their itineraries. At the same time, sites already frequented by pilgrims are more likely to be signposted and developed. In addition, new sites of religious significance may be developed as a result of new excavations or tourism initiatives. Such recent sites include the 'Jesus Boat' on the Sea of Galilee, the baptismal site on the Jordan (Yardenit) at Kinneret, and the 'Jesus Steps' near the Temple Mount (cf. Feldman 2007: 364-366). The diffusion of itineraries, web photos and postcards showing such sites further whet the pilgrims' desire to visit them.

THEMED ENVIRONMENTS

Over the last several decades, the waning of the power of the word and the rise of the image and the simulacrum throughout the West (Baudrillard 1994; Eco 1986: 1-58) have shaped the gaze and expectations of pilgrims (Urry 1995; Urry/Rojek 1997). Images and the desire for multi-sensory experience have found their way from Western mass culture into the heart of Protestant worship (Luhrmann 2004), as may be attested to by the proliferation of video screens and staged performances in churches, not to mention the taking of communion in cinemas, after a screening of Mel Gibson's *The Passion of the Christ* (Pinto 2004). One result has been the increased theming of the Bible, both in the Holy Land and elsewhere (Beal 2005; Rivera, Shani/Severt 2009; Rowan 2004; Shani/Rivera/Severt 2007; Shoval 2000), which is both a catalyst of those changes and a response to them.

Themed Environments in Protestantism

The phenomenon of theming has been widely discussed in the context of tourism. Gottdiener coined the term 'themed environments', which are "themed material forms that are products of a cultural process aimed at investing constructed spaces with symbolic meaning and at *conveying* that meaning to inhabitants and users through symbolic motifs" (Gottdiener 2001: 5). In academic literature, theming in tourism is identified as a secular activity, and is rarely discussed in the context of religious tourism. Shoval (2000) was among the very first to observe this new trend. He attributes the rapid growth of religious theming in the Holy Land to the North American and European origin of most incoming tourists to Israel. As such tourists "feel more comfortable in environments shaped by the new logic of franchising and theming", entrepreneurs and religious leaders have been "trying to take advantage of this concept to promote their businesses or ideologies" (Shoval 2000: 253).

Shani, Rivera and Severt (2007: 40), define religious theme sites (also known as 'Spiritual Theme Parks' and 'Bible Parks') as theme sites constructed "around religious contents [...] [whose] managers are driven by a religious ideology". To the best of my knowledge, Christian theme sites exist in Argentina, Germany, Poland, the United States, and Israel. In the Holy Land, two Protestant theme sites have been identified and will be discussed below: Biblical Resources Museum in Jerusalem, and Nazareth Village in Nazareth.

BIBLICAL RESOURCES MUSEUM

The first theme site in this context was the Biblical Resources Museum (henceforth, BR), over a quarter of a century ago. The location of the museum has changed several times. Between 1998 and 2006, it was located in the neighborhood of Ein-Kerem (the traditional birthplace of John the Baptist) in Jerusalem. The site has been recently relocated to Georgia, USA.[3]

BR was founded by Dr. James W. Fleming, a Biblical scholar and educator. Upon payment of an admission fee, visitors encounter several staged Biblical elements, including a threshing floor, a quarry, a goat's hair tent, a sheepfold, a watchtower, a water well, olive and wine presses, and a crucifixion site with Roman style crosses. The two highlights of the site are a replica of the tomb of Jesus and a Last Supper event offered as an optional meal to tour groups.

Fig. 2: Cross section of the replica of the tomb of Jesus at Biblical Resources Museum

Photograph: Amos S. Ron

The site – just like the Garden Tomb – is operated by non-Israeli Christian volunteers, who present themselves as devout Christians. While using volunteers is not cheaper than employing local salaried workers (Pinto 2004), it has invisible advantages, insofar as it suggests a comparison with well-established holy places (such as the

---

3   Quite often, themed environments shut down and are abandoned. Apparently, this phenomenon is so widely spread that there is an extensive web literature on it (cf. List of Defunct Amusement Parks).

Garden Tomb), and endows BR with the aura of spiritual sites of worship, rather than that of a commercial enterprise.

NAZARETH VILLAGE

Nazareth, located in the north of Israel, was the site of the Annunciation and the childhood home of Jesus. In the days of Jesus, Nazareth was a small village, inhabited by a traditional, mainly agricultural, Jewish population. Nazareth has become the largest Arab town in Israel today, and represents an important destination in most Christian travel itineraries to the Holy Land. Until the end of the 20th century, however, Nazareth had very little to offer the Protestant visitor. In the words of the Nazareth Village book, "this idyllic town has been transformed into a teeming city of 70,000... Horns blare from the cars and buses that jam the streets from dawn to dusk..." (Kauffmann/Hostetler 2005: 70). A typical Protestant tour of Nazareth lasts less than two hours, and includes a visit to the Church of the Annunciation and a short walk through a small Arab bazaar. The religious sites in Nazareth are mainly Catholic and Orthodox. In fact, the church setting of these sites repulse Protestant visitors who seek to spend their time in more natural and 'Biblical'-looking environments (Shoval 2000). Consequently, most Protestant tours regard Nazareth as a 'drive-through town' on their way to other Christian destinations, such as the Sea of Galilee or Jerusalem.

Toward the third millennium, serious attempts were made by the Israeli Ministry of Tourism to renew the appearance of Nazareth, especially in areas frequented by tourists. The plan, entitled *Nazareth 2000*, included the construction of new promenades and hotels, the repaving of the old bazaar streets, and the improvement of infrastructure (Cohen-Hattab/Shoval 2007). The main drive for the project was the anticipation of millions of Christian believers visiting the Holy Land and the city of Jesus for the new millennium, a hope which, in the end, was only partly fulfilled (Kliot/Collins-Kreiner 2003). These great expectations also stimulated private tourist development initiatives, the most prominent of which was Nazareth Village (henceforth, NV).

Established in 2000 by a local Protestant Arab, Dr. Nakhle Beshara, and supported by the Mennonite Mission Network, NV was designed to bring "to life a farm and Galilean village, recreating Nazareth as it was 2,000 years ago. It is a window into the life of Jesus, the city's most famous citizen" (site brochure). According to the site's founding director, D. Michael Hostetler, the concept of NV was inspired by three well-known heritage sites: Colonial Williamsburg in Virginia, Plimoth Plantation in Plymouth, Massachusetts, and Ecomusée d'Alsace in Ungersheim, France. In all three sites, theming is dominant. At NV, in return for an admission fee, visitors encounter costumed actors, staged buildings and streets, and artifacts. Such reconstructions also proudly proclaim their reliance on science.

The site itself includes a traditional rural area with traditional 'Biblical' artifacts, such as a threshing floor and well, newly built 'traditional' homes, streets, and an 'ancient' synagogue. When tourists come to the village, they encounter local[4] men, women and children dressed in traditional gear, performing traditional jobs, such as plowing, picking and olive crushing, manufacturing and repairing tools, weaving, winnowing, and more. The visitors also have the option of ordering a Biblical meal.

Fig. 3: A guided tour through Nazareth Village

Photograph: Amos S. Ron

Shoval wrote about the site at the time of its opening. His predictions – relying on preliminary market studies – were that North Americans would be very enthusiastic about the idea, whereas Europeans, in general, would fear that NV would be an '"American Production', that is, a site that would sacrifice authenticity on the altar of technological sophistication" (Shoval 2000: 258).

Almost a decade later NV receives visitors from several destinations; for the first quarter of 2008 about 30% of the visitors were of EU origin, while about 65% came from the U.S. (Roth 2008). These statistics, along with the presence of Christian theme parks in Poland, Germany and Argentina, seem to indicate that the appeal of

---

4   Since 2007 the site also receives regularly Christian (usually Mennonite) volunteers from Western countries, who come for a few weeks.

religious themed environments reaches much further than the North American Protestant market only.

COMPARING THE SITES

Both sites are located in important Biblical towns central to Jesus' mission; both depict their sites as Biblical, natural, agricultural, ancient, and Christian; both highlight archaeology and claim the scientific veracity of their reconstructions. NV and BR prominently expose contemporary rustic remains without identifying them as recent, and perform daily 'Biblical' practices, such as weaving and herding sheep, without framing them as staged. Thus, both sites accommodate themselves to the Protestant gaze and Protestant expectations. The sponsorship of the sites by non-profit, charitable Christian organizations and their partial staffing by devout volunteers serve to increase the sites' authority. In Bryman's (1999) terminology, both sites can be regarded as Disneyified environments, because in both one can easily identify the four trends of Disneyization suggested by Bryman: theming, dedifferentiation of consumption, merchandising, and emotional labor – defined as the "act of expressing socially desired emotions during service transactions" (Ashforth/Humphry 1993: 88-89, in Bryman 1999: 39).

Fig. 4: Science in the service of faith at Nazareth Village

Photograph: Amos S. Ron

Yet the relationship of the two sites to their local communities and their presentations of the past differ; BR is detached from the local community, and is staffed by Western Christians from abroad. At BR, guides are primarily instructors, and scientific cross-sections of models (see Fig. 2) and scholarly language are predominant. NV, on the other hand, was founded by members of the local community, and portrays itself as reflecting and contributing to the Christian community of Nazareth, which has endured throughout the ages. The majority of the staff are local Christian Arabs who also dress up in costumes and use primitive tools to play the roles of weavers, carpenters and shepherd girls.

As it is more oriented towards the local community, NV can be regarded as a form of an eco-museum which, according to Davis (2005: 370), emphasizes the relationship with the local population, and represents them and their heritage. BR, on the other hand, is more committed to the theme and less to the local community, which is reflected by the fact that the location changes every few years.

Both presentations accommodate the same orientalizing tendencies of the Protestant gaze. Whereas at BR, the global Westerner is perceived by the pilgrims as 'one of us', and presents a (pseudo-)scientific discourse, the physical features and accents of the NV narrators mark them as Oriental. The NV website, for example, portrays contemporary urban Christians as Biblical shepherd girls. Thus, they may convincingly play figures of the past in ways that would be perceived of as alienating make-believe, had they been performed by the Westerners of BR. Given the power of the Protestant orientalizing gaze, the best way for Arab Christians to find a place in conservative Protestant itineraries may be by portraying themselves as 'living stones' in a heritage site.

Both sites are very successful in terms of visitors' satisfaction (Hostetler 2005; Pinto 2004; Roth 2008). A possible explanation for this success is the dominant presence of three elements (see Fig. 5): theming, nature, and science. The theming of the sacred shapes the architecture, landscape, actors, performance, food, and souvenirs. By doing so, the sites fulfill the need for religious visualization, thus acting as alternatives to the traditional holy sites, which are sometimes perceived by Protestants as alienating and cold.

Significant resources are being invested in scientific research in order to get an accurate image of Biblical times. The fact that scientists – archeologists and others – have given the sites their seal of approval contributes to their reputation and increases their validity among the visitors. In addition, the scientific aura adds to the distinction made by the visitors between an ordinary theme park and such an authentic experience.

Nature is emphasized in two parallel narratives: the visual and the audio. The first narrative consists of natural elements that dominate the sites – trees, flowers, water and animals, all of which generate Biblical associations. The latter narrative is more evasive and depends greatly on the circumstances. In accordance with this narrative, the local guides are trained to emphasize nature by referring to relevant Biblical events through stories and parables.

An analysis of the two sites and their above-mentioned elements suggests that we are dealing with a contemporary phenomenon which can be called 'hyper-spirituality', to paraphrase Umberto Eco's *Travels in Hyperreality* (Eco 1986). The combination between spiritual context and meaning, on the one hand, and the active visitor participation, on the other, leads to a unique and enhanced experience that can be viewed as making a significant contribution to the spectrum of the religious spiritual tourist experience.

Fig. 5: Common Features of Protestant Theme Sites in Israel

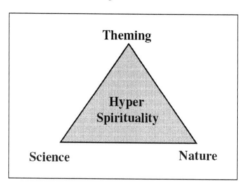

Conclusion

This article demonstrates how particular theological, aesthetic and orientalist considerations have always shaped the Protestant gaze, which directs the pilgrims' expectations in many informal and unrecognized ways. The popularity of pilgrim sites in Israel/Palestine is, to no small extent, dependent on the agents' capacity to construct sites to accommodate the Protestant gaze. Thus, this gaze will continue to be a powerful transformative force of the sacred space of the Holy Land, especially given the Israeli government's earmarking of Protestant – particularly Evangelical – pilgrims as an important market. As such themed sites proliferate, the Holy Land becomes increasingly fragmented into parallel sub-landscapes – Protestant, Catholic, and Orthodox holy lands (among others), each of them catering to a particular segment of the Christian market. The study thus supports a constructivist and relational view of the sacralization of space – ground is not holy in itself, but holy in relation to other sites, other gazes.

Yet the Protestant gaze itself evolves in accordance with historical and social circumstances: Since the mid-twentieth century, we are witnessing a decline in the authority of the written word and a rise in mediatized images as a source of knowledge (Baudrillard 1994; McLuhan 1962). Furthermore, identities (including religious identities) are increasingly mediated through cultural productions, including organized travel (cf. MacCannell 1976: 39–56). The last few decades also reflect the increased importance granted to multi-sensory experience – including experience while on the move – in identity formation, in general, and in American Protestant worship, in particular (Luhrmann 2004). The differences between sacred and profane spaces have also become blurred. Whereas in the past, places of worship were distinct buildings that drew people to leave the everyday world and enter a sacred space, now they are often nondescript, functional buildings that look like shopping malls and offices and that remind people of everyday life (Wuthnow 1998: 9). As the neighborhood church is being increasingly replaced by the 'Christian community center', where the place of worship is surrounded by franchised food courts, Christian book and music stores, and financial counseling services, the commodification of education and spiritual life is no longer anathema.

These processes, which have had a profound effect on American Protestantism (Coleman 2002; Luhrmann 2004; Wuthnow 1998), also lend greater religious value to theme sites as a means of contact with the holy (cf. Shoval 2000: 253). If Protestants initially sought to de-theme Christianity, and rely on the Word alone, looking at NV and BR, we see how the proliferation of images and simulacra by the heritage industry has effectively re-themed the Protestant Holy Land. Yet while Catholic theming – through the high drama of the mass, sumptuous vestments, darkened cathedrals, icons and incense (cf. Shoval 2000: 255) – remains threatening and 'idolatrous' (for Protestants), heritage museum theming is seen as spiritually neutral or, insofar as it employs advanced technology and convincing visualizations of the past, positive. Thus, theming reflects the return of the repressed ('Catholic') senses into Protestant pilgrimage through the portals of science, tourism and commodified entertainment.

The establishment of Protestant Holy Land theme sites, however, reinforces the preference of group tourists as a whole (who make up the majority of Protestant pilgrims), for planned, enclaval sites, and itineraries which emphasize safety and structure over adventure, risk and improvisation (Quiroga 1990; Schmidt 1979). Eventually, Protestants may (or might, depending on one's viewpoint) replace their visit to the traditional churches in town with a visit to NV, thus avoiding all contact with the Oriental Christians in the marketplaces and churches of Nazareth. Thus, the improvisation and uncontrolled nature of the marketplace, "pregnant with [...] possibility" (Chakrabarty 1991: 26, in: Edensor 2000: 333) and open to the criss-crossing flow of people, noises and smells (as well as improvised contact with local Christians), is eliminated. Some Protestant visitors may even substitute a theme park closer to home for the more time-consuming and expensive visit to the Holy Land. As Rowan reports with respect to the Holy Land Experience in Orlando, Florida, "one visitor to the Holy Land Experience suggested that it was better than the real thing, [thus, the term "hyper-spirituality"] not as 'smelly' as butcher's alley in Jerusalem's Old City – and much less crowded" (Rowan 2004: 262).

Over the past two decades, social studies have repeatedly asserted how territory is transformed through the power of media representations and the rapid movement of capital, ideas, and people across the globe. Scholars applying these perspectives to studies of contemporary tourism have, however, taken the hedonistic, often cynical, 'cool' pleasure-seeker (Bauman 1996; Urry/Rojek 1997) or postmodern tourist (Ritzer/Liska 1997) as their prototype. Highly mobile, living amidst a world shaped by representations and simulacra, this tourist seeks no authenticity, because basically, it is simply a game. Rather than seeking out the backstage of a foreign culture (MacCannell 1973, 1976), he delights in the play of surfaces, and seeks hedonistic pleasure. He inhabits a heterotopy where the original object counts for nothing, as all is simulation. Rather than seeking identity, truth, a place on which to stand, the postmodern tourist seeks to escape identity and stability, preferring play, movement, and constant change (Bauman 1996).

These analyses of tourism exclude the contemporary pilgrim or religious tourist, engaged in a more profound, more serious quest. Some scholars see the pilgrim as a prototype of the now passé and irrelevant modern (as opposed to postmodern) era (Bauman 1996). Such approaches tend to minimize the power of tradition, habitus, and religious beliefs. This article challenges the dichotomy of a postmodern tourist versus a modern (and pre-modern) pilgrim, by insisting on the contemporaneity of the religious tourist/pilgrim. The data on Protestant theming, while supporting many of the themes of globalization, show how global flows may be subject to constraints deriving from deeply rooted religious paradigms: theming may be acceptable, but it is the Bible that determines what kind of themes will be attractive to the traveler guided by faith. As Rowan (2004:

263) writes of visitors to the Holy Land Experience in Florida: "People are interested in constructing authentic relationships with a particular retelling of the past, and that past assists in the construction or reaffirmation of a sense of identity". Contemporary Protestant pilgrims consume religious theme sites not solely for amusement, but also to find meaningful relationships with God, Jesus, the Bible, the past, the future, themselves, and each other.

References

Abu el-Haj, Nadia. 2001. *Facts on the Ground. Archaeological Practice and Territorial Self-Fashioning in Israeli Society.* Chicago: University of Chicago Press.

Bar, Doron/Kobi Cohen-Hattab. 2003. "A New Kind of Pilgrimage: The Modern Tourist Pilgrim of Nineteenth-Century and Early Twentieth-Century Palestine." *Middle Eastern Studies* 39.2: 131-148.

Baudrillard, Jean. 1994. *Simulacra and Simulation.* Ann Arbor: Michigan University Press.

Bauman, Zygmunt. 1996. "From Pilgrim to Tourist – or a Short History of Identity." *Questions of Cultural Identity.* Eds. Stuart Hall/Paul du Gay. London: Sage. 18-36.

Beal, Timothy K. 2005. *Roadside Religion. In Search of the Sacred, the Strange, and the Substance of Faith.* Boston: Beacon Press.

Ben-Arieh, Yehoshua. 1989. *The Rediscovery of the Holy Land in the Nineteenth Century.* Jerusalem and Detroit: Magnes Press and Wayne State University Press.

Bowman, Glenn. 1992. "Pilgrim Narratives of Jerusalem and the Holy Land: A Study in Ideological Distortion." *Sacred Journeys: The Anthropology of Pilgrimage.* Ed. Alan Morinis. Westport, Conn.: Greenwood Press. 149-168.

Bowman, Glenn. 2000. "Christian Ideology and the Image of a Holy Land. The Place of Jerusalem Pilgrimage in the Various Christianities." *Contesting the Sacred: The Anthropology of Pilgrimage.* Eds. John Eade/Michael J. Sallnow. Urbana: Illinois University Press. 98-121.

Bryman, Alan. 1999. "The Disneyization of Society." *The Sociological Review* 47.1: 25-47.

Cardman, Francine. 1982. "The Rhetoric of Holy Places: Palestine in the Fourth Century." *Studia Patristica* XVII.1 – Historica, Theologica, Gnostica, Biblica, Critica, Classica: 18-25.

Cohen-Hattab, Kobi/Noam Shoval. 2007. "Tourism Development and Cultural Conflict: The Case of 'Nazareth 2000'." *Social & Cultural Geography* 8.5: 701-717.

Coleman, Simon. 2002. "Do you Believe in Pilgrimage? Communitas, Contestation and Beyond." *Anthropological Theory* 2.3: 355-368.

Coleman, Simon. 2004. "From England's Nazareth to Sweden's Jerusalem. Movement, (Virtual) Landscapes and Pilgrimage." *Reframing Pilgrimage. Cultures in Motion.* Eds. Simon Coleman/ John Eade. New York: Routledge. 45-68.

Coleman, Simon/John Eade. 2004. "Introduction: Reframing Pilgrimage." *Reframing Pilgrimage. Cultures in Motion.* Eds. Simon Coleman/John Eade. New York: Routledge. 1-25.

Collins-Kreiner, Noga/Nurit Kliot. 2000. "Pilgrimage Tourism in the Holy Land: The Behavioural Characteristics of Christian Pilgrims." *GeoJournal* 50.1: 55-67.

Collins-Kreiner, Noga/ Nurit Kliot/ Yoel Mansfeld/Keren Sagi. 2006. *Christian Tourism to the Holy Land. Pilgrimage During Security Crisis.* Aldershot, UK: Ashgate.

Davis, Peter. 2005. "Places, 'Cultural Touchstones' and the Ecomuseum." *Heritage, Museums and Galleries. An Introductory Reader.* Ed. Gerald Corsane. London/New York: Routledge. 365-376.

Eco, Umberto. 1986. *Travels in Hyperreality. Essays.* Orlando: Harvest/HBJ.

Edensor, Tim. 2000. "Staging Tourism: Tourists as Performers." *Annals of Tourism Research* 27.2: 322-344.

Eliade, Mircea. 1959. *The Sacred and the Profane. The Nature of Religion.* New York: Harcourt, Brace & World.

Feldman, Jackie. 2007. "Constructing a Shared Bible Land: Jewish Israeli Guiding Performances for Protestant Pilgrims." *American Ethnologist* 34.2: 351-374.

Gottdiener, Mark. 2001. *The Theming of America. American Dreams, Media Fantasies, and Themed Environments.* Second ed. Boulder: Westview Press.

Greenberg, Gershon. 1994. *The Holy Land in American Religious Thought, 1620-1948. The Symbiosis of American Religious Approaches to Scripture's Sacred Territory.* Lanham: University Press of America.

Guter, Yael. 1997. *Mormon – Christian Pilgrimage to Israel. Pilgrim's Experience,* MA Thesis, Department of Israel Studies, Bar-Ilan University (in Hebrew).

Halbwachs, Maurice. 1992. "The Legendary Topography of the Gospels in the Holy Land." *On Collective Memory.* Ed. Lewis A. Coser. Chicago/London: The University of Chicago Press. 191-235.

Hostetler, David Michael. 2005. Personal Communication (transcribed interview), 27 April.

Hummel, Thomas/Ruth Hummel. 1995. *Patterns of the Sacred. English Protestant and Russian Orthodox Pilgrims of the Nineteenth*

Century, London: Scorpion Cavendish (with the Swedish Christian Study Center, Jerusalem).

Kauffmann, Joel/David Michael Hostetler. 2005. *The Nazareth Jesus Knew.* Nazareth: Nazareth Village.

Keane, Webb. 2007. *Christian Moderns: Freedom and Fetish in the Mission Encounter (The Anthropology of Christianity, 1).* Berkeley: University of California Press.

Kliot, Nurit/Noga Collins-Kreiner. 2003. "Wait For Us – We're Not Ready Yet: Holy Land Preparations for the New Millennium – The Year 2000." *Current Issues in Tourism* 6.2: 119-149.

List of Defunct Amusement Parks. http://en.wikipedia.org/wiki/List_of_defunct_amusement_parks (accessed 31 Aug 2009).

Lock, Charles. 2003. "Bowing Down to Wood and Stone: One Way to be a Pilgrim." *Pilgrim Voices. Narrative and Authorship in Christian Pilgrimage.* Eds. Simon Coleman/John Elsner. New York: Berghahn. 110-132.

Long, Burke O. 2003. *Imagining the Holy Land. Maps, Models, and Fantasy Travels.* Bloomington: Indiana University Press.

Luhrmann, Tanya Marie. 2004. "Metakinesis: How God Becomes Intimate in Contemporary U.S. Christianity." *American Anthropologist* 106.3: 518-528.

MacCannell, Dean. 1973. "Staged Authenticity: Arrangements of Social Space in Tourist Settings." *American Journal of Sociology* 79.3: 589-603.

MacCannell, Dean. 1976. *The Tourist. A New Theory of the Leisure Class.* New York: Schocken Books.

McLuhan, Marshall. 1962. *The Gutenberg Galaxy. The Making of Typographic Man.* Toronto, Ontario: University of Toronto Press.

Markus, Robert A. 1994. "How on Earth Could Places Become Holy? Origins of the Christian Idea of Holy Places." *Journal of Early Christian Studies* 2.3: 257-271.

Monk, Daniel Bertland. 2002. *An Aesthetic Occupation. The Immediacy of Architecture and the Palestine Conflict.* Durham/London: Duke University Press.

Moore, Helen. 2003. "The Pilgrimage of Passion in Sidney's Arcadia." *Pilgrim Voices. Narrative and Authorship in Christian Pilgrimage.* Eds. Simon Coleman/John Elsner. New York: Berghahn. 61-83.

Obenzinger, Hilton. 1999. *American Palestine. Melville, Twain, and the Holy Land Mania.* Princeton: Princeton University Press.

Olsen, Daniel H./Dallen J. Timothy. 2006. "Tourism and Religious Journeys." *Tourism, Religion and Spiritual Journeys.* Eds. Dallen J. Timothy/Daniel H. Olsen. London/New York: Routledge. 1-21.

Pinto, Hanania. 2004. Personal communication (transcribed interview), 10 Dec.

Quiroga, Isabel. 1990. "Characteristics of Package Tours in Europe." *Annals of Tourism Research* 17.2: 185-207.

Rivera, Manuel Antonio/Shani Amir/Denver Severt. 2009. "Perceptions of Service Attributes in a Religious Theme Site: An Importance-Satisfaction Analysis." *Journal of Heritage Tourism* 4.3: 227-243.

Ritzer, George/Allan Liska. 1997. "'McDisneyization' and 'Post-Tourism'. Complementary Perspectives on Contemporary Tourism." *Touring Cultures. Transformations of Travel and Theory.* Eds. Chris Rojek/John Urry. New York: Routledge. 96-109.

Rogers, Stephanie Stidham. 2003. "American Protestant Pilgrimage: Nineteenth-Century Impressions of Palestine." *Koinonia Journal: The Princeton Seminary Graduate Forum,* XV (1): 60-80. Available at http://www.ptsem.edu/koinonia/assets/issues/15/stidman rogers2%20--%20for%20web.pdf (accessed 25 Aug 2009).

Ron, Amos Shlomo/Jackie Feldman. 2009. "From Spots to Themed Sites – The Evolution of the Protestant Holy Land." *Journal of Heritage Tourism* 4.3: 201-216.

Roth, Shirley. 2008. Correspondence with the author, 12 May.

Rowan, Yorke. 2004. "Repacking the Pilgrimage: Visiting the Holy Land in Orlando." *Marketing Heritage. Archaeology and the Consumption of the Past.* Eds. Yorke Rowan/Uzi Baram. Walnut Creek, CA: Alta Mira Press. 249-266.

Schmidt, Catherine J. 1979. "The Guided Tour. Insulated Adventure." *Urban Life* 7.4: 441–467.

Shani, Amir/Rivera, Manuel Antonio/Denver Severt. 2007. "'To Bring God's Word to All People': The Case of a Religious Theme-Site." *Tourism* 55.1: 39-50.

Shoval, Noam. 2000. "Commodification and Theming of the Sacred: Changing Patterns of Tourist Consumption in the 'Holy Land'." *New Forms of Consumption. Consumers, Culture and Commodification.* Ed. Mark Gottdiener. Boulder, CO: Rowman and Littlefield. 251-263.

Silberman, Neil Asher. 2001. "If I forget Three, O Jerusalem: Archaeology, Religious Commemoration and Nationalism in a Disputed City, 1801-2001." *Nations and Nationalism* 7.4: 487-504.

Sizer, Stephen Robert. 1999. "The Ethical Challenges of Managing Pilgrimages to the Holy Land." *International Journal of Contemporary Hospitality Management* 11.2/3: 85-90.

Todd, Janey R. 1984. "Whither Pilgrimage. A Consideration of Holy Land Pilgrimage Today." *Annales de la Commission Des Pélerinages Chrétiens,* Jerusalem: Notre Dame Center. 20-54.

Urry, John. 1995. *Consuming Places.* London: Routledge.

Urry, John. 2002. *The Tourist Gaze.* Second ed. London: Sage.

Rojek, Chris/John Urry, eds. 1997. *Touring Cultures. Transformations of Travel and Theory*. New York: Routledge.

Werblowsky, Raphael J. Zwi. 1988. *The Meaning of Jerusalem to Jews, Christians and Muslims*. Jerusalem: Israel Universities Study Group for Middle Eastern Affairs.

Wuthnow, Robert. 1998. *After Heaven. Spirituality in America Since the 1950s*. Berkeley: University of California Press.

From Themed Space to Lifespace

Scott A. Lukas

In 1994 testimony was taken up by the US Senate that focused on the nature of theming at the proposed Disney's America theme park near Manassas, Virginia (Potential Impact 1994). The park would have included reconstructions of a Civil War-era fort and many other landmarks representative of this era of American history. The proposed theme park, itself, is an interesting object for anthropological analysis, but what is more curious about the controversy surrounding Disney's America is the nature of the discourse under consideration. Some critics attacked the park from a public works perspective, but most interesting were the many historians and anthropologists, including Mike Wallace, who attacked the plan because it was envisioned as a theme park (Wallace 1996). For them, the idea of representing history and culture as a theme park was tantamount to blasphemy. There are many other such examples in which critics have portrayed the theme park or themed space as an illegitimate way of representing culture and history (Lukas 2007a, 2007d, 2008, 2009). "What is paramount is not just that these spaces had controversial subject matters as their narratives, but that they were materialized – they were given a more vivid way to tell their controversial stories" (Lukas 2008: 214). They were situations in which narratives took form, and were played out, through themed spaces.

This paper focuses on the themed space as a cultural form with specific emphasis on the ways in which themed spaces have become the subject of heated political, representational and consumerist debates within anthropology and the social sciences. The myriad of themed spaces, including theme parks, themed casinos, themed restaurants, and other lifestyle spaces, reflects two interesting yet often contradictory cultural interpretations. The supporters of themed spaces claim that consumers of theming rely on these many spaces for self-fulfillment, identity construction and fantasy escapism. Critics of these spaces utilize them in their own ways, often pointing to the negativity of their representational forms, the political contexts of their cultural displays, and the seemingly conformist nature of their quotidian forms (Bryman 2004; Fjellman 1992). This paper aims to look at these two competing visions of theming and bring them into closer proximity and dialogue. First, the writing will consider the nature of authenticity and the ways in which it is endemic in both theming and the cultural criticism of theming. A specific focus is Bass Pro Shops Outdoor World. Following this is a discussion of cultural relativism and how it relates to the emic-level analyses within themed spaces. This is developed through an analysis of Six Flags AstroWorld. Next is an analysis of the political debates that have been applied to theming. This is developed through analysis of the discourse at an international conference on theming held at Walt Disney World. The chapter concludes with a discussion of how theming has been transformed in recent years, specifically focusing on Legends at Sparks Marina, located in Sparks, Nevada. The concept of the lifespace is developed in order to consider the emergence of a new, post-authentic cultural world.

Authenticity: A Curious Tension

Authenticity has been defined as "worthy of acceptance or belief as conforming to or based on fact; conforming to an original so as to reproduce essential features; made or done the same way as an original; not false or imitation; true to one's own personality, spirit, or character" (Merriam-Webster 2009). This definition, as it is played out in cultural means, is particularly significant in connection with the themed space. While an employee trainer at Six Flags Astro-World theme park in Houston, Texas, the author experienced many instances in which employee training philosophy was directed by the desire to produce the most authentic forms of theming (Lukas 2007b). As it was reflected at AstroWorld, authenticity included in-park references to all of these definitions of the concept: Employees were asked to dress, speak and act out the part. Patrons were guaranteed certain experiences, including jousting festivals and dining experiences that were purported to replicate the experiences of history and culture referenced in the theming. At AstroWorld numerous attempts were made to create an authentic experience, but many of these did not sit well with critics.

Unlike the theme park worker or the patron, the critic often fails to find authenticity within themed spaces. Extreme attention is given to minute details that may be incorrect, exaggerated or represented in an incorrect cultural context. Critics may also use the very claim that a park is aiming at an authentic experience to attack the basis of the theming (cf. Schatzer 2004). Acting out a medieval tournament and meal, for example, can never be authentic. For critics the approximations of material culture, behavior, and activities that are common to themed experiences are false approximations.[1]

In 2007 the author undertook ethnographic research at Bass Pro Shops Outdoor World in Hammond, Indiana. During this time, these fieldnotes were recorded:

"This 35,000 square foot space is unlike other outdoor adventure stores that I have visited. While Cabela's, Sheels and REI establish the essence of similar key signifiers of outdoor, nature and adventure, Bass Pro Shops Outdoor World is alone in scale, level of detail and the depth of the connections made by the theming throughout the space. I am not a hunter, so my immediate sense upon entering this place is of the disconnection that I feel, but I quickly realize that while this place does not relate to my interests, it does speak to the many others who enter this space. I could begin a study of consumer authenticity at any number of the micro spaces within the store: the camping center with life-sized figures, the roaring indoor streams complete with real fish and fake bears, the mannequin outdoors people above on precarious perches, the themed bathrooms that play on irony and camp, and the tens of thousands of products that speak to the life world of the outdoor enthusiast."

"There is a more significant place that invites me – an image, simulation and reconstruction. Near the door a perfect hunter's table is laid out. Two duck decoys are flanked by timbers and photos of an unknown hunter's children. In one image a boat approaches the shore of a lake, in the other a young boy proudly displays two fish that he has caught. Clearly, this fictitious family is meant to connote to us the bucolic, familial and the sublime. Next to those two photos are the other trappings of this hunter's life: a rifle, gunpowder, cleaning

---

1   One Disney text on Imagineering offers that "heightened reality", not reali-ty, is the true focus of theming: "Heightened reality is a staple of the Im-agineering toolbox, giving us the artistic license to play more directly to our emotional attachments to design details rather than to strict adherence to historical accuracy. [...] take the things people 'know' from the world around them, select the ones that suit the story you wish to tell, and com-bine them into something that is entirely new but that seems oddly famil-iar" (Imagineers 2005: 23). Thus, it would seem according to Disney's mis-sive on theming, that any discussion of authenticity as related to theming is inherently problematic. Disney, quite clearly, states that it is not produc-ing historical or cultural accuracy in its theme parks and other themed spaces, it is heightening reality and focusing on the emotional attachments that people have to places and cultures. In 2008, while conducting re-search at Europa-Park in Rust, Germany, the author encountered a similar sentiment. The park's lead architect expressed that their design decisions related to theming are based on stereotypes, not accurate portrayals of places and cultures in the world. This focus recalls Wayne Curtis' reflection that the authentic is "something that looks as you imagine it might" (Lukas 2007c: 82).

equipment, a pelt and a curious note reading, 'Go to Bass Pro and Pick Up Shells'.

My gaze extends upwards beyond the archetypal hunter's table. Above is a wall flooded with duck decoys and antlers from an unidentified species, as well as a few taxidermy models. The wall displays patinaed panels of a red hue that also appears to be chipping and decaying. Just next to a few more images of hunters holding turkeys around their necks is an oddly placed surveillance camera, reminding us of the curious tension of authenticity at play here.

Knowing our place in the scheme of things seems to be a defining condition of the authentic (Guignon 2004: 13). For the hunter the various dioramas, displays, product demonstrations, animal and nature simulations and the texts deployed throughout the store offer a clear sense of the authentic. While the outdoor enthusiast is never just an outdoor enthusiast – s/he is many people, at once – the strong urges and affective regimes of Bass Pro Shops Outdoor World remind the visitor that he or she shares with others a place in this world. As I leave the shop I have the clear sense that authenticity lies in a precarious balance between traditional worlds (like those represented in the images on the hunter's table) and consumer ones."

Fig. 1: Bass Pro Shops

Photograph: Scott A. Lukas

As Holtorf has argued, in the case of material culture, the concept of an authentic past is highly problematic (2005: 112-129). Beyond the material and into the realm of the ideational, there are similar reasons that one should be suspicious of monolithic constructions of the authentic experience (Guignon 2004; Heidegger 1964). Authenticity, like the complex and changing themed worlds in which it deployed, is evanescing. We can, theoretically, "own ourselves" in consumer themed spaces such as these, but what is the outcome of such "self-possession" (Guignon 2004: 7)? Is it a post-authenticity that, like the other formulations of postmodernism, suggests a necessary reformulation of our concepts of space, self and society (Gergen 1992; Harvey 1991; Jameson 1992; Klein 2002; Lyotard 1984)?

Everyday Life and the Themed Space

The issue of authenticity highlights the significant role that experience plays in the discourse surrounding theming. While popular critics of theming often focus on material, architectural and consumerist constructions, social scientists have pointed to the in-situ, existential, quotidian, identity-based and psychological aspects of these spaces and they have stressed the aspect of social practice to be studied in its own right. Indeed as rhetorician Derek Foster's work on themed love hotels in Japan suggests, the contexts of themed spaces must be understood beyond mere academic critical ones:

"So, far from critiquing such establishments for their patent artificiality, we ought to recognize that the love hotel 'isn't the mimicry of a thing; it's a thing'. Everything in the environment is self-consciously fabricated and obviously fake. The themed spaces of love hotels are not meant to be something else but exist simply to connote it, to allude to it so that the essence of such far-off (or far-out) places might attach itself to patrons, corporeally, for the duration of their short stay." (Foster 2007: 170)

Foster's emphasis on the everyday and the social role that theming plays in Japan is indicative of the classic anthropological emphasis on cultural relativism and emic-level analysis. Anthropology stresses the values of understanding cultures in their indigenous terms. As Foster illustrates, love hotels are meaningful cultural forms for many Japanese, even in the face of their clearly fabricated and overdetermined nature.

For many patrons and workers of themed spaces, theming may provide senses of meaning, excitement, even agency, but few take theming to a existential level. During the early years of operation at Disneyland, there was one such worker who did. A young boy, when asked to portray Tom Sawyer on Tom Sawyer Island, took the part so seriously that he took on an aggressive persona. Much like the character in the novel, he attacked other kids who visited the attraction (Capodagli/Jackson 1999: 133). This case signifies a situation in which theming goes beyond the surface level of dramaturgy and into psychological and existential realms. According to a guidebook on extending Disney theming and customer service principles to non-Disney venues, "The final phase of building a performance culture is to give employees the freedom to begin living it" (Disney Institute 2001: 98). The worker at Tom Sawyer Island who lived his thematic role too closely suggests the development of a deeper connection between the theme and a worker and/or patron.

Lived theming helps illustrate the situation in which the thematic constructs of the corporation become internalized, even personalized, in the individual. This phenomenon refers to the "movement of the material elements of theming into the realm of the immaterial. It refers to situations in which workers or patrons of themed spaces psychologically take on the characteristics, values, or attitudes that are connoted by the particular themes of the venues" (Lukas 2007e: 295). Much like the fan culture evident with *Star Trek*, *Star Wars* and other popular shows and forms of media, theming has attracted its own followers. Magazines like *Tiki Magazine* illustrate how personally individuals have taken what appears to be a superficial construction in *tiki* (Tiki Magazine 2009). In contexts like these we can begin to understand how *tiki*, or any other form of constructed culture that we call theming, is more than the figurines, thatched bars, and island music that could be associated with the form. As people begin to associate more clearly with the nuances of the culture or situations being themed, it becomes more likely that, similar to Civil War reenactment aficionados, individuals will develop a deep and lasting connection to the worlds being simulated. As lived theming becomes more common in the world, further applications of cultural relativism will, no doubt, be warranted.

Yet the challenge of such applications to the venue of the themed space is that theming involves the approximations of cultures, people and places, and thus it is within the shorthand versions of cultures in which anthropologists commonly emphasize critiques (Lukas 2009). Critics of popular culture point to the stereotypes, revisions, inaccuracies and omissions of culture that themed spaces like Epcot promote (Van Eeden 2007). As Van Eeden points out in her study of the Lost City theme park complex in South Africa, a combination of such stereotypes, revisions, inaccuracies and omissions of culture results from the rather overdetermined image of Africa that is itself produced in the world of video games, motion pictures and the colonialist imaginary (ibid.). What sorts of resolutions to this conundrum can be had?

While working at the Six Flags AstroWorld theme park, I became familiar with the contradictions that developed between the pleasures of patrons and workers and the critical models of anthropology. In particular, my work with one rides manager helped inform a critical ethnographic tradition that balanced these two worlds (cf.

Marcus 1998; Rabinow/Marcus 2008; Tyler 1987). While working together in the park, the rides manager and I had a conversation regarding the design of the newest themed ride – the Mayan Mind Bender. The manager, while acting fully immersed within both his work world and his pleasure world – he would often comment on the joy of working specifically in a themed environment – on one occasion expressed outrage with the ride's theming. The Mayan Mind Bender was a recycled ride in that it was purchased from another park and then rethemed with a Mayan narrative. For the rides manager this was tantamount with treason: "How can they call this Mayan? The glyphs aren't even Mayan, and many of the other details... they also got those wrong." When this manager went to upper management and expressed his concerns with these inaccuracies, he was told that these constructions were all in fun. In retrospect, upper management should have appreciated this manager's concerns. He, like some of the devout park workers, showed characteristics of internalizing the thematic and other narratives expressed in the park. Simultaneously he showed signs of applying a critical analysis of the Mayan theming that approximates the critiques of anthropology. Individuals like this manager illustrate a potential middle range approach to the challenges of the anthropology of theming.

Constituent and Processual Theming

Theming has had a profound impact on world cultures. Whether one looks at the local pub down the street or the newest theme park, the person is likely to discover the explicit or implicit effects of theming. The "theme park form" suggests that theme parks have impacted culture in four main ways: They have affected *showing* by instituting new forms of architecture, geography and space; they have influenced *doing* by offering new social forms, relationships and self-directed programs; they have affected *knowing* by producing new understandings of culture and the world at large; and they have influenced *telling* by introducing new narratives and understandings of the world (Lukas 2008: 240-245). In sum, these effects have been transformative, not just in the world of theming specifically but within the world of consumer culture generally. As previously discussed, for some critics the nature of this transformation is especially problematic. From their point of view, the theme park form, in all of its impacts, will move cultures down the path of inauthenticity and simulation, will produce undesirable social forms such as Disneyization and McDonaldization (Bryman 2004; Ritzer 2007), and will ultimately challenge, if not negate, other forms of culture, such as museums and even historical reenactments.[2] Indeed, many of these criticisms are real concerns, but one fundamental problem with them is the static nature of their foundations. Few cultural critics have had substantial, emic-level experiences within theme parks and themed spaces, and thus their criticisms assume a monolithic construct, essentially negating constituent and processual understandings of theming.

There is, however, an interesting development within the world of theme parks and themed spaces. There are four specific transformations that respect the culturally constituted and non-static nature of theming. First, there is the movement of the theme park to the meta level. A theme park can be seen and interpreted as "text", as something people variously read, interpret, and recreate (Lukas 2008: 212-245). As such, it moves from a material realm to an immaterial one. The many examples of homemade, backyard roller coasters, theme park video games, the defunct Virtual Magic Kingdom, theme parks in Second Life, fictional accounts of theme parks including *England, England; Civilwarland in Bad Decline;* and *Utopia* (Barnes 2000; Child 2002; Saunders 1997) and numerous fan and enthusiast pages on the Internet, project a secondary text that has rarely been considered in the accounts of theme parks. Primarily because theme parks have been seen as hegemonic structures, not as culturally constituent objects, many critics (Bryman 2004; Fjellman 1992) have failed to grasp the unique and at least occasionally even curiously counter-hegemonic and meta constructions of theme parks. What is most profound in this first transformation is the degree to which these texts transform, and are transformed by, the theme park and themed space.

Next, there is the issue of the tropes that are now emerging as new foundations for theming. While at the SATE (Storytelling, Architecture, Technology, and Experience) theming conference in Orlando, Florida, I had the opportunity to hear a presentation on the design of Hard Rock Park in Myrtle Beach, South Carolina. The park closed in 2008, and was reopened and renamed Freestyle Music Park in 2009. What was curious about the park's approach to theming was how it referenced cultural and historical topics in unconventional ways. In contrast with how history is sometimes used as a rather static and aesthetically simple trope in many theme parks

---

2   At the 2007 SATE conference in Orlando, Florida, one of the common topics was the interplay of theme parks and museums (King 1991). A number of the designers representing major museums in the United States indicated that the circumstance is not merely that museums are competing with theme parks for the revenue of visitors but that museums are actively embracing many of the technologies, techniques, and design patterns made popular in theme parks.

(such as the Western Village archetype that proliferates many of them) was how Rock n' Roll, as one example, was conceived as a more subcultural, less conventional thematic construct than we might expect. *Nights in White Satin* is used on a psychedelic ride through the Sixties, while the concepts of rebellion, anti-authoritarianism, and even bad taste (as exemplified in restrooms and the signage of park attractions) are used to convey a much different sense of theming. In this and in other examples, theming has moved into a more "dark" territory (Foley/Lennon 2000; Lukas 2007a). *Dark theming* (summarized in Table 1) indicates the movement of theming into the realm of unconventional tropes, new approaches to material construction and abandonment of purely modernist sensibilities. Irony, ambiguity and what Georges Bataille offered as the 'low' are now found in more themed spaces than in the past (Lukas 2005, 2007a: 276-285). Like Hard Rock Park's unconventional approach to telling the past, themed spaces in many Asian countries, Scandinavia, and the United States, have rewritten the ways in which a space presents its narratives. In Japan there are toilet-themed restaurants and cannibalistic sushi, in Latvia, there are hospital-themed restaurants, and in many cultures there are literally dark-themed venues (in which patrons eat in complete darkness), death or grave-themed establishments, and there is the excess and toilet humor at Bon Bon Land in Denmark (Bon Bon Land 2010; Lukas 2005, 2007a; Web Urbanist 2010).

Third, there is growing reflexivity within the non-academic worlds of theming, including those of park design and architectural firms. In the case of Disney resorts and theme parks, theming has always been a conscious and often critical process. In one example from a Disney Imagineering text intended for a popular readership, the concept of theming is addressed in explicit terms:

"When we use the term [theme], we are more interested in what something means than what it looks like [...] 'Theme' is a noun rather than a verb. It is sometimes mistakenly taken to mean applying ornament to an object to make it appear to belong to a particular time or place, such as the architecture or propping found in Main Street, U.S.A." (Imagineers 2007: 41)

In the late 1990s, designers responsible for the Polynesian Resort at Walt Disney World began experimenting with new work models that paralleled, on a normative level, the cultures in which the theming was based. Disney management attempted to inculcate the traditional island values associated with the South Pacific in their workplace structure, including specific values that were stressed among workers and patrons (Lukas 2007b: 195). Further evidence of more reflexive understandings of theming were noted during the author's visit at the SATE theming conference in Orlando, Florida.

Table 1: Dark Theming Characteristics

	Traditional Theming	Examples	Dark Theming	Examples
Nature of Themes	Clean, happy, uncontroversial	*Pirates of the Caribbean* (Disney). Death and violence is fun.	Dark, morbid, controversial	Hitler's Cross (Mumbai, India)
Nature of Space	Sacred, pure, clean	Cinderella Castle (Disney)	Profane, unpurified, dirty	Hard Rock Park
Role of the Carnivalesque	Reduced to a desexed consumerism	Masquerade Show in the Sky (Rio All-Suite Hotel and Casino). Carnival is depoliticized.	Present and glorified	Bon Bon Land (Denmark). Sexuality, body parts, defecation are among the themes.
Semiotics of Content	Simplified	Hall of Presidents (Disney). World history, including the Vietnam War, is reduced to jingoistic simplicities.	Complex	Eden Camp (England). Patrons are asked to look at the complexities of World War II.
Presence of Death and Violence	Limited	Haunted Mansion (Disney); limited to a consumerist macabre.	Explicit	Museum of Tolerance (Los Angeles)
Role of Patron	Experiences pleasure, non-contemplative	Disney's Animal Kingdom. While issues like poaching and deforestation are raised, the emphasis is on consumption and pleasure.	Contemplative, asked questions	Imperial War Museum (England). The patron is asked to think deeply on the nature of war and violence.

Quite surprising and promising was the critical discourse on theming expressed by practitioners that paralleled the same discourse often expressed by anthropologists and academics. One architectural firm, while in the process of discussing a new theming complex in Egypt, referenced the complex discourses of theming that had previously used Egyptian cultures as a subject. According to the architects, there was a conscious effort to negotiate the complex and constructed history of Egypt as a nation and the often-stereotyped and overused construction of Egypt as a simulacrum, such as at the Luxor Casino in Vegas. The firm actually referenced the Luxor Casino as something that they would explicitly avoid as a model on which to base their project (WATG 2010).

Fig. 2: Adventurer's Club

Photograph: Scott A. Lukas

A second context was the work of the Goddard entertainment firm and its design work related to the Georgia Aquarium. The firm spoke of efforts to build the narrative of sea life at the aquarium through various forms of theming, architecture, decor, and technology. Towards the end of the presentation, firm lead Gary Goddard offered a missive for the theming individuals gathered at the SATE conference. He spoke of the complacency within the theming industry and, much like cultural critics and anthropologists, bemoaned the forms of representation within the theming industry: "We must abandon the Hollywood boulevards and New York City streets [that have become the archetypes of the theme park and themed space]" (Goddard 2008).

Last, there is an expansion of the nature of theming beyond its bounded materiality and geography. The first transformation of theming (the meta level) has in turn, resulted in a movement of theming into the level of the life world – its most intimate and potentially influential transformation. While attending the SATE conference, I was particularly taken with a conversation held at one of the now closed nightclubs of Pleasure Island, called the Adventurer's Club. What was most interesting about this gathering – which was intended to be a social mixer for the conference participants – was the opportunity to comment on theming in situ, something that is rather uncommon in academic studies of theming. As conference participants looked over the elephant stools, wrecked pipe organ, rooms of masks and somewhat-in-jest adventurer's spoils, they discussed the irony that one of the most interestingly themed spaces at Disney would soon be closed. They debated the merits of theming, considered the irony of it and spoke about the challenges that designers face as they confront the issues of authenticity, creativity, and patron satisfaction. The most sobering thing about the conversations was how cognizant the designers and architects are of the fact that their decisions about theming are not simple choices about accurately re-presenting another culture, people, or event, but rather, perhaps like anthropologists, they understand that any choice made is always a partial and political one. The sum of these transformations within the world of theming suggests the analytical need to produce more grounded, constituent and processual accounts of theme parks and themed spaces. It also suggests the necessity for a reformulation of themed spaces – a phenomenon which I will tentatively attempt to classify as *lifespace*.

Lifespace: The Transformation of the Themed Space

> "Rousseau [notes that] self–discovery is not a matter of *finding* an entity that has been there all along. It is a matter of *making* the self in the course of the search." (Guignon 2004: 69)

Through Henry Jenkins' concept of convergence culture, media subcultures, and fandom are given new and expanded meaning. As multiple media forms proliferate, as synergies of media become the norm, and as "consumers are encouraged to seek out new information and make connections among dispersed media content", a new form, convergence culture, is given shape (Jenkins 2006: 3). A similar transformation has begun to take root within the world of theme parks and themed spaces. The "lifespace" represents the emergence of a new form of consumer space. Like theme parks and themed spaces in general it utilizes theming, consumer immersion, and storytelling to project a narrative onto consumers, but what is most curious about this new form is the degree to which it breaks with the past. In addition to being more ubiquitously found in cities and communities throughout the world, it is characterized by a number of shifts in form and approach, summarized in Table 2.

The lifespace represents transformations in the ways in which the consumer is oriented to the world (Lukas 2008: 243-44). Whereas in the past themed spaces purported to take the consumer into new and exotic worlds, in the present the lifespace takes the consumer on a more inward and reflexive journey in which the orientation of the space is decidedly focused on the lifeworld of the individual. Whereas the themed environment in restaurants, shopping malls, and spas presented its own theming somewhat self-consciously as a stage backdrop for the event in which the customer was supposed to participate, the lifespace has successfully integrated its themed elements: The spatial and geographic boundedness of themed environments is extended in favor of permeable spaces. Coupled with this shift is a new understanding of leisure itself. No longer will the theme park represent a pilgrimage away from work and everyday life. Instead, life and work are blurred, and the consumer is asked to think of consumer life as being adhered to and even identical with everyday life. Perhaps most significant in this new world is the way in which authenticity, this archetype of theming, is turned on its head. In its place is the world of post-authenticity in which originals and copies comingle and in which meaning itself is produced in continual "loops" (Baudrillard 1983; Ferrell/Hayward/Young 2008: 130). In Table 2, the theme park form is compared to the lifespace. A series of twelve issues are considered. These include life orientation (how does the form orient itself to the individual and culture), berm (how bounded is the space), reflexivity (how does the space reference its own constructs), and others.

Table 2: Characteristics of Lifespace

Issue	Theme Park Form	Lifespace
Life Orientation	Outward Exotic	Inward Familiar
Cultural Communication	The door of the world	The mirror of the self
Material Culture (Architecture, Geography, Décor)	Unfamiliar Cabinet of curiosities Grand Tour	Familiar Contemplative Atmospheric
Berm	Bounded park (Tilyou's Steeplechase park in Coney Island, New York)	No berm: space is permeable; a transgression of spaces literal and figurative (Starbucks, 'third place')
Transformation	Go to the place; Van Gennep's rite de passage; change is spatially located	Lifelong and adaptive: individuals carry with themselves a sense of agency, affect, values
Reflexivity	Sense of the authentic even when it is purely simulation	A wink, ambivalence, camp and kitsch, self-flagellation, self-awareness
Status of the Brand	Part of the show (from the ride into the branded merchandise store)	Brandlessness and erasure (Celebration, Florida); Roberts' lovemark (an expression of the self and less an outward material manifestation; the lovemark is a fusion of the devotional focus of religion and the economic focus of consumerism; the inward modes of religion are connected not to spirituality but to consumption itself, 2004)
Civics & Politics	Coney Island: social mixing; Disney's 'Thatcherean individualism and iso-lationism'; apolitics	Civic orientation through consumerism: 'Starbucks Civics': drink coffee, read a brochure & change the world!
Theme	People, place, culture	Trope, idea, feeling, affect

Issue	Theme Park Form	Lifespace
Pedagogy	Teach about the value of something (electricity in the world's fair) or certain values (American democracy)	Museum of Tolerance, Seattle Music Experience Museum: micro-politics, looming issues, social change begins with the change of the self, lifestyle politics
Copy	Concern for authenticity	Post-authenticity: a comingling of most aspects of the world through traces and intertextuality
Leisure	Separation from work	Incorporation of work into life: complete blurring of it (Home Depot and the do-it-yourself movement in UK/US)[3]

In 2009 the author began preliminary research at Legends at Sparks Marina, an upscale shopping mall located in Sparks, Nevada (Legends at Sparks Marina 2009). This open-air mall is a unique shopping destination that combines elements of shopping malls, theme parks and themed venues. Like many consumer spaces in the United States, Legends at Sparks Marina reflects the emerging tendency of the lifespace. This tendency is described in the author's fieldnotes:

"The first store built at the Legends, Scheels, gave some indication of the lifestyle tendencies of this open-air shopping complex. Sheels, like Bass Pro Shops Outdoor World and Cabela's, is marketed to the sports enthusiast. Inside the monumental space (300,000 square feet) of the store, one finds the typical trappings of any sports store, but much larger, and, compiled with this scale are attractions that resemble the insides of a theme park – virtual race car games, expansive diorama and décor and a large and impressive mountain of taxidermy. Scheels was the anchor store, and now the many other shops have taken root – The Gap, the Old Farmer's Almanac General Store, Guess, Off Broadway Shoes, Michael Kors and many others.

---

3   While work and home are indeed blurred in many of these new venues, it should be emphasized that forms of alienation and hegemony (of the sorts identified by Gramsci, Marx, Horkheimer and Adorno) are still quite pronounced. If anything, this blurring of these two life domains should inspire us to look at the increasing forms of illicit and latent alienation within our world.

On first glance Legends may appear to be like any other outdoor mall where the focus is primarily on consumption, but something different is at play. According to the publicity department, "It's [...] a walking history tour, integrating land and hardscape features that reflect the history and pop culture of Nevada [...] The Legends at Sparks Marina honors legends of Nevada in athletics, science, technology, politics and art, recognizing the people that have helped make the area truly unique and legendary" (Legends at Sparks Marina 2009). Throughout the outdoor mall, numerous features point to the efforts of the designers to have this mall stand out as something different than another shopping center. The parking lot features theming based on Mark Twain, the numerous landscape features point to the state of Nevada's important flora and fauna, and strewn next to many of the stores are historical plaques that detail the contributions of famous leaders from the state. One of the most interesting ones, tucked somewhat away from the main stores and near the parking lot, is a memorial sign for George Ferris, the inventor of the Ferris wheel who lived in Carson City, Nevada as a child.

Fig. 3: Legends mall

Photograph: Scott A. Lukas

As I am pursuing the displays at Legends, I am struck by the sense of the different narrative that is at play here. Were I in a theme park, I could go ride a thrilling roller coaster. While I cannot do that at Legends, I have the sense that this place owes its sense of geography, attention to thematic sculpture, themed parking lots and landscape architecture to the theme park form. Were I in a shopping mall, I would only think about the next consumer store that I would visit and perhaps set my sights on a restaurant that would suit my liking, but at Legends I have the feeling that I am being asked to do more than consume and eat. I am asked to reflect – inwardly – on what the state of Nevada means. Basque sheepherders, the desert tortoise, sagebrush, the Comstock mine, the Pony Express, Chinese railroad laborers, the Virginia and Truckee Railroad, Naval Air Station Fallon, Mark Twain, Lake Tahoe, Governor John Sparks, Sarah Winnemucca, Wovoka, the Ichthyosaur, Pyramid Lake, desert bighorn sheep, bristlecone pine, Jedediah Smith, and buckaroos are juxtaposed throughout the mall – either through historical plaque, sculpture, water or outdoor feature, or other artistic display. The lifespace, like the theme park and the themed space before it, intends for us to have a pleasurable time, but the emphasis here is on a lasting effect that we can take home with us."

While the lifespace is a preliminary concept intended to inspire more theoretical exploration, it does, in the present, allow researchers to consider the ways in which the theme park and the themed space have started to transform contemporary consumer space. If the theme park could still be conceptually understood as 'that place down the street that looks nothing like our everyday spaces', the innocuous theming of lifespace has not only become pervasive beyond shopping malls and housing developments, it may already have taken root in your very backyard.

References

Barnes, Julian. 2000. *England, England.* New York: Vintage.

Baudrillard, Jean. 1983. *Simulations.* New York: Semiotext(e).

Bon Bon Land. n.d. "Bon Bon Land." http://www.bonbonland.dk/ (accessed 29 Mar 2010).

Bryman, Alan. 2004. *The Disneyization of Society.* London: Sage.

Capodagli, Bill/Lynn Jackson. 1999. *The Disney Way: Harnessing the Management Secrets of Disney in Your Company.* New York: McGraw-Hill.

Child, Lincoln. 2002. *Utopia.* New York: Doubleday.

Disney Institute. 2001. *Be Our Guest: Perfecting the Art of Customer Service.* New York: Disney Editions.

Ferrell, Kevin/Keith Hayward/Jock Young. 2008. *Cultural Criminology: An Invitation.* London: Sage.

Fjellman, Stephen. 1992. *Vinyl Leaves: Walt Disney World and America.* Boulder: Westview.

Foley, Malcolm/John Lennon. 2000. *Dark Tourism.* Florence, KY: Cengage.

Foster, Derek. 2007. "Love Hotels: Sex and the Rhetoric of Themed Spaces." *The Themed Space: Locating Culture, Nation, and Self.* Ed. Scott A. Lukas. Lanham, MD: Lexington. 167-181.

Gergen, Kenneth J. 1992. *The Saturated Self.* New York: Basic Books.

Goddard, Gary. "Architecture." Presentation at the 2008 Theming Entertainment Association SATE conference. 18 Sep 2008.

Guignon, Charles. 2004. *On Being Authentic.* New York: Routledge.

Harvey, David. 1991. *The Condition of Postmodernity: An Enquiry into the Origins of Cultural Change.* London: Blackwell.

Heidegger, Martin. 1964. *Being and Time.* New York: HarperOne.

Holtorf, Cornelius. 2005. *From Stonehenge to Las Vegas: Archaeology as Popular Culture.* Lanham, MD: Altamira.

Imagineers, The. 2005. *The Imagineering Field Guide to the Magic Kingdom.* New York: Disney Editions.

Imagineers, The. 2007. *The Imagineering Field Guide to Disney's Animal Kingdom.* New York: Disney Editions.

Jameson, Fredric. 1992. *Postmodernism: Or, the Cultural Logic of Late Capitalism.* Durham, NC: Duke University Press.

Jenkins, Henry. 2006. *Convergence Culture: Where Old and New Media Collide.* New York: New York University Press.

King, Margaret. 1991. "The Theme Park Experience. What Museums Can Learn from Mickey Mouse." *The Futurist* 25.6: 24-31.

Klein, Naomi. 2002. *No Logo.* New York: Picador.

Legends at Sparks Marina. 2009. "The Legends at Sparks Marina: Northern Nevada's First and Only Outlet Center." Available at http://www.experiencelegends.com/post/sections/61/Files/The _Legends_Fact_ Sheet.pdf (accessed 5 Nov 2009).

Lukas, Scott A. 2005. "The Theme Park and the Figure of Death." *InterCulture* 2. Available at http://www.fsu.edu/~proghum/int erculture/pdfs/lukas%20theme%20park%20death.pdf (accessed 2 Apr 2010).

Lukas, Scott A., ed. 2007. *The Themed Space: Locating Culture, Nation, and Self.* Lanham, MD: Lexington.

Lukas, Scott A. 2007a. "A Politics of Reverence and Irreverence: Social Discourse on Theming Controversies." *The Themed Space: Locating Culture, Nation, and Self.* Ed. Scott A. Lukas. Lanham, MD: Lexington. 271-293.

Lukas, Scott A. 2007b. "How the Theme Park Gets Its Power: Lived Theming, Social Control, and the Themed Worker Self." *The Themed Space: Locating Culture, Nation, and Self.* Ed. Scott A. Lukas. Lanham, MD: Lexington. 183-206.

Lukas, Scott A. 2007c. "Theming as a Sensory Phenomenon: Discovering the Senses on the Las Vegas Strip." *The Themed Space: Locating Culture, Nation, and Self.* Ed. Scott A. Lukas. Lanham, MD: Lexington. 75-95.

Lukas, Scott A. 2007d. "The Theming of Everyday Life: Mapping the Self, Life Politics, and Cultural Hegemony on the Las Vegas Strip." *Community College Humanities Review* 27: 167-192.

Lukas, Scott A. 2007e. "Key Terms." *The Themed Space: Locating Culture, Nation, and Self*. Ed. Scott A. Lukas. Lanham, MD: Lexington. 295-296.

Lukas, Scott A. 2008. *Theme Park*. London: Reaktion.

Lukas, Scott A. 2009. "Anthropology in a Simulation World: When Fieldwork Engages Pop Culture." *Anthropology News* 50.1: 20.

Lyotard, Jean-Francois. 1984. *The Postmodern Condition: A Report on Knowledge*. Minneapolis: University of Minnesota Press.

Marcus, George E. 1998. *Ethnography through Thick and Thin*. Princeton, NJ: Princeton University Press.

Merriam-Webster. 2009. Online Dictionary. http://www.merriam-webster.com/Dictionary.

Potential Impact of Disney's America Project on Manassas National Battlefield Park, Hearing Before the Subcommittee on Public Lands, National Parks and Forests of the Committee on Energy and Natural Resources. 21 Jun 1994. United States Senate. US Government Printing Office.

Rabinow, Paul/George E. Marcus. 2008. *Designs for an Anthropology of the Contemporary*. Durham: Duke University Press.

Ritzer, George. 2007. *The McDonaldization of Society 5*. Thousand Oaks, CA: Pine Forge Press.

Roberts, Kevin. 2004. *Lovemarks: The Future Beyond Brands*. New York: powerHouse Books.

Saunders, George. 1997. *CivilWarLand in Bad Decline*. New York: Riverhead Trade.

Schatzer, Mark. 2004. "Historical Fiction: How Do Medieval-Themed Restaurants Get It Wrong?" *Slate Magazine*, 6 Oct, 2004. Available at http://www.slate.com/id/2107363/ (accessed 2 Apr 2010).

Tiki Magazine. 2009. "Tiki Magazine." http://www.tikimagazine.com/ (accessed 2 Apr 2010).

Tyler, Stephen A. 1987. *The Unspeakable: Discourse, Dialogue, and Rhetoric in the Postmodern World*. Madison: University of Wisconsin Press.

Van Eeden, Jeanne. 2007. "Theming Mythical Africa at the Lost City." *The Themed Space: Locating Culture, Nation, and Self*. Ed. Scott A. Lukas. Lanham, MD: Lexington. 113-135.

Wallace, Mike. 1996. *Mickey Mouse History and Other Essays on American Memory*. Philadelphia: Temple University Press.

WATG. 2010. "Wimberly Allison Tong & Goo." http://www.watg. com/index.cfm (accessed 2 Apr 2010).

Web Urbanist. 2010. "15 of the Strangest Themed Restaurants: From Buns and Guns to Cannabalistic Sushi." http://weburbanist. com/2008/08/10/15-of-the-strangest-themed-restaurants-from-buns-and-guns-to-cannabalistic-sushi/ (accessed 2 Apr 2010).

Transhistorical Action:
Performance and Social Experience

Themed Environments – Performative Spaces:
Performing Visitors in
North American Living History Museums

CAROLYN OESTERLE

In North America, historically themed environments range from week-end-encampments on former battlefields or other historical sites to carefully restored or recreated homesteads or villages in open-air museums, and include some highly artificial simulations of histori-cal settings in theme parks, resorts, public places, malls, and restau-rants. In many of these simulated environments, displays of material culture are enlivened by "costumed interpreters"[1] who are engaged in period tasks and rituals, impersonating historical figures and skillfully interpreting history to a very diverse group of visitors, as well as by a range of participatory activities for the visiting public.

Regardless of these historical environments' differences in au-thenticity, objective, scientific standards, and interpretation policy, they are all stages for history, or what performance theorist Richard Schechner has called "large environmental theaters" (Schechner 1985: 79). There are a number of ways in which the axioms of environmental theater are realized in the themed environments of liv-ing history museums,[2] proving not only that living history pheno-mena may be assessed in terms of theatrical experience but also showing how spatial arrangements may generate and engineer the

---

1 Terms for performing staff vary greatly due to the organizations' philoso-phy and perspective on living history: most commonly they are referred to as "costumed interpreters", but also as "cultural informants" (Schechner 1985: 81), "costumed guides", "costumed characters", "re-enactors", "re-creators", "actor/guides", "actor/interpreters", "demontrators" (Goodacre/ Baldwin 2002: 111).

2 While my study focuses on living history programs in North-American mu-seums, I hold that the general approach also applies to other historically themed environments in theme parks and other public spaces, as well as to reenactments within the "unofficial 'folk' living-history movement" that nonetheless attract spectator-participants (Carlson 2000: 243).

"live performance" of both staff and visitors involved in the programs.

A myriad of studies[3] have addressed the importance of staging (or *mise en scène*), historical accuracy of the overall production and analyses of interpretive style (for example, the debates about *first* or *third person interpretation*[4] and the general interaction between staff and visitors) with regard to their effectiveness in bringing history to life[5] – mostly from a curatorial point of view. Evaluations of visitor experience are usually based on surveys that address visitor satisfaction in terms of how expectations were met or how visitors enjoyed the respective interpretive style, and on interactional data as witnessed or reported by staff (cf. Goodacre/Baldwin 2002: 91). A few studies have explicitly assessed visitor experience (cf. Snow 1993; Goodacre/Baldwin 2002), but even though the authors of these studies dedicate separate chapters to the motivations, perceptions, and interactions of visitors, they draw a distinct line between "performers" and "visitors" when discussing the performative aspects of living history – which points to the underlying assumption that the "living" in living history is done by trained staff while visitors are merely required to watch or interact with them, have fun, and extract historical meaning and knowledge from these interpretive performances.

In contemporary performance theory, however, and especially in theatrical genres such as environmental theater, the audience takes center stage in that they are – via "feedback loop" (Fischer-Lichte 2008) or direct participation – actively involved in the performance. My argument therefore follows a different path from conventional understanding of audiences at a performative history event based on the assumption that the performative experience of staff and vis-

---

3   Cf. among others Goodacre/Baldwin 2002; Hochbruck 2008b; Magelssen 2006, 2007; Schindler 2003; Snow 1993.

4   *First person interpretation* refers to the "act of portraying a person from the past (real or composite). [...] Through the portrayal of a character, [first-person interpreters] create for the visitor the illusion that their historic personage has returned to life" (ALHFAM 2007). In *third person interpretation* "the interpreter maintains a historical distance and is analytical and descriptive of the period being represented [...] looking at the past from an objective viewpoint and within a context relative to events before and after the period being interpreted" (ibid.).

5   The paradoxical quality of "Living History" or of "bringing history alive" has been much debated (cf. Hochbruck 2008b). The distinction between 'past' and 'history', however, seems a useful one for solving this dilemma. I will therefore refer to the 'past' for "the sum total of human experience, inchoate, incomprehensible, and elusive", and to 'history' for "a construct, a selective interpretation of part of that experience" (Yellis 1992: 52).

itors in living history environments may be different in degree, but not in kind. This requires a different terminology: whereas I hold on to the functional term 'visitor' as opposed to 'staff', I attribute the 'performing' aspect to both groups, thus referring to them as 'performing staff' and 'performing visitors',[6] respectively. Furthermore, my assumptions on visitors' potential experiences are not only grounded in visitor surveys or staff-reported re-/interactions, but are further deduced from theoretical findings in performance theory, as the living history experience is, at its core, *theatrical* experience.

By addressing the medial and material qualities of living history as well as its aesthetic and semiotic effects, an aesthetics of the performative might be able to account not only for the phenomenon's attraction and affective impact, but also for its transformative power. I therefore contend that historically themed environments are more than just stages for the past. As performative spaces they are also stages for the contemporary selves of both staff and visitors: liminoid spaces that *may* engender cultural learning and – ultimately – transformations of the self.

Environmental Theater

For living historians and museum officials with an 'orthodox' understanding of theatre and a strong dedication to historical accuracy, the idea that any serious interpretation of history might be considered 'theater' touches on a raw nerve.[7] Rather than accepting theatrical performance as a valid mode of transmitting historical knowledge, they categorize their own interpretations as an "outgrowth of history or a mode of pedagogy that, if anything, *borrows* techniques from theater and performance" (Magelssen 2007: 105).

In his assessment of contemporary American theater, however, Schechner has contended that its "new mainstream" consists of exactly those performative phenomena "found as practice in popular

---

6   In her *Performing Consumers*, Maurya Wickstrom has raised a similar claim for consumer experience at malls, theme parks, and other consumer venues (Wickstrom 2006). I would like to thank Scott Lukas for this reference.

7   A large number of museum officials as well as living historians deny the idea that their interpretatorial work may be theatrical; see quotes in Carlson 2004: 3; Magelssen 2007: 107-116. Likewise, visitors enjoying performances at theme parks, in museums, or at street fairs are usually not aware of their activitiy's connection to 'theater' (Schechner 1994: xvi). Many scholars, however, agree with Schechner and reaffirm the notion that "history museum interpretation is ultimately theater" (Carson 1998: 47), among them Snow 1993; Carson 1998; Carlson 2000, 2004; Magelssen 2007; Hochbruck 2008a.

entertainments, theme parks, and site specific performances" (Schechner 1994: xv):

"This 'new mainstream' ranges across the gamut of performance from the educational to the avant-garde, from crass commercialism to experimentation, from small-scale operations to vast enterprises. I am talking about the Disney theme parks and their imitators; the hundreds of 'restored villages' and 'living museums' that entertain and educate millions; re-enactments of the Civil War and other 'real life' events; renaissance pleasure fairs, processions, and street carnivals [...]." (ibid.: xv)

Schechner's claim may best be understood if one takes a closer look at his "Six Axioms for Environmental Theater" (1967, revised 1989) which, although developed in the very different social and aesthetic context of the 1960s and 70s, still prove current and useful for an assessment of today's living history phenomena (cf. ibid.: ix). According to the first axiom, environmental theater is "a set of related transactions": There are three primary transactions
- among performers,
- among members of the audience,
- and between performers and audience (Schechner 1994: xxiii),

supplemented by four secondary interactions
- between production elements,[8]
- between production elements and performers,
- between production elements and spectators as well as
- "[b]etween the total production and the space(s) where it takes place" (ibid.: xxiv).

Theatrical transactions between any of the above-mentioned elements are highly influenced by spatial arrangements, the principles of which are propounded in the second and third axiom: Environmental theater creates space or makes use of found space in its spatial entirety. When the entire space of a location opens up to the performance, performer and audience space coincide and allow for a number of possible transactions.

"Once fixed seating and the automatic bifurcation of space are no longer present, entirely new relationships are possible. Body contact can occur between performers and spectators; voice levels and acting intensities can be varied widely; a sense of shared experience can be engendered. Most important, each scene can create its own space, either contracting to a central or a remote area

---

8   The production elements that may "serve either as background for performers or as independent performing elements" are scenery, costumes, lighting, sound, make-up, etc. (Schechner 1994: xxv).

or expanding to fill all available space. The action 'breathes' and the audience itself becomes a major scenic element." (Schechner 1994: xxix)[9]

When geographical space becomes performative space, demarcations between "performers" and "spectators" are blurred. In fact, spatiality fosters whole-sense-involvement – "no one is 'just watching'" (Schechner 1994: xxix) – and this, in turn, engenders audience participation, an aspect of theater Schechner had heavily experimented with. His fourth axiom deals with spectator focus transformed from the single-focus of the proscenium to a "flexible and variable" one (xxxvii). The overall environment prestructures the audience's focus and, at the same time, grants them the freedom to move about, explore and performatively transform space on their own. In its final two axioms, environmental theater grants all production elements their own language, to the point of contradiction, implicitly dismissing both the authority of the verbal text as starting point or goal of the production (xl-xli), and the exclusive authority of actors/directors over the production. Ultimately, Schechner's concept of performative space as well as his emphasis on the dehierarchization of performing elements aims not only at the concept of audience participation but at its integration into the performative whole. Thus,

"to stage a performance 'environmentally' means more than simply to move it off of the proscenium or out of the arena. An environmental performance is one in which *all the elements or parts* making up the performance are recognized as alive. To 'be alive' is to change, develop, transform; to have needs and desires; even, potentially, to acquire, express, and use consciousness." (Schechner 1994: x)

When viewed in this light, living history – a history that is meant to 'be alive' – is more than trained performer-interpreters conveying knowledge to visitors: it is a format in which the transactions of all people involved account for the performance of history.

Visitor Performance

With their decades of experience, living history museums have made great advances in creating naturalistic simulations of past landscapes or settlements. Visitors are often surprised by the "convin-

---

9   As recent findings in performance theory have laid out, audience participation via feedback loop is crucial to any performance (cf. Fischer–Lichte 2008). In forms of environmental theater, the audience's co–performance is further abetted by spatial arrangements.

cing scenic illusion" (Snow 1993: 160) of these historical environments. Preserved, restored or recreated buildings, artifacts, and landscapes not only provide the environment with an ambiance feel but constitute the physical setting for the staging of a history that is peopled with 'real' human beings in period gear and often further enlivened by all kinds of rare-breed animals and plants.

The experience is a multisensory one. Unlike traditional museums that rely primarily on the visuals and sounds of multimedia installments in their displays of material culture, living museums offer visitors involvement in historical culture, "directly through sight, sound, smell, touch, taste" (Kelsey 1991: 72). In Old Sturbridge Village, for example, visitors may "listen to the blacksmith's rhythmic hammering, or smell the aroma of bread baking in a fireplace oven" (Old Sturbridge Village 2009d), in the exploratory exhibit of an 1830s household they can "open drawers, sit on the beds, and try on clothing" (Old Sturbridge Village, Fitch House).

Fig. 1: The Fitch House at Old Sturbridge Village, MA

Photograph: Carolyn Oesterle

At Plimoth Plantation, free-ranging hens and live-stock in corrals spread a pungent smell; visitors can explore the small houses where open fireplaces belch out smoke and heat. As advertised in brochures, leaflets and web pages, the strong appeal to the senses involves the visitor in an atmosphere that engenders its own kind of physical-sensorial performance: Fabrics may be felt, animals touched, people spoken to.

Many institutions have recognized that "visitors desire higher levels of participation in the historic environment than mere spectatorship" or communication with performing staff (Magelssen 2006: 299), so they increasingly employ forms of *second person interpret-*

ation.[10] The most commonly used devices for visitor participation of this kind are hands-on activities where visitors do not only observe costumed workers demonstrating historical crafts such as spinning, basket making, or candle dipping, but where they can try their own hands at these crafts or help with period chores under the guidance of specially trained staff (e.g. "Help churn butter" or "Try your hand at Ploughing with Oxen", Old Sturbridge Village 2009c).[11]

Visitors are further encouraged to take part in social-cultural activities and events. At Old Sturbridge Village, visiting children are invited to play period games, and, especially in their night programs, many of the museums offer historical dinners (e.g. "Eat like a Pilgrim", Plimoth Plantation 2009b), and period plays, music, or dances (e.g. the program "Terpsichorean Etiquette (or the Do's and Don'ts of Dancing)", Old Sturbridge Village 2009a). In the recently established "Worship In Plimoth Colony" event, visitors are summoned to "follow the drumbeat to the Fort/Meetinghouse" to "become part of the congregation" in psalm-singing and listening to a reading from the Geneva Bible (Plimoth Plantation 2009a).

In hands-on activities and cultural performances, visitors usually partake in the experience "as themselves" (cf. Magelssen 2006: 301); they appropriate the past in an experiential, predominantly physical and sensorial way from a contemporary non-historical-role-playing perspective. The rhetoric of orientation materials and specific props, however, guides visitors towards certain roles. In an attempt to spatialize time, the past is referred to as a "foreign country" (Lowenthal 1985) or "other world", implicitly casting the visitor in roles as either foreigner, traveler or time traveler: "Upon entering the 1627 village, you have traveled back in time and are immersed in the sights, sounds, smells, and ideas of the past... a place both familiar and foreign" (Plimoth Plantation 2008: 12; cf. The Colonial Williamsburg Foundation 2009: 2). Just as a tourist would explore a foreign destination, the visitor is thought to wander the 'foreign' sensescapes of history.

---

10 'Second person interpretation' is "a relatively recent term in the living history field" that has been introduced by Scott Magelssen for activities that "allow[] visitors to pretend to be part of the past and offers possibilities of co-creating the trajectory of the historiographic narrative with the staff" (Magelssen 2006: 298f.). In museum materials, however, visitors' participation in museums is most often referred to as 'hands-on activities' or 'immersion experiences' (cf. Mount Vernon 2009a; Plimoth Plantation 2008: 12; Sherbrooke Village 2009; Menare Foundation 2009).

11 There has been a trend in living history museums to establish special centers for hands-on activities (e.g. Hands-On Crafts Center at Old Sturbridge Village; Hands-on History Room at Mount Vernon's Education Center; Plimoth Plantation Family Discovery Station).

In his environmental theater, Schechner had used *opening ceremonies* to induce audience participation. Likewise, museums make use of initiation procedures as they channel visitors through temporal space. At Plimoth Plantation, visitors are encouraged to embark on their "journey into this fascinating and sometimes conflicting history" and asked to "[g]et ready to step into the 17th century" (Plimoth Plantation 2009d); at Colonial Williamsburg, the footpath from the visitor center to the historic area leads through a tunnel with a creek – the sound of gurgling water and crickets, and the idyllic sight of a duck-weed covered pond may shape the experience and heighten the anticipation for whatever pastoral version of history one expects. In a peculiar tongue-in-cheek sort of initiation, visitors at Louisbourg (Nova Scotia) used to be "stopped at the gate and instructed to proceed only after an informal search, conducted in French. If you reply in English, a wary eye is kept on you as you proceed" (cf. Schechner 1985: 89); similarly, at Plimoth Plantation, an older brochure welcomed Spanish and French visitors "if unarmed" (ibid.).

Closely linked to the spatial arrangement of time, another metaphor has been used with reference to the museum visitor, especially in those museums that make heavy use of *first person interpretation*: the metaphor of the "anthropologist-for-a-day" (cf. Carson 1991: 28; Anderson 1984: 51). Visitor performance is linked to the work of social anthropologists who – by means of intensive field studies including participant-observation methods – investigate the culture and social organization represented by performing staff in the exercise of their chores as well as in in their interactions with each other or other visitors. Introductory films and other media encourage visitors to approach performing staff and initiate communication like at Plimoth Plantation: "Remember, at Plimoth you're the explorer" (Plimoth Plantation 2009d), or at Old Sturbridge Village, "Where Everyone Is an Explorer of the Past" (Old Sturbridge Village 2009c).

Some museums engage visitors in part-time role-play. Colonial Williamsburg, for example, makes use of visitor participation in the two-hour audience-interactive street performance "Revolutionary City":[12] Here, the visiting crowd comes to represent colonial street crowds at political events or church congregations. In the reenactment of a period play, the audience is called upon to impersonate an 18th century audience that would comment on the play with emphatic "Huzzahs!", "Boos!", and "Encores!". In the "Order in the Court" program in which the visitors represent the court audience,

---

12 For a detailed description of this program see Martine Teunissen's article in this volume.

some of the visitors are cast in the roles of those standing trial. Whereas these kinds of participatory programs work with uncostumed visitors, some of the more recent museum programs provide visitor immersion experiences that involve period costumes. At Colonial Williamsburg, costume rentals are available for children at the visitor center.[13] In the "Discovery Camps" program at Old Sturbridge Village, participating children dress up and "take on the roles of real Sturbridge children from the 1830s. They play the games, do the chores, and participate in classroom lessons" (Old Sturbridge Village 2009b). At Sherbrooke Village, so-called "live-in costumed" programs have performing visitors spend one or more nights within the historical environment (Sherbrooke Village 2009). If and how costuming shapes visitors' actual performances cannot be assessed easily. As new findings in theatre studies have shown, however, costume "does far more than decorate the surface of the body" (Monks 2010: 3): Rather, with its various effects and functions, costuming "comes with risks and possibilities for the bodies and psyches of actor and audience alike" (ibid.) as it co-produces and forms the represented identities. Accordingly, costuming for visitors is likely to shape and enhance their immersion experiences and influence their actions (cf. Weldon 2009).

Fig. 2: Costumed visitors at Colonial Williamsburg

Photograph: Carolyn Oesterle

---

13 Visitor research and evaluation at Colonial Williamsburg has shown a strong interest in costume rentals for adults, also (Graft 2009). Even though this interest has been acknowledged by the site management, it has not (yet) been realized due to logistics as well as authenticity concerns (Weldon 2009).

Immersion opportunities of a different sort have been established at the Living History Museum Conner Prairie (Indiana), where the program "Follow the North Star" features the Underground Railroad, which tells the story of the risky journey made by slaves escaping to freedom. After being introduced to their roles as runaway slaves, participants hike "on rough terrain" across trails where they "encounter not only a slave sale but also a wide range of people, including a belligerent transplanted Southerner, a reluctantly helpful farm wife, a slave hunter motivated by financial rewards, a Quaker family and a free black family". Throughout this dramatic experience, participants are "treated as slaves and are told to keep their eyes down and not to speak unless spoken to" (Conner Prairie 2009). A similar Plantation Life and Underground Railroad two-day-program ("The Bridge") has been designed for The Historic Button Farm Living History Center in Germantown, Maryland, which has participants changed into slave clothing, blindfolded, and transported to a plantation where they have to "conduct authentic plantation tasks before making the harrowing journey to freedom" (Menare Foundation 2009).

The range of activities and events that rely on active and participatory visitor performance is growing, but varies greatly according to the museum's interpretive policy. In general, museum officials and affiliated historians have acknowledged that "seeing action and – better yet – participating in it holds great attraction" (Chappell 2002: 156). Consequently, many living museums have agreed on using "as much action, surprise, and excitement as useful to stir interest and activate thinking" (Chappell 2002: 121) and have become part of a venture that opens the "living" in living history to visitors, experientially as well as intellectually.

For visitors, these themed environments are spaces of choices (cf. Schechner 1994: 30f.): As they organize their own focus, degree and mode of interaction within the historical environment, they have become performing visitors who not only influence and transform performative space (e.g. by gathering in crowds, creating atmospheres, etc.), but also exert a strong influence on the transactions of performing staff. As in general theater, the experience depends not only on the visitors' general interest in the production's subject matter, but also in their curiosity, their willing suspension of disbelief and their willingness to fully immerse themselves in the experience, in short: to "let go" (cf. Yellis 1992: 57). This leads to a highly subjective and contingent experience: The visitors can choose to remain distant and entertainment-oriented, or they can enter into the challenge by willingly assuming roles becoming participant-observers (in the ethnological sense), explorers in the unknown of history, and above all actors in a performed game, or play.

There are a number of factors, however, which restrain the experiential choices of performing visitors from the outset and counteract any view of autonomous visitor transactions. Even where active participation is invited, visitor behavior is usually in accordance with museum expectations as prescribed by detailed instructions in orientation material (cf. Magelssen 2006: 300) and controlled by performing staff. While performing visitors are, of course, allowed to behave as they wish "few opt for ruining what is considered to be an agreed upon game" as "to go against the grain and voice alternative histories, or to question the agenda of the institution (or to assume a character not assigned by the interpretive staff), would make one a spoilsport" (Magelssen 2006: 300; cf. Snow 1993: 171).

Some of the living museums have employed strict policies on visitor clothing; in Plimoth Plantation, for example, visitors are asked not to appear in costume so that other visitors may not be confused and mistake them for performing staff (Magelssen 2006: 301). Even though performing space usually *is* visitor space, visitors may further be barred from certain spaces or excluded from some experiences for curatorial reasons or due to requirements of safety, hygiene, law or insurance (Goodacre/Baldwin 2002: 101, 107; Yellis 1992: 55). There is no way of "avoiding anachronisms and the intrusion of today's values, political and aesthetic" (Schechner 1985: 88), so that theatrical contingency is inevitably restrained. And yet: As participatory activities are on the increase they create the prerequisites for a theatrical emergence of new and unexpected meanings and the specific phenomenological operations involved in theatrical experience.

Somatic Experience and the Orders of Perception

As various advertisements of living museums suggest, "rich living history experiences" (Menare Foundation 2009) and "glimpse[s] into our shared past will jolt and affect you in ways that reading a book or watching a movie [...] cannot" (Conner Prairie 2009). In theater performances in general, the medial qualities of presence and co-presence, the sense of community, touch and liveness (cf. Fischer-Lichte 2008: 38-74) as well as the material conditions of performative space and atmosphere, the physicality and involvement of all senses, and the temporal qualities of performance (cf. ibid.: 75-137) promote a special aesthetic experience unparalleled by other media. In environmental theater, where performance space is shared space and audience participation is encouraged, many of these qualities are of even greater importance. The medial and material qualities of performance distinguish the living history experience from other popular history presentations and render the themed environment a space that plays on the physiological and affective responsiveness of visitors.

It is acknowledged "that the total representation of even a small community for so much as a moment in the past is impossible" and that visitors' sensations neither "are of", "resemble nor were possible in the past" (Yellis 1992: 55; Magelssen 2007: 55) – yet, historical representations are nevertheless being implanted into visitors' bodies and senses.

Performance theory has spelled out how bodies in theater are affected by atmospheric space where not only visual but also "acoustic, thermal, tactile, olfactory, and brain-wave maps can [...] be drawn" (Schechner 1994: 15). Erika Fischer-Lichte has further stressed how especially acoustic and olfactory production elements "intrude on and penetrate the perceiving subject's body" and "make them become aware of their own corporeality" (Fischer-Lichte 2008: 116, 119): "Through its atmosphere, the entering subject experiences the space and its things as emphatically present. [...] The spectators are not positioned opposite to or outside the atmosphere; they are enclosed by and steeped in it" (ibid.: 116).

In a very compelling assessment of today's themed consumer environments, Maurya Wickstrom has identified the way in which store designers make heavy use of theatrical effects by creating

"experiential environments through which the consumer comes to embody the resonances of the brand as feelings, sensations, and even memories. As if we were actors in the theatre, as consumers in branded spaces we loan the brand's character the phenomenological resources of our bodies. We play out its fictions, making them appear in three dimensions, as if they were real. Embodied, the story the brand is telling feels real." (Wickstrom 2006: 2)

The same could be stated for the experiences in the themed environments of living museums. Those involved in the interactions and activities come to embody the resonances of historical representations as feelings and sensations; thus, by loaning specific versions of history "the phenomenological resources of their bodies", they bring history "alive" in three dimensions.

Bodies and environment are thus not only carriers of meaning for fictive, historical bodies and environments but are somatically perceived as "real bodies" and "real spaces" within the larger shared space (cf. Fischer-Lichte 2008: 34). This perception in turn initiates (re)actions in visitors that are not only acted out in the imagination, but which in their physical presence may be perceived by all performers involved and may influence the progress of the performance. This energetic embodiment and the foregrounded present reality of the experience finally account for "theatre's ability to exercise an immediate sensual effect on the audience and trigger strong, even overwhelming affects" (ibid.: 94).

In its three-dimensional "liveness", the aesthetic experience of living history creates a new sense of authenticity: Its constructedness known, performed history nevertheless "feels real" (cf. Wickstrom 2006: 2).

"A special empathy/sympathy vibrates between performers and spectators. The spectators do not willingly suspend disbelief. They believe and disbelieve at the same time. This is theater's chief delight. The show is real and not real at the same time. This is true for performers as well as spectators and accounts for that special absorption the stage engenders in those who step onto it or gather around it." (Schechner 1985: 113)

One of the core features of "Living History" is thus that it acts upon the theatrical tension between "reality" and "simulation", between the corporeal authentic experience and the meaning-carrying theatrical simulations that together foster immersion into what is perceived as representation of the past. Where the proscenium stage had granted the "orthodox theater-goer" a certain kind of distance, its removal in the "in-and-out experience of environmental theater" causes a quite literally dramatic change in the modes of theater perception (Schechner 1994: 18; cf. Magelssen 2007: 104).

"In restored villages as in environmental theater generally, the domain of the performance surrounds and includes the spectator. Looking at becomes harder; being in, easier. Where there is no house, spectators are thrown back on their own resources for whatever assurance they need to maintain who and where they are." (Schechner 1985: 98)

For visitors as participating "co-subjects", performative space is therefore a space of indeterminacy where the "collision and disruption of frames" plunges them into situations where they have "to make choices and evaluations about each frame" and "decide whether to treat the situation as a theatrical or social interaction" (Fischer-Lichte 2008: 48).

In this state of "perceptual multistability" the participating visitors are not only cast between different orders of perception, the order of presence (perception of one's bodily being-in-the-world) and the order of representation (perception of the absent referent, here: the past) (ibid.: 147f.), but between different positions and identities.

"Perceptual multistability ensures that neither of the two orders can stabilize themselves permanently. With each shift, the dynamic of the perceptual process takes a new turn [...] Each turn allows for new perceptual content that contributes to the stabilization of the newly established order and, effectively, helps generate new meanings." (ibid.: 150)

Participants are cast "in between", in a liminal/liminoid space which is – according to anthropologist Victor Turner – the seedbed of cultural creativity, of self-reflexivity, and of transformation (Turner 1982: 28; cf. Fischer-Lichte 2008: 174f.).

The co-presence and performance of visitors in the environmental theaters of history add yet another dimension to the transformative power of the experience. When the staging of history is released as a performance in which new roles are assigned to visitors, they are not just observers of versions of history from which they try to distill historical meaning. Rather, visitors are considered integral parts and active producers in the production of historical meaning who influence and negotiate the performance by their physical presence, their perceptions, reactions, and interactions. It is these negotiations that push the aesthetic experience of living history into the social and political realm and lead to a peculiar situation in the hermeneutical process: performing visitors "generate meaning in a performance by virtue of the peculiar fact that they themselves partake in creating the process they wish to understand" (cf. Fischer-Lichte 2008: 155). Processes of understanding and creation of historical meaning therefore rely not only on matters of staging, but on the emergent performance of participants from which they may gain some insight into the past as much as into their own lifeworlds and their understanding of themselves.

The Transformative Power of Living History

Drawing on the efficacy of theatrical performance, historically themed environments and their modes of interpretation must then be seen as building the framework for powerful and fascinating cultural activities that establish "strong and convincing relationships with the past" and provide viable bases for historical learning (Goodacre/ Baldwin 2002: 198). Indeed, direct personal experience and emotional relevance have been anchored as crucial principles in teaching and learning theories (cf. Gudjons 2008a, 2008b).

Yet, however great the transformational potential may be, there are considerable flaws. In a Plimoth Plantation exhibit, a wall chart hints at an ambivalent attitude towards living history's implications: "A well-researched, carefully executed living history presentation is a compelling experience. It seems 'real.' This is both the advantage and the danger of living history" (Plimoth Plantation 2009c). How and why would an anticipated 'realness' of the living history experience be dangerous?

In a different context, Schechner had classed performance as an inherently "amoral" enterprise, "as useful to tyrants as to those who practice guerilla theatre" (Schechner 1995: 1); whereas transformation is thought to be part of any performative practice, morality or what I would call ethical or critical considerations are extrinsic to the practices themselves. Whereas an analogy with a tyrant's propaganda machine might be a little overstated within the context of US living history museums, the basic idea still applies. If performative means are efficacious in terms of individual and collective transformation, then, of course, their use as instruments of intentional historiography or hegemonial indoctrination is definitely a practical possibility. Given the surpassing credibility of museums (Reach Advisors 2008), people tend to believe that what they see and experience is 'authentic' and close to what they conceive of as 'historical truth'. The danger then consists in an uncritical absorption and internalization of sanitized versions of history that may be based on privileged knowledge, prevalent stereotypes, or worse, outright propaganda.

Flaws of a different kind are exemplified in Colonial Williamsburg's "Revolutionary City" program. As crowd reactions to the "Court of Tar and Feathers" scene show, identification procedures within the theatrical process may lead to unreflecting group dynamics: When an English loyalist is accused of having threatened the patriots, the visitor crowd usually all too readily agrees that this man deserves to be tarred and feathered; rarely, individual visitors protest openly, identifying the practice as actually contradicting the very basic rights the patriots had been fighting for. The scene's developers, however, had aimed at exactly this: critical reflection (cf. Weldon 2009). Thus, the visitors' actual experiences in these theaters of history may "not have the effects for which they are designed", and visitors may "read into them unwarranted assumptions" (Goodacre/Baldwin 2002: 97, 102). Theatrical efficacy may – consciously or unconsciously – reinforce stereotypes visitors have derived from popular culture, or reproduce, sustain, and even naturalize certain ideologies even where staging strategies may aim at challenging and critical attitudes towards history.

If history education's main purpose is not only to "get some sense of the past" but to establish a critical view of one's own relationship with the past – including the understanding that different versions of the past (histories) are constructed according to the perspectives and ways in which the past is presented or staged (cf. ibid.: 168) – then performative activities alone will certainly not reach that goal.

For this reason already, first person interpreters in many museums are seconded by mediators ("Red T-shirting"; ibid.: 12) who contextualize the observed actions for visitors to engender an effective learning experience. Visitor participation, too, needs mediating facilities. Participants must be given the opportunity to critically reflect on what has been presented and what they have been involved in. In the Underground Railroad pilot project at Historic Button Farm Living History Center, for example, the immersion experience is followed by a workshop in which the experience is distilled "through break-out sessions and activities focused on personal growth, group collaboration and problem solving" (Menare Foundation 2009). The combination of direct personal experience and critical reflection proves efficacious in terms of historical understanding and individual self-assessment, especially where clashes between a participant's somatic experiences and his or her preconceptions reveal existing biases.

Another interesting approach has been offered by theater scholar Scott Magelssen. In his critique of the rather limited roles offered to the visiting public in interactive programs, he has proposed second-person interpretation "as a more active historiographic mode" (Magelssen 2006: 303). Based on the works of theatre and performance theoreticians such as Augusto Boal he opts for programs that grant visitors the roles of characters "faced with social and political choice" (ibid.: 311) – roles that, so far, have been reserved for performing staff.

"Visitors to living museum sites ought to be given the roles of documented historic personages (developed characters) in singular, stageable situations. They should be presented period information and led to make choices based on their understanding of their role and the sensibilities, relationships, ethics, knowledge, curiosity, and creativity unique to each visitor. The outcome(s) of the performance should hinge on these choices, which would generate discussion and, in turn, further restagings." (ibid.: 304)

I think this approach is promising if risky, and time will tell if some of the institutions involved do, indeed, open themselves to these dehierarchized, less controllable negotiations about the past, which may engender a deeper understanding of historical dispositions than many, albeit excellent, presentations of trained staff-interpreters.

As the "still emerging 'world of environmental theater'" opens up "formerly stodgy museums to playful, interactive, and participatory exhibits" (Schechner 1994: xv-xvi), I am convinced that the interpretive potential of performing visitors may be tapped further by new programs that provide quality insights into historical culture and engender strong impacts on the social and cultural self.

References

Association for Living History Farms And Museums (ALHFAM). 2007. "Definitions Project." http://www.definitionsproject.com/definitio ns/def_full_term.cfm (accessed 9 Nov 2009).

Anderson, Jay. 1984. *Time Machines. The World of Living History.* Nashville, TN: American Association for State and Local History.

Barnes, Arthur. 1985. "Living History. Its Many Forms." *The Colonial Williamsburg Interpreter* 6.3: 1-2.

Carlson, Marvin A. 2000. "Performing the Past. Living History and Cultural Memory." *Inszenierungen des Erinnerns,* Paragrana 9.2. Eds. Erika Fischer-Lichte/Gertrud Lehnert. Berlin: Akad.-Verlag. 237-248.

Carlson, Marvin A. 2004. *Performance. A Critical Introduction.* Second ed. New York: Routledge.

Carson, Cary. 1991. "Living Museums of Everyman's History." *A Living History Reader. Volume 1: Museums.* Ed. Jay Anderson. Nashville, TN: American Association for State and Local History. 25-31.

Carson, Cary. 1998. "Colonial Williamsburg and the Practice of Interpretive Planning in American History Museums." *Public Historian. A Journal of Public History* 20.3 (Summer): 11-51.

Chappell, Edward A. 2002. "The Museum and the Joy Ride. Williamsburg Landscapes and the Specter of Theme Parks." *Theme Park Landscapes. Antecedents and Variations.* Eds. Terence Young/Robert Riley. Washington, DC: Dumbarton Oaks Research Library and Collection. 119-156.

Conner Prairie. 2009. "Follow the North Star." http://www. Conner prairie.org/events/follow_the_north_star (accessed 18 Oct 2009).

Fischer-Lichte, Erika. 2008. *The Transformative Power of Performance. A New Aesthetics.* New York: Routledge.

Goodacre, Beth/Gavin Baldwin. 2002. *Living the Past. Reconstruction, Recreation, Re-Enactment, and Education at Museums and Historical Sites.* London: Middlesex University Press.

Graft, Conny. 2009. "Colonial Williamsburg. Guest Research and Evaluation." 15 Sep 2009. Email.

Gudjons, Herbert. 2008a. *Handlungsorientiert lehren und lernen: Schüleraktivierung, Selbsttätigkeit, Projektarbeit.* 7., aktual. Aufl. Bad Heilbrunn: Klinkhardt.

Gudjons, Herbert. 2008b. *Pädagogisches Grundwissen: Überblick – Kompendium – Studienbuch.* 10., aktual. Aufl. Bad Heilbrunn: Klinkhardt.

Hochbruck, Wolfgang. 2008a. "Im Schatten der Maus: Living History und historische Themenparks in den USA." *Living History im Museum. Möglichkeiten und Grenzen einer populären Vermitt-*

lungsform. Eds. Jan Carstensen/Uwe Meiners/Ruth-E. Mohr-mann. Münster/New York/München/Berlin: Waxmann. 45-60.

Hochbruck, Wolfgang. 2008b. "Living History, Geschichtstheater und Museumstheater. Übergänge und Spannungsfelder." *Living History in Freilichtmuseen. Neue Wege der Geschichtsvermittlung.* Ed. Heike Duisberg. Ehestorf: Freilichtmuseum am Kiekeberg. 23-35.

Kelsey, Darwin P. 1991. "Harvests of History." *A Living History Reader. Volume 1: Museums.* Ed. Jay Anderson. Nashville, TN: American Association for State and Local History. 69–72.

Lowenthal, David. 1985. *The Past Is a Foreign Country.* Cambridge: Cambridge University Press.

Magelssen, Scott. 2006. "Making History in the Second Person. Post-touristic Considerations for Living Historical Interpretation." *Theatre Journal* 58.2: 291-312.

Magelssen, Scott. 2007. *Living History Museums. Undoing History Through Performance.* Lanham, MD: Scarecrow Press.

Menare Foundation. 2009. "Hands on History." http://www.mena re.org/handsonhistory.html (accessed 18 Oct 2009).

Monks, Aoife. 2010. *The Actor in Costume.* Basingstoke: Palgrave Macmillan

Mount Vernon. 2009a. "Mount Vernon. Discover the Real George Washington." Brochure.

Mount Vernon. 2009b. "Teachers and Students." http://www.mount vernon.org/learn/teachers_students/index.cfm/ss/114/(accessed 18 Oct 2009).

Old Sturbridge Village. 2009a. "Daily Event Listing." http:// www. osv. org/activities_events/MapGuide.php (accessed 18 Oct 2009).

Old Sturbridge Village. 2009b. "Old Sturbridge Village. Discovery Camps." Brochure.

Old Sturbridge Village. 2009c. "Welcome to Old Sturbridge Village. Where Everyone Is an Explorer of the Past." Program: Saturday, 26 Sep, 2009.

Old Sturbridge Village. 2009d. "Our Museum." http://www.osv. org/museum/index.html (accessed 18 Oct 2009).

Plimoth Plantation. 2008. "Plimoth Plantation." Brochure.

Plimoth Plantation. 2009a. "Calendar of Events." Leaflet.

Plimoth Plantation. 2009b. "Eat Like a Pilgrim." http://www.pli moth.org/dining-functions/theme-dining/pilgrim.php (accessed 18 Oct 2009).

Plimoth Plantation. 2009c. "Interpreting the Past." Exhibit *Thanks-giving: Memory, Myth & Meaning.* Wall chart.

Plimoth Plantation. 2009d. "Plimoth Plantation. Two Peoples. One Story." Orientation film.

Reach Advisors. 2008. "Authenticity and Museums." *Museum Audience Insight: Audience Research, Trends, Observations from Reach Advisors and Friends.* 7 Apr 2008. http://reachadvisors. typepad.com/museum_audience_insight/2008/04/authenticity-an. html (accessed 8 Dec 2009).

Schechner, Richard. 1985. *Between Theater and Anthropology.* Philadelphia: University of Pennsylvania Press.

Schechner, Richard. 1994. *Environmental Theater. An Expanded New Edition Including "Six Axioms For Environmental Theater".* New York, NY: Applause.

Schechner, Richard. 1995. *The Future of Ritual. Writings on Culture and Performance.* London: Routledge.

Schindler, Sabine. 2003. *Authentizität und Inszenierung.* Heidelberg: Winter.

Snow, Stephen Eddy. 1993. *Performing the Pilgrims. A Study of Ethnohistorical Role-Playing at Plimoth Plantation.* Jackson: University Press of Mississippi.

Sherbrooke Village. 2009. "Hands On History." http://museum. gov.ns.ca/sv/handsonhistory.php (accessed 18 Oct 2009).

The Colonial Williamsburg Foundation. 2009. "Colonial Williamsburg. A Revolutionary Adventure." Brochure.

Turner, Victor. 1982. *From Ritual to Theatre. The Human Seriousness of Play.* New York: Performing Arts Journal Publications.

Weldon, Bill. 2009. Interview. Colonial Williamsburg, 8 Sep 2009.

Wickstrom, Maurya. 2006. *Performing Consumers. Global Capital and Its Theatrical Seduction.* New York: Routledge.

Yellis, Ken. 1992. "Not Time Machines, But Real Time. Living History at Plimoth Plantation." *ALHFAM Proceedings of the 1989 Annual Meeting 12 (1992):* 52-57.

Staging the Past in the Revolutionary City:

Colonial Williamsburg

MARTINE TEUNISSEN

> "More than 200 years ago, the pursuit of
> equality, freedom & independence began a
> movement that continues to shape the world...
> Welcome to the Revolutionary City!"
> (www.history.org)

Since 2006, Colonial Williamsburg has been staging an extended living history program, shown on a daily basis: The Revolutionary City. This two-hour theatrical performance on the Duke of Gloucester Street depicts several events from 1774 to 1781 in first person interpretation.

Is this new theatrical program a reinforcement of Americanist values, or does it provide a more critical approach? In order to evaluate the program it is important to be aware of the challenges it faces in representing the past. In addition, it is important to understand Colonial Williamsburg's message in its historical context. This study will discuss the creation-process and outcome of this *Revolutionary City* program, set within the context of Williamsburg's revolutionary history. My focus is not so much on what has actually happened in the past, or how historians have reconstructed it, but how the past is reconstructed and represented *in the museum itself*. This paper offers a reflection on the themed environments of Colonial Williamsburg with regard to both the history of the program and the structural and theatrical devices at play in its creation and performance.

A representation of the past and its interpretation by an audience is always shaped by the needs of contemporary culture. An institution like Colonial Williamsburg has to create a balance between the expectations and interests of different groups, such as academic historians, business managers, educational managers, and the public. The interaction between these different elements determines the limits and possibilities of a reconstruction of the past in the public sphere.

The History of Colonial Williamsburg's Restoration

In times of rapid modernization at the beginning of the 20th century, Dr. Goodwin convinced millionaire John D. Rockefeller Jr. to help restore Williamsburg's past glory. It was a time in which industrial change was rapidly distancing all known pasts, creating an historical consciousness amongst Americans that expressed itself in the recognition and glorification of the Revolutionary period on a national scale (Lowenthal 1985: 13-15).

In the late 1920s and early 1930s, Rockefeller began to purchase buildings to recreate the town's physical presence in the 18th century. The restoration of Williamsburg was pursued with an insistence on accuracy and authenticity, but concurrently aimed to reproduce an ideal picture of the birth of the nation (cf. Greenspan 2002: 11). Thus authenticity in this case is related to the physical presence of the past, but not to the representation of the most complete social picture of the past including every player, rich or poor, black or white, male or female. Williamsburg's 'pastness'[1] manifests itself then as a material construction (old material and recreations) which is combined with pre-understandings of nostalgic stereotypes about progress and American heroism.

Colonial Williamsburg started as a "shrine to Americanism", attracting well-educated visitors from a high socio-economic class who particularly liked the standards for house building, furniture and gardens (Rentzhog 2007: 48-49). Obviously, this 'snob-appeal' left little room for the representation of the history of the lower classes.

In the 1940s, Colonial Williamsburg's focus lay on "the story of a community that helped to create American democracy" (Carson 1998b: 15). In particular, soldiers were invited to Colonial Williamsburg to encourage their patriotic feelings. Through radio programs the general public was indoctrinated by the idea that people were fighting in World War Two for the same principles their ancestors had at Jamestown, Williamsburg and Yorktown (cf. Greenspan 2002: 14, 45, 60-65). The idea of freedom for all mankind is a mission the United States still strives for today (cf. Foner 2002: 58). The unique political significance of Colonial Williamsburg becomes a red thread traceable throughout its entire restoration history.

Until the 1950s, Colonial Williamsburg displayed an elite history and promoted the story of creating American democracy. The story of women and African Americans, however, was still ignored. During the mid-century, due to the increasing size of the restored area, Colonial Williamsburg took on an expanding ideological role and began

---

1   For a concept of pastness cf. Cornelius Holtorf in this volume.

promoting democracy on an international scale. The Cold War helped to entrench the glorification of American freedom, although Williamsburg's role in this should not be overblown (Carson 1998b: 31). In the 1960s we begin to see the introduction of more 'ordinary' citizens incorporated in the representation of the past (Greenspan 2002: 121-122).

By the late 1970s, Colonial Williamsburg had turned itself into a social history museum, which strove for a more complete picture of 18th century life. The civil rights movement in the 1960s added to this awareness in general. Tate's research report *The Negro in Eighteenth Century Williamsburg*, published in 1965, helped to recreate the story of the other half of Williamsburg's population: the story of black people (cf. Tate 1965).

In 1977, the first major formalized interpretive framework was created, *Teaching History at Colonial Williamsburg, A Plan of Education*. *Teaching History* focused on three basic themes: *Choosing Revolution*, *Becoming Americans*, and *The New Consumers* (Carson 1998a: 37). It was intended to serve as a broader interpretation, and included the stories of 'ordinary' people – women, children, slaves, and servants. Its effect was slow and it received much criticism from the management not because of its focus on social history, but for its focus on theatrical interpretation. A critique voiced in the 1980s was that Colonial Williamsburg could be compared with Disneyland and seen as *just* a period theme park or quaint tourist stop (cf. Greenspan 2002: 149). This continuing line of criticism has much to do with Colonial Williamsburg's dual incarnation as a business *and* as an educational institution – targeting visitor satisfaction collides with serious education, as critics are quick to point out.

BECOMING AMERICANS

In 1998 a new interpretive framework was developed and published in a guidebook for Williamsburg. The program, *Becoming Americans: Our Struggle to be both Free and Equal* is a program which aims to display the dynamic story of cultural transformation which occurs as various people's transition from immigrants to Americans, and implicitly the story in which American society transforms from a colony to a republic. This involved many, sometimes paradoxical, stories about the diversity of people, customs, values, ideals, and beliefs. The sub-themes, "from subject to citizen" (referring to the change from a monarchical to a republican society based on freedom and democracy), and "our struggle to be both free and equal", further underline this complexity (Wood 1992: 169). Altogether, the storylines are meant to represent a total view of 18th-century Williamsburg, the transformation of Virginia, and the story of how

America came into being. In addition to creating a better under-standing of America's past, the interpretational program is sup-posed to help the visitor to think about race, culture, citizenship, nationhood, and the reshaping of American identity (cf. Carson 1998a: 9-10).

Is *Becoming Americans*, a theme still central in Colonial Wil-liamsburg's current interpretation programs, the long expected criti-cal approach to American history? The six underlying storylines, *Taking Possession*, *Enslaving Virginia*, *Buying Respectability*, *Rede-fining Family*, *Choosing Revolution*, and *Freeing Religion* "illustrate six representative issues, each of which brings historical perspective to values and attitudes that still provoke controversy in American society" (ibid.). The increased emphasis on the diversity of people and their experiences is paralleled in historiographical research, and may be regarded as a counter-reaction to celebratory American-ism (Appleby/Hunt/Jacob 1994: 1). In theory, there is indeed room to show how the revolutionary promise of freedom and equality began to be partially obtained by some, while remaining unfulfilled for many, thus representing the darker side of the American experi-ment.

However, even though the intentions appear noble, the story-lines tend to follow an optimistic account of the democratization of colonial society focusing on equal possibilities to strive for a better life. Also, practical application displays the difficulties involved in representing a 'total' history. The most complete story of 18th cen-tury Williamsburg is quite difficult and complex for visitors to com-prehend. In addition, interpreters have had difficulty incorporating the new storyline into their presentations.

When the interpretative program was tested with Colonial Wil-liamsburg's visitors, *Choosing Revolution* came out as the most pre-valent trend in discussed topics (cf. Korn 1994). The interpreters also appeared to favor this theme. Evaluative research concluded that less is indeed more, and that it would be beneficial if the *Choosing Revolution* theme was put into stronger focus, performing it in first person interpretation, increasing the number of African American interpretation programs, and increasing the number of interpreters in general (ibid.). These recommendations have been implemented in the creation of the *Revolutionary City* program since then.

Comparing this evaluative research with the intentions of this program is an illustration of the ever conflicting tension between theory and practice. Theory propagates a representation of the past that is as inclusive as possible, but evaluative research touches upon the difficulty of applying all these storylines in practice, and favors an incorporation of all the diverse narratives into one suc-cessful storyline – *Choosing Revolution*. One has to bear in mind, of course, that a published guidebook will always be, and always must be more comprehensive than what is or can be shown in practice. For a theatrical program such as *Revolutionary City*, it means that selection and simplification are necessary in practice. Whether the degree of simplification is appropriate depends on the story being told, and the different dynamics of genres of every single reconstruction and representation of the past, and is thus a variably determining factor in interpretive narratives. Cary Carson has described the difficulty of applying the new interpretive framework as

"often it is nigh on impossible to introduce new 'software' – a new interpretation – into an environment where the 'hardware' – what museum visitors see – remains unchanged. The same people in the same places, wearing the same costumes while doing the same activities with the same objects, are strongly inclined to revert to the same methods and messages that have served them well in the past." (Carson1998a: 42)

The physical structures at Colonial Williamsburg: the Capitol, the Governor's Palace, and the houses of the rich represent the lives of the upper class and push history making towards a particular political juncture. To present social history, revolutionary changes are needed.

Colonial Williamsburg and Performance Art

Steps towards a more engaging performance were taken in 1998 by introducing *Days in History*, a historical theatre program acted out on the streets like a soap series on TV, and the introduction of *Days to Remember*, both based on actual historical events (from 1774-1776). *Days to Remember* was used as a thematic thread in determining the weekly schedule (Rentzhog 2007: 352-353). A chosen theme, either political, cultural, or religious, was introduced to the visitor on arrival, and talked about in the houses, at the market, in church, and in the taverns. The story developed throughout the day and concluded, in Carson's words, with a "dramatic finale – an angry demonstration, a militia muster [or] a torchlight parade" (Carson 1998b: 51). The introduction of *Days to Remember* produced a new coherence between the many parts of the Williamsburg story, and gave the visitor an engaging and comprehensive historical experience. The 'dramatic end' incorporated theatrical ploy by creating a plot line with protagonists and antagonists to tell the story. Nuanced stories with an open end or unresolved outcome are more difficult to tell from this perspective. This does not seem to be a problem for the *Becoming American* theme as it focuses on clashing interests and their inherent drama – for "those were the encounters that profoundly reshaped American identities and American values" (Carson 1998a: 10). To Williamsburg's educators,

"history museum interpretation is ultimately theatre, but to admit that openly was too scary until 1997. Fifty years of 'professionalization' thundered against it. A thousand jabs and jibes from journalists and academics warned that any conjunction between education and entertainment was spelled D-I-S-N-E-Y no matter what." (Ibid.: 46)

These thoughts are unfortunately still vividly alive today. As Carolyn Oesterle has argued, "for living historians and museum officials with an 'orthodox' understanding of theatre and, at the same time, a strong dedication to historical accuracy, the idea that any serious interpretation of history might be considered 'theater' touches on a raw nerve" (Oesterle in this volume: 159). Nevertheless, Williamsburg has transformed itself into a performing arts organization, and has arguably been influenced by a Disney-like approach. In the late 1990s, Williamsburg visitor data revealed that "America's premier historic site had gradually aged into a 'mature travel destination' for 'senior citizens'" (Carson 2001: 2). Visitor satisfaction numbers in 1999 and 2000 fell short of prognoses, and after 2001, as in many other open-air museums, visitor numbers began to drop. The management consultants that Colonial Williamsburg subsequently hired to revitalize their core business leaned heavily on the Disney model for guidance (ibid.: 2-14).

Financial pressures and their accompanying budget cuts produce different outcomes in different museums, and tend to dramatically influence plans for updating exhibits, catering for the visitor, and producing a level of intellectually challenging historical interpretation. For an operation as grand as Colonial Williamsburg, which used to have more than one million visitors a year and a staff of 3,500 people, dropping visitor numbers were a serious problem (Rentzhog 2005). Williamsburg needed to make a huge financial investment to reinvent itself, and has not yet attained financial success: they still have an actual or operating deficit. This deficit has been fluctuating and increased exponentially with the 20 million dollar *Revolutionary City* program that was launched in the spring of 2006. With the recent economic crisis it is to be seen how much money will be left for live interpretation.

Thus, on the one hand the change towards performance art seems to be brought about for business reasons: visitor numbers and visitor satisfaction. On the other hand, when educators are asked to develop a program, they will do so with the means granted to them. They are often not very concerned about or aware of financial pressures. Although there is an apparent causal link between business and education, it is difficult to gauge how much influence the one has on the other. Nevertheless, one assumes that if Williamsburg's scholars had not been convinced of the merits of a theatrical approach to produce a worthwhile historical experience, they would not have gone through with it. As Carson has acknowledged: "theater and arts administration don't come naturally to historians and curators" (Carson 2001: 17). The bureaucratic departmental approach based on university organization is not necessarily beneficial when organizing historical productions of this nature, but to Carson, and many others working at the Foundation, the museum does not need to resemble the university, and should help visitors in making "creative use of scholarship to see themselves and their own personal stories in historical perspective" (ibid.).

In Europe, we see a similar development towards using performance art in museums and historical sites to negotiate a personal encounter with history. As Mark Wallis (director of *Past Pleasures* in England) has indicated, "increasingly, most visitors want to learn the history of the site or object via interaction with a costumed guide/docent/interpreter. The old days of pedagogy in Great Britain have mostly gone, and are largely being replaced by costumed storytelling and historical drama in its various forms" (Wallis 2009).

The Revolutionary City Program

The development in social historical narratives and political positionings are at least potentially resolved in the creation of the *Revolutionary City* program. The new interpretive program promised to bring together "the two halves of the Williamsburg story", the one celebrating Williamsburg's nation-making role, the other representing its social history (Carson 2005). The *Becoming American* storyline and its sub-themes form its primary intellectual framework. The program attempts to elucidate Williamsburg's role in the process of becoming American. It also strongly positions the visitor in his role as a citizen, and endeavors to encourage the visitor to become an *active* citizen. To achieve active citizenship, actor interpreters invite the public to join in and identify with 'their' (the historical character's) struggles, a form of structural positioning which further implies that in order for democracy to work participation is needed. The program makers believe that an explicit connection between freedom and democracy promotes civic involvement (Carson 2004), and this is echoed in the formal and structural elements found in the dramatic delivery of various scenes.

The concept of 'education in citizenship' is recognizable in the American school education rationale that history should contribute to democratic civic participation.[2] Bill Weldon, the director of *Revolutionary City* in Colonial Williamsburg's Historic Area, points to "provocation", "entertainment" (or edutainment), and "challenging thoughts", as the main goals of the program (Weldon/Graft 2006). The aspect of provocation is based on Freeman Tilden's argument that "the chief aim of interpretation is not instruction, but provocation" (Tilden 1977: 9). The program is also shaped by Tilden's principle that "information as such is not interpretation: information is revelation based on interpretation" (ibid.: 32). In the late 1970s, executive president Charles Longsworth argued that "puzzlement, confusion, ambiguity, and uncertainty" should be welcomed, because "it is the tension of these debates that provides the intellectual zest that stimulates the creation of a lively learning environment." At that time, it was visionary thinking (Carson 1998a: 34). The *Revolutionary City* program illustrates the change of paradigm which has occurred in how Colonial Williamsburg teaches history. It is 'revolutionary' for Colonial Williamsburg's history, not only in terms of the means of presentation, but also in the inclusive history that is being represented. The increased emphasis on the diversity of people and their experiences is also apparent in historiography as a reaction against celebratory Americanism. Arthur M. Schlesinger (*The Disuniting of America*), and the work of Joyce Appleby, Lynn Hunt, and Margaret Jacob (*Telling the Truth About History*) have, however, brought forward concerns with the destruction of a unifying American identity and the lack of a single narrative of national history as a consequence of the "increased emphasis on the diversity of ethnic, racial, and gender experience" (Appleby/Hunt/Jacob 1994: 1). Thus, Colonial Williamsburg's role in educating for citizenship could be perceived as rooted in liberal social and academic concerns and beliefs, and should be placed in the context of its history in which it has promoted ideals of democracy and liberty for a long time, although not necessarily with a particular liberal slant.

In the fall of 2006, the *Revolutionary City* program consisted of fourteen scenes, focusing on political events, socio-economic relationships, family life, the position of slaves, war, and religion. These fourteen scenes were presented over two days, *Collapse of Royal Government*, presenting seven events from 1774 to 1776, and *Citizens at War*, presenting another seven events from 1776 to 1781. From this classification it is clear that politics and war provide the primary narrative thread within the overall storyline and determine the other stories which are told within its referential frame. The main focus is *Choosing Revolution*, with other *Becoming American*

---

2   Arguably, it finds its European equivalent in the new Dutch National History Museum that is currently being planned in the Netherlands.

storylines incorporated into it. I will highlight only two scenes here: one told from the elite perspective, and one from the perspective of the marginalized people of Williamsburg.[3]

A DECLARATION OF INDEPENDENCE. JULY 25, 1776

The public gathers in front of the Capitol, greeting the marching soldiers and waiting for news. The Declaration of Independence is read aloud by different actors: men, women, citizens, and slaves. They all verbalize the violations and injustices the British Government has inflicted on them, "posing taxes without our consent", "abolishing our most valuable laws", "destroying the lives of our people" and "bringing war upon us". These violations are the justification for dissolving all ties with Great Britain and declaring Americans as citizens of free and independent states. There is great irony in this scene, since slaves and women read aloud controversial aspects of the declaration. A black actor interpreter, portraying a slave, yells that "all men are created equal!" The scene also presents the debatable unity of Americans (in the past and present) which is reinforced by the actors reading parts together, "Our (humble) repeated petitions have been answered only by repeated injury" and "we mutually pledge to each other, our lives, our fortunes and our sacred honor".

The irony in this scene, and the way the Declaration is read, are provocative and unexpected. This should make visitors think critically about the document as a product of its time. In this scene, the focus is mostly on drama and the shock-effect, and not on authenticity. Nevertheless, the scene is also celebratory in its implied connection between freedom and democracy. Experiencing the scene, one hears loud cheering and jingoistic support for the American cause from the assembled visitors. The scene ends with a third person interpretation providing hindsight information about Virginia's Declaration of Rights and the American Bill of Rights. Here, third person interpreters acknowledge that freedom in this case would have applied only to white males, and thus that the document was inconsistent in the context of the society in which it was produced. They ask the public what it means to be citizens in a republic, inviting them to go back in time and to join the Revolutionary City as citizens of the 18th century. The whole scene is intended "to provoke people to rethink their preconceptions as well as to rethink the pos-

---

3   To get a brief video impression of the program, see the compilation of film footage I have shot of the *Revolutionary City* program (Teunissen 2007). For a detailed program of Colonial Williamsburg's *Revolutionary City*, cf. appendices 1 and 2.

sibilities of citizenship" (Weldon/Graft 2006), and as such reflects the politicized process of citizen education previously mentioned.

RUNNING TO FREEDOM. APRIL 20, 1781

This scene illustrates that during rebellious times all social ranks had to think about taking sides. The program attempts to highlight the difficulties and emotions involved in these decisions. By portraying three slaves (Juba, Kate, and Ive) who argue about the possibilities the British might give them in gaining freedom, the program tells the story of the other half of Williamsburg's population in the 18th century.

Juba cares about freedom, but doesn't believe the British can guarantee his freedom. He finds it more important to be alive and to be fed well than taking the risk of gaining freedom, or losing everything. Ive is not sure whether the English will give her freedom, but she is willing to take the risk. Historically, the British emancipated slaves who left their American masters and joined their side, but only men could join the army. Ive seems to be aware of this fact, and even questions what will happen to women and children. But she desires freedom so much that she decides to align herself with the British in the hope of securing freedom for herself and her son. Kate takes a middle position which is expressed in the performance in her position between Juba and Ive. She too desires freedom, but she is unsure about running away. She is pregnant and decides to wait for the return of her partner Daniel who has joined the British in their fight against the rebels, hoping that they will escape and obtain freedom together. The farewell between Ive and Kate draws the public into the scene emotionally, and gives visitors an opportunity to identify with the characters as 18th century slaves – a dramatic strategy which relates strongly to the tradition of social history which the Williamsburg organizers are committed to.

The Development of the Program as Historical Theater

It becomes apparent, then, that the program favors an interactive theatrical process, focusing on provocation. Theatrical techniques force the audience to see things they might not want to see; they are provoked and stimulated to think critically about past-present relations. A traditional museum or open-air museum environment allows the audience more choice as to the degree to which they engage with each exhibition, and is therefore more passive and less demanding from the visitor than a theatrical environment. The interactivity in these scenes, however, is limited to an intellectual provocation by addressing people as visitors of the 18th century (Declaration of Independence) in so-called second person interpretation.

Theater, or theatrical methods have a culturally determined set of expectations, causing visitors to have different attitudes towards receiving theater and first person interpretation. As Oesterle has argued, the theatrical performance is a highly subjective and contingent experience, and "visitors can choose to remain distant and entertainment-oriented, or they can enter into the challenge by willingly assuming roles becoming participant-observers (in the ethnological sense), explorers in the unknown of history, and above all actors in a performed game, or play" (Oesterle in this volume: 166). Even though the experiences of visitors may vary greatly in their level of participation, the performative and liminal space where the visitors find themselves is argued to stimulate self-reflexivity and transformation (ibid.: 169f.).

The way people learn in a staged historical environment has not yet been thoroughly researched. Nevertheless, in terms of education, studies of the learning process indicate that "after 48 hours, people remember only 10% of what they read, 20% of what they hear, 30% of what they see, and 90% of what they do" (Sternberg 1993: 34). In *The Art of Participation*, Susan Sternberg has emphasized the on-going challenge of museums to motivate people in their learning experience, and has called for interactive and participatory approaches (ibid.). This experience is further underscored by the outcome of my evaluation of the *Revolutionary City* program which shows that 'engagement' and 'provocation' in historical performances work well to promote critical thinking and to increase understanding (Teunissen 2008a). Since a learning process involves both intellectual and emotional aspects, the use of 'edutainment' can be legitimized. With the adaptation of theater or performance art, Williamsburg endeavors to "make visitors *feel* as well as *comprehend* its inspirational message" (Carson 1998a: 17).

The performances are based upon scripts, carefully developed by dramatists and historians, and character scores which are developed by the actor interpreters themselves. In addition, the actor interpreters get ten weeks of training in historical background, staged and improvisational acting, and rehearsing the scenes. At Colonial Williamsburg, historical context is provided by means of booklets, readers, and lectures that constantly update actors with information (Schneider 2006). Further, the library provides possibilities for individual research, both with the use of primary and secondary sources. Actor training focuses on the interpreter's interactions with the public and on improvisation skills to prepare them for both staged and non-staged interpretation.

Character Scores

In order to make the historic recreation as accurate as possible, the program makers and live interpreters use character scores to improve their performances. According to Roth, character interpretation is the "envelope in which the interpretive message is delivered" (Roth 1998: 57). A character score consists of a biography and character analysis. Once a historical character has been chosen, actor-interpreters can base their portrayal on objective, external facts and on internal, subjective criteria.

Objective, external criteria include hard factual information: name, age, date of birth, place of birth, residence, family, education, religion, and occupation. Subjective or internal criteria are described by the *Revolutionary City* program makers as "consist[ing] of the qualities that define how you relate to life, how you act and react toward the world you inhabit. These are not hard facts, but are subject to interpretation, to possible change, and difference of opinion" (Colonial Williamsburg 2006). Other examples of subjective or internal criteria include character details that may not be ascertained by facts (where someone comes from, 'the strongest cultural influences', 'community connections', the character's present, 'immediate circumstances', social life, 'physical existence', temperament, (dis)interests, political situation, and the character's future, wishes, opportunities, obstacles, fears) and presuppose a super objective: the primary motivation in life (either conscious or unconscious) of the chosen character. Objective as well as subjective criteria are not always known, and require in-depth character analysis, and a thorough investigation of colonial Virginian life in all its aspects. To develop and reconstruct the characters, the *Revolutionary City* program makers refer to three sequential steps of development: investigation, inference, and invention.

Investigation refers to the use of historical records to find information. The *Revolutionary City* program makers take this research seriously, exhorting actors to "be as thorough as possible in researching all accessible documentation related to your character. If any information can be known about an individual, you as the interpreter of that person are obliged to find and use it!" (Colonial Williamsburg 2006). They also caution extreme care in using subjective material. Actor interpreters are allowed to do research during 'paid' time, but usually also do at least some investigation outside working hours.

Inference refers to filling in the factual gaps that remain after historical investigation. It implies the interpretation of "biographical information from the demographic historical record" (Colonial Williamsburg 2006). This method is applied to both objective and subjective criteria, and seeks to answer questions regarding which values and beliefs people had within the same gender, race, age, class, or religion, and aims to 'flesh out' individual characters through the use of data acquired from similar groups where more adequate historical documentation is available. Inference is, at its best, a disciplined and holistic understanding of the social framework in which a character might find him or herself, and provides an essential link in performance history between investigation and invention.

The third step of development is invention. This only applies in the *Revolutionary City* program to complete documented factual information. This is often necessary for slave characters about whom few 'hard' facts are known. For example, Art Johnson, who plays Juba, has invented his family relations; a mother Sarah and a sibling Caesar. He has further embellished the narrative of Juba by casting him as unmarried, and the father of a 14 year old son, John. Juba learned to read and write on his own and is an agnostic. Although the *Revolutionary City* makers try to avoid the invention of subjective material regarding values or beliefs, it is very difficult to fully develop a slave character without this. In an attempt to simulate and recreate life in the past, every detail has to be filled in, in a similar way to how film producers attempt to create a complete and detailed 'reality' on the screen. In film, however, characters are never required to engage with and counter questions from their audience. Colonial Williamsburg and other performative historical groups are required to develop an intensely detailed and multisensory informative and translatable view of the 18th century, weaving known and interpreted historical data into a composite experience of the past.

Following this methodology, the *Revolutionary City* program directors and actor interpreters try to create characters that are historically as accurate as possible. Nevertheless they are influenced in their performance by the actor director, and their own way of portraying a given role. To Mark Schneider, "authenticity is from top to bottom knowing everything from the historical character" and this means "research, research, research" (Schneider 2006). Acting true to character and history is not only knowing everything about the character, and using the vernacular of the time period, but also trying to look physically like the historical characters. Of course, this is often quite impossible (though the use of costumes and wigs does a good job).

Revolutionary City can be seen as a collage with several themes in the fore- and background. The past is brought to life in a metaphoric and provocative way. It is necessarily metaphoric, because one has to be selective to get a message across. The scenes chosen are the ones that carry the *Becoming American* story best. In achieving educational aims with the *Becoming American* story, the *Revolutionary City* program should be seen in connection with other presentations in the historic area; tours through the houses, encounters with the craftsmen, meetings with historical characters, additional or evening programs, and the guidebook among others serve to both establish and underwrite the larger narratalogical frame of the 'Becoming American' thread. Moreover, the performances try to forge a connection to the framework of knowledge which most Americans would have learned in school about the past, and it is this framework that the *Revolutionary City* tries to amplify, confirm, and contest.

Does Theater Challenge 'True' History?

A theatrical piece, unlike an academic treatise, relies on a sense of heightened drama to create and propel the story. It usually begins by setting the scene, rising to a climax, and culminates with a conclusion or the moral of the story. In this sense, while the dramatic story is finished, the retrospective qualities involved in reliving history mean that one is constantly confronted with the element of historical continuity which works against any truly satisfying conclusion. While the theatrical piece needs a form of conclusion for its structural coherence, history is never finished. As such, the theatrical element requires definitive protagonist and antagonist roles in order to promote a coherent dramatic structure and ideas. In the pursuit of a finite theatrical structure with an historically accurate content, the practical constraints of time and visitor attention spans require dramatic protagonists and antagonists to articulate larger historical positions. These roles should not be read in the classical sense of a protagonist with good will per se, but more as a subtle means of dynamic interaction between the characters, providing the scene with different perspectives positioned in opposition to each other. This method is perhaps most clearly seen in the scene *Running to Freedom* in which the three aforementioned characters perform a protagonist, a middle and an antagonist role. The particular nature of theatrical performance in an historical setting determines the choice of starting point, evolution of plot, and the conclusion of historical events. Almost by default, it influences the *way* historical characters are portrayed.

There is enough conflict present in the 18th century to show diverse opinions and facilitate dramatic and climactic conflict. Nevertheless, the idea of a necessary protagonist and antagonist in the scenes can lead to exaggeration and magnification. To engage the public, one often has to start with a stereotype in order to aid recognition and identification. The motives of characters need to be clear and understandable. Hence, the best portrayals of historical characters are often those that develop from an easily identifiable stereotype into a more in-depth character.

The use of theater can cause confusion as well. Ideas expressed by actor interpreters, for instance, about the low status of women, are sometimes mistaken by visitors as the interpreters' own opinion. Another issue is clarity in first and third person interpretation. African American interpreters in third person interpretation are sometimes seen as slaves, whereas they could be craftsmen, explaining an 18th century craft in a 21st century manner. 'Breaking character' in first person interpretation can be disturbing when it is obviously done for crowd control, but when done at the end of a scene, like in *Declaration of Independence* it gives visitors the possibility to place the scene in a context and it may open space for questions beyond time and character borders.

In addition to the danger of stereotypes, exaggeration, and confusion, the use of theater entails a focus on a more personal story. The specific attention on individual actors gives human agency a more prominent role than economic or social processes. This focus on human agency is reinforced by the *Revolutionary City's* purpose to educate in citizenship. The focus within the larger ideological framework is therefore also centered around the role any individual could play in the American experiment. Potentially, this emphasis on personal agency can negate a comprehensive understanding of historically systemic frameworks which would have played an important role in the larger historical context.

As a learning device theater is not always received positively. Theater involves the danger of mixing fact and fiction (see Hendry and Salazar in this volume), and the use of it in museums is often criticized as being too focused on entertainment. Handler's criticism that Colonial Williamsburg simulates an 'authentic' past that bedazzles visitors with theatrical entertainment seems to have some foundation (Handler/Gable 1997). However, if one considers the difficulties that are involved in every representation of history (the social and cultural constraints in which a representation takes place) it appears that no presentation of history can truly escape struggles with authenticity. Indeed, the use of theatre to stimulate visual and interactive learning is becoming an increasingly popular and pedagogically accepted method for the teaching and comprehension of history.

The intellectual framework behind Colonial Williamsburg's representations indicates the institutional commitment to historical research. Compared to other museums, Colonial Williamsburg is a notable exception in providing a large annual budget for research. With such effort and money put into research, we can assume that Colonial Williamsburg does its best to present thoroughly researched history.

Carson has spoken of Colonial Williamsburg as a novel. It is a story in which historians have connected the factual 'dots' that are known, and, based on these dots, they have developed an interpretive storyline which serves as a foundation for the performances. The performances are interpretations based on historical research, but they are *not*, nor are they intended to be, fully authentic. The history presentations in Colonial Williamsburg should be seen as a model, never complete, but somewhere near the historic 'truth' (Carson 2006). Therefore, museums should not present themselves as authorities of authenticity, even when their representations are supported by academic research.

The Role of the Public

Performance is not a one-way matter. How the program is received by the public can be quite different from its intentions.[4] In "An Evaluation of the Revolutionary City" I have shown that all interviewees were engaged with the *Revolutionary City* experience (Teunissen 2006). Another satisfaction survey showed that 56% of those who attended the program while visiting Colonial Williamsburg found it both involving and engaging, versus 39% of those who did not attend the program (Colonial Williamsburg Foundation 2007: 7).[5] Both surveys showed that in terms of education, the program does indeed stimulate visitors to think about past-present relations. Also, 42% of the visitors who visited the *Revolutionary City* versus 26% who did not visit were inspired to learn more about history. One aspect of this renewed or awakened interest in America's past was an increased understanding and appreciation of Williamsburg's role in the birth of democracy in America, which was singled out as important by 58% of the visitors to the program as opposed to only

---

4 For a theoretical analysis of the diverse ways in which the public can be involved I refer to Carolyn Oesterle's article in this volume.

5 Drawing from online surveys, a newspaper article also stressed visitor satisfaction with the *Revolutionary City* program, quoting several visitors as follows: "the march with the militia to the courthouse on Wed., June 7, nearly moved [us] to tears", "I had tears in my eyes as I watched the birth of democracy in this country", "[we were] part of the action", "[I interacted] with the drama with genuine support and enthusiasm", "[I] also really appreciated the 'tar and feather' segment, appreciated the importance of freedom of speech" (Vaughan 2006).

40% of those who had not attended while visiting Colonial Williamsburg (Colonial Williamsburg Foundation 2007: 7). These figures show that the *Revolutionary City* program is better at stimulating education than other, less theatrical parts of Colonial Williamsburg.[6]

The figures mentioned above seem to underline the *Revolutionary City*'s achievements. The program seems to be quite successful in achieving its main aim: 30% of the visitors attending this program are inspired to reflect on their own responsibilities as citizens, versus 16% of those who did not attend. Still, the *Revolutionary City* program should be seen in the context of American society. The outcome of the historical process in which American democracy is celebrated today demands an Americanist interpretation. Although Americans are provoked to be critical about their past (the Revolutionary promise was delayed for many people, democracy was not established from one day to the other) they seem less provoked to be critical about the present where the glorious cause of America is still being (often uncritically) celebrated.[7]

Conclusion

Stimulating Americans to rethink citizenship shows that Colonial Williamsburg's educational aims are not represented without a particular set of convictions. The museum wants to change people's minds. Even when the historical facts are correct one can criticize a representation of the past in pushing the story in a certain direction. As Noel Salazar, Judith Schlehe, Michiko Uike-Bormann, and Joy Hendry (in this volume) have argued, many themed environments, whether museums or theme parks, provide a feeling of national identity, the illusion of a continuity between past and present, and even a feeling of "healing". This all seems to be partly true for Colonial Williamsburg. However, *Revolutionary City*'s revisionist history presentation includes facts from history that do not suit the dominant civic culture of educated white Americans, thus actively preventing the exclusion of certain groups from the collective memory. The *Revolutionary City* program is breaking the pattern of the White Anglo Saxon Protestant (WASP) orientation on a grander scale. This inclusive history is in itself revolutionary for Colonial Williams-

---

6   In 2010, further research results will be published that emerged from the ongoing work of the "Performance, Learning and Heritage project" at the University of Manchester and from the international conference held in Manchester in 2008, where the results of the evaluation of the *Revolutionary City* program were presented as well.

7   For more information on how the program was received by the public, I refer to *Evaluation of the Revolutionary City* (Teunissen 2008a).

burg's history. It is an attempt to move out of the celebratory mode of presenting history to provide a more critical version of the past. The criticism that living history sites only show a sanitized and romanticized history no longer applies to Colonial Williamsburg. The *Revolutionary City* program has taken the lead on a grander scale in showing a complex and more inclusive past.

The inclusion of all levels of society in the *Becoming American* story and in the *Revolutionary City* program seems to aim at a new patriotism and an American ideal of democratic values. Still, the historical narratives show different sides of the story and try to communicate an understanding that the so-called American experiment did not appear from out of nowhere, and that some of its promises remain unfulfilled today. Clearly the past is used, or at least perceived, as a means to validate and promote American values, but does this make the actual historical presentations less 'true'? It is the compilation of 'true' facts that attracts criticism. I have already shown that it is impossible to achieve an objective representation of the past. One can argue that some versions of the past are better than others, but by what criteria? Should the goal be inclusiveness, or the stimulation of critical thinking? Selection remains necessary, and this selection is based on the aims that are to be achieved.

Since Colonial Williamsburg aims for education in citizenship it necessarily maintains its focus on values of patriotism, freedom, and democracy. Here, patriotism is deliberately more inclusive, the *Becoming American* storyline involving, as it does, all levels of society. Social history is incorporated into an understanding of Americanism and Patriotism. In taking this position, Colonial Williamsburg is an active contributor to the assumption of shared experience and memory as the basis of American identity. The continuous interaction of Colonial Williamsburg with its visitors alters the representation of the past. The representation of the past in Colonial Williamsburg is a clear example that historical performances are sensitive to and constrained by current culture. Nevertheless, it shows that public historians can play a vital role in challenging selective views on the past and in promoting a more critical approach to the general public.

Appendix 1: The Revolutionary City Program, Day 1

Collapse of Royal Government, 1774–1776

A number of events occurred in Williamsburg that were pivotal to the evolution of Virginians from subjects of a distant monarch to citizens of a self-governing republic. These events eventually led Virginians to declare that the colonies were no longer under British rule but free and independent states of America. Join us today for Revolutionary City™ to experience the difficult choices facing the townspeople.

In between the timed events listed here, meet on the street with some of the people of Williamsburg and learn how these changes touch their lives.

10:45 a.m.   MAY 26, 1774   *Enemies of Government: Governor Dunmore Dissolves the Assembly*
Lord Dunmore, the royal governor, arrives at the Capitol most unhappy with the House of Burgesses for their protesting the closing of Boston Harbor by the British government. What will he do? How will the burgesses react to his announcement? What does this mean for the people of Williamsburg? *[Capitol, West Balcony]*

11:10 a.m.   APRIL 15, 1775   *A House Divided!*
Ariana Randolph, a loyalist mother, warns her daughter Susannah that her father's loyalty to the British king may require the family to leave the colony for England if American protests grow more violent. *[In front of Wig Shop]*

11:20 a.m.   APRIL 29, 1775   *The Gale from the North!*
On April 21, Governor Dunmore ordered the removal of gunpowder stored in the Magazine. When some patriots threatened retaliation against the governor, Peyton Randolph, Virginia's most influential politician and president of the Continental Congress, negotiated a truce. A week later, as Randolph prepares to return to Philadelphia, devastating news from Lexington and Concord arrives in Williamsburg.
[In front of Raleigh Tavern]

11:35 a.m.   SEPTEMBER 3, 1775   *A Court of Tar and Feathers*
The men who answered Virginia's call to arms for the defense of American liberty were proud, brave, and spirited. They were bound together by the ties of honor and love of country. Any who would challenge their rights and liberties had better beware.
[In front of Raleigh Tavern]

Noon   NOVEMBER 17, 1775   *Liberty to Slaves! Dunmore's Proclamation*
Enslaved people gather to consider the royal governor's offer of freedom to slaves who will take up arms with the British against their rebel masters. Should they leave their homes and families and endanger their lives for this one chance for freedom? Will the governor honor his offer? What will happen if they are captured and returned to their masters?
[Behind the Coffeehouse Archaeological Site]

12:15 p.m.   MAY 15, 1776   *The Citizen Soldier!*
Alexander Hoy, a 30-year-old carpenter who has fallen on hard times, and his wife Barbry engage in a public argument about his enlisting in the army. His wife is concerned that he is too old and that the family can't survive without him. *[In front of Raleigh Tavern]*

Conclusion.

12:25 p.m.   MAY 15, 1776   *Resolved: Free and Independent States!*
The representatives of the free men of Virginia pass resolutions for independence from Great Britain and prepare to establish a republican form of government.
[Begins in front of Raleigh Tavern and moves to Capitol, South Wall]

Appendix 2: The Revolutionary City Program, Day 2

Citizens at War, 1776–1781

Many tests and trials befall the people of Williamsburg as they create a new self-governing society. Several key events move the people of Virginia towards founding a new democratic republic. Join us for Revolutionary City™ and experience the turmoil and challenges that confront the citizens of Virginia while creating a new society and government in the midst of war.

In between the timed events listed here, meet on the street with some of the people of Williamsburg and learn how these changes touch their lives.

10:45 a.m. JULY 25, 1776 *A Declaration of Independence!*
The Declaration of Independence is read to the citizens of Williamsburg. This news arrives only a few weeks after Virginia's representatives have adopted their own Declaration of Rights and a Constitution for the new state. *[Capitol, West Balcony]*

11:05 a.m. JULY 14, 1779 *The Cost of Freedom!*
On a hot summer morning, a confrontation with a merchant draws a crowd of angry protestors to complain about the high price of goods and collapse of Virginia's currency. If remedies are not put in place immediately, they argue, they will all be ruined.
[In front of Raleigh Tavern]

11:15 a.m. SEPTEMBER 15, 1780 *In Desperate Circumstance!*
Barbry Hoy, a camp follower whose soldier husband was captured in the siege at Charleston, seeks work at the Raleigh Tavern. She tells the story of the war in South Carolina and of the grim defeats of the Americans. *[In front of Raleigh Tavern]*

11:30 a.m. APRIL 20, 1781 *The Town is Taken! The British Occupy Williamsburg*
The American turncoat British General Benedict Arnold seizes Williamsburg with British forces under his command. He raises the British flag over the Capitol and announces the rules of occupation. *[Capitol, South Wall]*

11:45 a.m. APRIL 20, 1781 *Running to Freedom!*
A group of enslaved people hear about freedom offered by the British for service to the army. They debate whether they should leave home, as have more than 600 former slaves who left their rebel masters in the Carolinas to follow the British northward.
[Behind the Coffeehouse Archaeological Site]

Noon SEPTEMBER 28, 1781 *The Promised Land, or A Matter of Faith*
An African American Baptist preacher talks about his hopes for the future in a new society where all citizens are equal and where there will be no state church connected to the government like the Church of England had been. A young soldier confronts him with questions of faith in the face of war and world-changing events.
[Behind the Coffeehouse Archaeological Site]

Conclusion.

12:15 p.m. SEPTEMBER 28, 1781 *On to Yorktown and Victory!*
The General addresses his men and the citizens of Williamsburg as he prepares to leave for Yorktown. *[In front of Raleigh Tavern]*

All programs are weather permitting.
Times listed are approximate.

References

Appleby, Joyce/Lynn Hunt/Margaret Jacob. 1994. *Telling the Truth about History.* New York/London: W.W. Norton.

Carson, Cary. 1998a. *Becoming Americans. Our Struggle to be Both Free and Equal.* Williamsburg: Colonial Williamsburg Foundation.

Carson, Cary. 1998b. "Colonial Williamsburg and the Practice of Interpretive Planning in American History Museums." *The Public Historian* 20.3: 11-51.

Carson, Cary. 2001. "Lights, Cameras... Colonial Williamsburg." Winterthur Conference, September 21-22. Draft 20 Mar 2002: 1-19.

Carson, Cary. 2004. "Government BY and For the people: Making those two mighty conjunctions the benchmarks of our new approach to 'Becoming Americans.'" 10 Dec 2004. Email to Jim Horn.

Carson, Cary. 2005. "Revolutionary City = Bagdad Outside the Green Zone". 15 Nov 2005. Email.

Carson, Cary. 2006. Interview. Colonial Williamsburg, 1 Dec 2006.

Colonial Williamsburg. 2006. "Outline Character Scores Revolutionary City."

Colonial Williamsburg Foundation. 2007. "Colonial Williamsburg Guest Satisfaction: Issues and Insights 2006, Year-End Summary." Prepared by Southeastern Institute of Research in conjunction with Guest Research.

Foner, Eric. 2002. *Who Owns History? Rethinking the Past in a Changing World.* New York: Hill and Wang.

Greenspan, Anders. 2002. *Creating Colonial Williamsburg.* Washington/London: The University of North Carolina Press.

Handler, Richard/ Eric Gable. 1997. *The New History in an Old Museum. Creating the Past at Colonial Williamsburg.* Durham/London: Duke University Press.

Korn, Randi. 1994. "An Evaluation of the 'Becoming Americans' Theme." Prepared for Colonial Williamsburg by Randi Korn & Associates.

Lowenthal, David. 1985. *The Past Is a Foreign Country.* New York: Cambridge University Press.

Rentzhog, Sten. 2005. "Challenges and Opportunities of a Changing Future." *Conference Report 2005. Association of European Open Air Museums 22nd Conference.* Turkey Provincial Museum, Finland.

Rentzhog, Sten. 2007. *Open Air Museums: The History and Future of a Visionary Idea.* Stockholm: Carlssons Bokförlag/Osterund: Jamtli Förlag.

Roth, Stacy. 1998. *Past into Present: Effective Techniques for First-Person Historical Interpretation*. London/Chapel Hill: University of North Carolina Press.

Schlesinger, Arthur M. 1998. *The Disuniting of America: Reflections on a Multicultural Society*. New York/London: Norton.

Schneider, Mark. 2006. Interview. Colonial Williamsburg, 17 Nov 2006.

Sternberg, Susan. 1993. "The Art of Participation." *Theatre in Museums. Technical Information Service's FORUM. Occasional Papers and Readings on Museum Issues and Standards: Perspectives on Museum Theatre*. Washington, D.C.: American Association of Museums.

Tate, Thad W. 1965. *The Negro in Eighteenth Century Williamsburg*. Williamsburg: Colonial Williamsburg Foundation.

Teunissen, Martine. 2006. "An Evaluation of the Revolutionary City." Evaluative report, November 2006, Department of Educational Program and Evaluation, Colonial Williamsburg. Unpublished manuscript.

Teunissen, Martine. 2007. *The Revolutionary City. An Impression*. http://www.youtube. com/watch?v=X7eDI_zpDZU (accessed 20 Apr 2010).

Teunissen, Martine. 2008a. "Evaluation of the Revolutionary City (Colonial Williamsburg): A Programme of Theatre as a Valuable Tool for Interpretation." *On the Future of Open Air Museums*. Ed. Inger Jensen. Ostersund: Jamtli Förlag.

Teunissen, Martine. 2008b. "Representation of the Past in Public Spheres. Experiencing the Past: The Reconstruction and Recreation of History at Colonial Williamsburg." Mphil Thesis Public History, Department of History, Leiden University. Unpublished manuscript.

Tilden, Freeman. 1977. *Interpreting Our Heritage*. Chapel Hill: University of North Carolina Press.

Vaughan, Steve. 2006. "'Rev City' Fans Laud Living History Ideal: Comments in Response to Summer of Surveys." *The Virginia Gazette* 4 Oct.

Wallis, Mark. 2009. "'The New You.' Best Practice in Historical Live Interpretation." Conference talk. *Staging the Past: Themed Environments in Transcultural Perspectives*, Freiburg, 23-25 Apr.

Weldon, Bill/Conny Graft. 2006. Internship meeting, 22 Sep.

Wood, Gordon S. 1992. *The Radicalism of the American Revolution*. New York: Vintage.

"The New You":
Best Practice in Historical Live Interpretation

Visitors to Berlin's Brandenburg Gate have their visas stamped by a grim-faced soldier wearing the immaculate uniform of the Soviet army, watched by a gum-chewing G.I. But this is the 21st century: the Berlin Wall fell two decades ago and there is no tension in the air – today there is a holiday mood, because the line of people having their visas stamped are not nervous East Germans but tourists having fake documents 'inspected' by an actor in costume. This is an initiative (some say Disneyesque stunt) intended to give an impression of the divided city during the Cold War. Perhaps if the tourists suspend their disbelief enough and ignore the fact that the wall – that most potent symbol of division – is no more, they may get something out of it. Certainly this initiative is in keeping with the *zeitgeist* – the urge to experience the uniqueness of the places we visit on our travels...

Further east in Russia, visitors to Moscow's Red Square can be photographed next to look-alikes dressed as Czar Nicholas II and his nemesis Lenin, whilst in St. Petersburg you can be bear-hugged by Peter the Great or hold the dainty hand of Catherine the Great for a souvenir snapshot. Increasingly tourists can find appropriately bedecked historical characters (at varying levels of historical authenticity) in many heritage sites around the world, all eager to be photographed and appropriate (in some measure) to their historical surroundings. It is similar to standing next to the Horse Guards in London's Whitehall, as they sit astride their patient mounts for photographs, or posing with a 'Beefeater' at the Tower of London or Swiss Guard at the Vatican: similar, but not the same, because – in the cited cases of Berlin, Moscow and St. Petersburg, those in costume represent people from a vanished age. Although the Horse Guards, Beefeaters and Swiss Guards do not go into battle in their elaborate fancy dress, their forebears did; thus they represent a long and unbroken historical tradition and, in many cases, are still in the armed forces: they are not 'playing a game of make believe' and are therefore authentic. They are simultaneously 'then' and 'now'.

But what if you want more in the way of engagement than merely posing for a photograph with the real soldier in 'fancy dress uniform' or the pretend 'person from the past', or even more than the limited interaction involved in having your 'papers' stamped at the Brandenburg Gate? What if you want to discover the unique history of the site you are visiting but do not want the traditional guided tour, or do not have time for one, or perhaps, want something tailor-made to your particular interests or adapted to those of the different ages in your group? What if you want to *talk* to the historical personage to discover their unique view on the place you are both standing in, to find out what it meant to them, in 'their' time? To find something that is not in the guidebook, for instance. To feel that, to some extent, you are stepping back in time?

Increasingly there is another path to understanding the history and significance of the place you have come to see which does not involve the traditional guide, guidebook, graphic panel or audio guide, or does not only involve these forms of interpretation. Many museums, galleries and historic sites around the world – recognising the value of what is, in essence, costumed storytelling – offer interaction with professional or amateur costumed guides/docents/ actor-interpreters (call them what you will). As part of the visitor experience, either as the core offer or on special occasions, and often as an 'added value' attraction, running in conjunction with the more traditional interpretation. This move is so widespread and so much a part of our currency that it was parodied in an episode of *The Simpsons,* where Homer works in 'colonial' costume in a site clearly modelled on Colonial Williamsburg.

In America the granddaddy of all sites that employ historical interpreters (and for the rest of this paper I shall use this ugly but accepted term) is indeed the Colonial Williamsburg Foundation in Virginia; though you may find costumed interpreters in forts, farmhouses, mills and monuments throughout the United States; but the largest and most famous, next to Williamsburg in public perception and visitor numbers, are Conner Prairie, Mystic Seaport, Old Sturbridge Village, Jamestown and Plimoth Plantation – all wellestablished sites – whilst the use of costumed live interpretation takes place regularly in Canada, from Newfoundland to British Columbia, and in Australia, notably at Sovereign Hill in New South Wales. In the last couple of decades this inter-war North American 'invention' (if we discount its 19th century genesis in Skansen, Scandinavia) has spread to the European continent, with varying degrees of success; some countries have taken to this form more readily than others. It may be that this form of interpretation has grown so rapidly since 1987 in Great Britain because of the Anglophone countries' shared language and heritage: the so-called 'special relationship'... Who knows?

However, it is needless for me here to list all the sites in the various European countries that use costumed live interpretation, as I would much rather briefly examine why it works – and when it does not.

I am firmly convinced that, as little children, many if not most boys think about knights when they visit castles, whilst their sisters may well dream of princesses – a gender truism acknowledged by the Disney Corporation in making their films and products. Of course, children now are growing up without having to merely imagine such storybook characters; they can meet them face to face. And if you study these encounters, as Professor Tony Jackson continues to do at Manchester University, you will see how positive it can be for future recall of facts: Costumed interpretation – in the right hands and for the right people – can be a wonderful pedagogic tool and many statistics exist to support this view.

When we grow up we may well encounter people dressed as knights and princesses at historical sites, and this is invariably shocking on some level: their presence certainly affects our visit – and can make or mar it. Encountering costumed interpreters can be exciting and attractive but simultaneously ludicrous and embarrassing – principally I believe because you, the adult visitor, fear being singled out by them to do something, or perhaps your own historical knowledge is not as detailed as theirs, and you dread being belittled in public (young children have not yet learnt embarrassment so they enter into such encounters more readily). I imagine most of us have, at some stage, been pounced upon by an out-of-work actor and made to participate in his or her 'reality' – and we still cringe at the memory. London's long-vanished Museum of the Moving Image was the classic example of this...

I have seen adult visitors humiliated at some sites, and at others children pushed towards the costumed characters like sacrificial lambs by embarrassed parents who opine that having people in costume on site is interesting for (and aimed at) the children. Well, responsible costumed interpretation, *carefully researched and executed,* is good for *everyone* who chooses to use it and is not just for the children, or should not be.

It should never be the *only* form of interpretation on site, however, as some people remain uncomfortable with it, and especially with 'first person' character interpretation, because it is so often badly done. But again, I believe that if care is taken, a first person encounter can be just as memorable as a traditional third person guided tour. In fact the Colonial Williamsburg Foundation neatly sums up the differences between the two styles thus: "Third person interpretation is the most efficient form of oral data transfer, but first person is the most effective."

So if a site wishes to use costumed interpretation as a way of communicating information that is not in the guidebook, or that would not be read in a densely-written graphic panel, and instead desires the flexibility of a human 'historical' encounter over the rigidity of an audio guide script, then there are several steps that must be followed in order to achieve success. Ignoring these steps will, almost invariably, lead to disaster – embarrassment, bad word-of-mouth etc. I offer the following advice based on my lifetime's experience – you do not have to take it but you can learn to avoid the pitfalls, if you choose.

To set out my credentials, I should mention that I have been professionally engaged in the field of costumed historical interpretation since 1977, but a decade later brought my company, Past Pleasures Ltd, over to the UK from the US, where I had worked for a number of years at (amongst other places) Colonial Williamsburg. I still work with them as a consultant, and recently trained their actor/interpreters for the ground-breaking *Revolutionary City* programme (see Teunissen in this volume); now they have commissioned me to re-interpret their main exhibition buildings. Past Pleasures Ltd holds Europe's largest contract for daily costumed interpretation (with Historic Royal Palaces) and I travel internationally advising sites that use, or are considering using, costumed interpretation.

To them – and to you – I say that the first step is *recruitment.* Find the right person and you will have won half the battle. And by the 'right person' I mean someone who is enthusiastic, a good 'people person' with bundles of wit, energy, humour and charm, yet possessing a strong seriousness of purpose, respect for research, the site and its visitors, a deep passion for history and the ability and desire to communicate it. Someone who is active, not passive. Someone the visitors actively enjoy and want to spend time with. Do not on any account hire a bully, a boor, a bore or anyone with a raging ego – they will not be a team player and will refuse to take advice and direction, and will often be divisive in the changing room. Worst of all, they will lack the key quality that every costumed interpreter must possess: empathy.

The right people *do* exist, but to the surprise of many curators, site managers, education officers etc. they are not necessarily recruited from the acting profession – though dramatic techniques and skills are necessary tools for the trade. I have often found that teachers make ideal costumed interpreters... But whoever they are and whatever their background, I urge you to make the recruitment process difficult – just as you would for someone applying to enter another field of human endeavour. Just because 'dressing up in costume' looks easy – and when you watch your charges delighting your visitors – it looks like fun as well, do *not* assume that it *is* easy! A good costumed interpreter (whether in first or in third person) has to combine the skills of a host, a storyteller, an entertainer, an expert, a psychologist, a guardian (of the site and its artefacts), a tour guide, a stand-up comedian (when and if appropriate), a therapist and a counsellor. It is not – or should not be – an easy job, preferable to working in a bookshop or stacking shelves in a supermarket. It is a (relatively) new profession and deserves respect because it is very hard to do well and very easy to do badly.

The second step is *training*. Ensure your recruits are trained in the variety of interlocking disciplines, the patchwork quilt that is costumed interpretation. These include, but are not limited to, vocal techniques, body language, reading their audience, how to move in period costume, how to improvise convincingly in character, how to select and digest the appropriate research, how to engage the visitors and interact with them, as well as other site staff, how to deal with problem visitors – even how to pose for a photograph.

Amazingly there is nowhere in the world where you can train to be a costumed interpreter – but shouldn't there be? After all, you must train to be a journalist, a teacher, a plumber, a doctor – would you let untrained people loose on your magazine, classroom, sink or body? So why would you let untrained (or at the very least unassessed) people in costume loose in your museum, gallery or historic site, with all the attendant risks that brings?

Therefore I am in the middle of discussing with a client the establishment of a Live Interpretation Training Academy. It is time for professionalism in this emergent field, without squeezing out those amateurs (re-enactors and the like) that burn with passion for their hobby and often have a great deal of practical knowledge to impart.

The third step is *costuming*. Whether your recruits will be working in the first or third person, or a mixture of the two (which can be very effective if done well; again, this is a training issue) they must obviously wear appropriate period attire – so somebody connected with the site has to decide what it should be. Therefore many questions must be asked and many matters considered before scissors cut through cloth (or indeed before the cloth is purchased!). Apart from the most obvious ones of gender, interpreters' age and time period to be interpreted, other vital questions must be asked before producing the appropriate period outfit. For example, is the interpreter to represent someone from the town or the country? Are they fashionable or do they despise the current modes? Are they widowed? What is their profession, or are they gentry, with no profession... I suggest involving the interpreter (to a limited extent) in this discussion, because he or she will be the one wearing it. But the final decision as to what outfit is worn, what colour or colours the clothes are made of and what fabric they are made from, as well as what accessories they carry (if any) must be yours.

Then you must ensure that the outfit is made to the most exacting museum standards and that the interpreter understands how to wear it in the correct period manner, and what each item represents and means. The period clothing worn on site should be just that – clothing, not costume! *Nothing* cheapens or debases a site – nor undermines staff morale – more than fancy dress. And what will your visitors think if you allow staff to wander around wearing a pair of old curtains? Doing reproduction period clothing properly costs a great deal of money, energy and time but it pays huge dividends.

The fourth step is *assessment.* Always make time to assess your interpreters on the information that is being given out to your visitors. This achieves two desirable goals: they will feel valued (and continue to enjoy their job) and you will know that your site is providing the best, most up-to-date information. The bonus is that your visitors enjoy their encounters with your interpreter(s), will tell their friends and – most importantly – come back! Regular assessment combined with involving your staff in the latest developments on site will ensure maximum enjoyment and productivity for all. Communication is the key to everything in life, and lack of it is the cause of all of life's problems...

Remember that interpreters are only human and will have good and bad days. They are not animatronics and can get lazy or bored and make stuff up. Do not let them. Let them see you on 'the floor' and they will respect you all the more.

Following the steps I have outlined above *should* ensure excellence and make your site a shining example of best practice in live, costumed, historical interpretation. But there are no guarantees.

History's Pure Serene: On Reenacting
Cook's First Voyage, September 2001

VANESSA AGNEW

> Much have I travell'd in the realms of gold,
> And many goodly states and kingdoms seen;
> Round many western islands have I been
> Which bards in fealty to Apollo hold.
> Oft of one wide expanse had I been told
> That deep-brow'd Homer ruled as his demesne;
> Yet did I never breathe its pure serene
> Till I heard Chapman speak out loud and bold:
> Then felt I like some watcher of the skies
> When a new planet swims into his ken;
> Or like stout Cortez when with eagle eyes
> He star'd at the Pacific – and all his men
> Look'd at each other with a wild surmise –
> Silent, upon a peak in Darien.
>
> John Keats,
> "On first looking into Chapman's Homer", 1816

He'd seen many places – real and imagined – but there were things the young John Keats couldn't know. When at last he entered those uncharted realms to breathe what he called "the pure serene" it was not from the prow of a ship; it was via a book, and a translated one at that. It was on reading George Chapman's 17th-century translation of Homer, the poet said, that new vistas opened to him. He likened his adventures in reading to the discoveries of astronomers and conquistadors gazing in silent wonder at new planets and Pacific seas. Apparently, the doing of a thing was not the same as the telling of it, nor experience tantamount to understanding.

We were book people ourselves – a handful of readers and writers among a crew of doers. But our journey was a journey in reverse, a journey from the book to the ship, from reflection to experience. We'd signed on as ordinary seamen and supernumeraries so as to voyage back in time. For a moment, the gap between the present and the past seemed no wider than a gap in the reef. The passage might be treacherous but still we imagined we'd breach it. We'd re-enact Cook's first voyage, test his equipment and navigation, eat lemons, and smoke the decks. We thought we'd stare down the Pacific from an island peak and a fighting top and find an understanding of the past so rich and thick and incontrovertible it'd come to be called the "pure serene" of history itself.

Duly, we learned our way round that wooden world. We obeyed orders. We lived on oatmeal, hard tack, and salt meat; we slept in hammocks. We maneuvered our *Endeavour* through coral shoals and pirate waters. We scrubbed the decks and boats in time for the captain's rounds. We found that a ship has no business with dirt; it's not a sentimental or private place; it's indifferent to joy, mourning, and other niceties of the land. We found that the voyage brought sickness, mental breakdowns, and evacuations. There was bewilderment and ignorance. And afterwards, I came to wonder what, in fact, it was that we had learned about history during our six weeks before the mast.

My first sight of the ship comes unexpectedly. With a day to go before signing on, I'm walking along the Cairns Esplanade and there, beyond the mangrove flats, is the ship working its way up the coast, its bare masts and rigging hatched on the sky. Later it occurs to me that the ship must have an engine. It might be 18th century to the eye, but the ship is entirely of our time and place. I remind myself not to say "boat" and to refer to the ship as "she" but my mind careens between the past and present, the sea and the shore. Try as I might, it is my lubberly self that keeps resurfacing.

I recall an earlier ship and one of Samuel Wallis's midshipmen doing his homework. He saw a puff of smoke on the horizon then heard the canon's report. Penned in the margins of his notebook is a sum calculating the distance of the ship in the offing – around three miles, he reckoned. I, too, await the sound that will tell me how far it is from then till now.

We go aboard to find that the ship is crushingly small. By day, the hammocks are taken down and the sea chests become mess benches. We are sent aloft, sent below, sent on deck. This perpetual motion unmoors us: there's no place to settle, no corner of the ship to call our own. Many hours are spent, as they say, "standing by to stand by". It's unprofitable time. I run and fetch a book but then I'm absent from my bracing station and get a dressing down from the captain o' the top. Next time, I carry a book with me, but have no place to put it when we come to wear ship. I try and learn to be idle – to liberate myself from the need for productive activity. Soon I'm too tired to do anything anyway and I stop wondering why ordinary seamen rarely put pen to paper: they had no time. The ship is crawling with people, but its spaces remain hermetically sealed. The Great Cabin and the wardroom, mere feet from where we eat, sleep, and work, remain out of bounds. Power, I'm reminded, is managed by the regulation of movement and here we have no jurisdiction over space or matter.

The order comes to go aloft. We climb onto the rough tree rail – this in itself seems foolish – then carefully step onto the shrouds. The captain o' the top shows the way, scuttling up the rigging and along the yard, and grasping lines with his toes. I creep up to an overhanging section of rigging that's 50-odd feet above the deck. It's the futtocks that connect the shrouds to the fighting top, a platform three-quarters of the way up the mast. Hanging backwards and climbing fast, we hook our elbows into the futtock lines and haul ourselves up. There are cautionary tales about falling from the futtocks and each of us determines *never* to fall. Then, at last, we flop onto the fighting top, giddy with relief.

But it's the yard-work I really hate. We're shown how to clip onto a fixed rope and feel with our toes for a line looped beneath the yard. We sing out a warning; then step onto the footrope and reach for the sail. Our topman tells us it's quite safe; we just have to lean out farther over the yard. "Counterbalance", he says. But I don't like it, not a bit. The slightest movement sets everyone wobbling and the footrope comes so low that the yard rides up somewhere near my neck. The scale of the rigging seems somehow wrong: below deck where there's little headroom, I'm an ergonomic fit, but here I'm Lilliputian.

We're set to furling. The gasket, we learn, must first be prepared: this short rope is looped over the yard and used to tie up the sail. Then we pull on the swathes of canvas. I know this feeling: it's like hauling a futon upstairs while dangling by one's feet from the banister. The immense sail has to be rolled into the top part of itself. Tugging with one hand and holding with the other, we stuff the sail into the "skin" and tuck in the little ratlines. When we all have a purchase on our bit of sail, we give the fat sausage a shake to settle it. Then the gasket loop is passed behind and under the sail. The gasket tail is fed through the loop, pulled tight, and secured with three half hitches. It sounds straightforward but my gasket loop is hanging down somewhere by my feet and I can't lean far enough over the yard to reach it.

We make Cooktown. Everyone wants to go ashore but it's decided that the botanists and BBC camera crew are to be landed first. We begin to feel that the botanists are being given preferential treatment and that the hierarchies of the Cook voyage are being re-animated on this one. In Cook's day, privilege was part of the natural order: seamen may have grumbled, but it was not motivated grumbling. We, on the other hand, feel our sense of entitlement and complain volubly.

Of course, in June 1770, everyone went ashore at Endeavour River because of the beating the ship had taken on the reef. The crew had to offload the stores, ballast, anchors, and cannon, while the carpenters floated the ship with barrels and repaired the hull. The seamen, too, needed attention. With their bleeding gums and swollen limbs, a dozen or so men were suffering from scurvy. Lieutenant Gore was sent to look for fresh provisions, returning with palm cabbages, yams, and tasty plantains. Cook found time in this flurry of work to climb the highest hill and inspect the estuary, mangrove swamps, and sandy shoals. The sight made him ill when he contemplated the difficulties of reaching the open sea.

While on land, Cook's astronomers observed an immersion of Jupiter's moons and used this to calculate their position. Our navigators attempt to do the same using the lunar distance method. They spend hours consulting tables and wrangling numbers to finally put our position somewhere up the coast. Still they are glad to have us in the right hemisphere and, in their minds at least, Nevil Maskelyne's *Nautical Almanac* trumps John Harrison and his longitude-finding watch.

Endeavour River is one of the great accomplishments of Cook's voyage – a triumph of ingenuity and leadership over limited resources and natural adversity. At the same time, it reminds us of the constraints on the Europeans' intellectual apparatus, especially their difficulties in interpreting the new. It was here they first saw a kangaroo, which they likened to a greyhound crossed with a hare or a deer. The naturalist Joseph Banks said he didn't quite know how to describe the animal, "nothing certainly that I have seen at all resembles him" (Beaglehole 1962: II: 85). They were also puzzled by the fruit bat. Quoting a sailor for his "Seamanlike a stile", Banks said, the bat was "about as large and much like a one gallon cagg [barrel], as black as the Devil and had 2 horns on its head, it went but slowly but I dared not touch it" (ibid.: 84). Banks found the sailor's description as amusing as we find his. I wonder what this means for the historicity of our own analogies.

Most puzzling to Cook were the local Aborigines. He tried to communicate with them but they seemed disinterested in the visitors, either fleeing when they saw the sailors or accepting "trifles" without real enthusiasm (cf. Nugent 2009). Had it not been for the intervention of the Polynesian Tupaia, who facilitated some of these cross-cultural exchanges, there might have been no contact at all. But this didn't stop Cook and Banks describing the people in terms of what they were apparently *not*: their hair *wasn't* "woolly or frizzled", their features *weren't* "disagreeable" (Beaglehole 1955: 395); they seemed to have "*no* Idea of traffick" and "*never* would understand our signs" (emph. added. Beaglehole 1962: II: 125). My friend Jonathan says there's a name for the habit of cataloging what's not there: it's called litotes, he says. Homer did it, so did 17th-century voyagers like William Dampier (Lamb 2001: 247).

Joseph Banks obviously knew the classics and he had no trouble circulating Dampier's views on Aborigines: Aboriginal people from the Top End to Tasmania were all the same; apparently, they were stuck at a low level of development and unable to advance to the rank of cultivator. At the same time, he pointed out that they knew things that Europeans did not: they had, for instance, an intimate knowledge of the local flora and fauna, even naming their plants. As a namer of plants himself, this was concessionary. And yet Banks's contradictions also gave him away. He insisted that the land was uninhabited and this depiction of Australia as a kind of *terra nullius* opened the way for British imperial interests. Before long, Banks would be appearing before a House of Commons Committee to call for the colonization of New Holland (cf. Agnew 1998).

Cook, meanwhile, had taken possession of the eastern seaboard from a rather unprepossessing island off the northernmost coast of Queensland. It's clear from his journals that they landed on the island, not specifically in order to claim it, but "in order to be better informed" (Beaglehole 1955: 387). The men climbed a hill two or three times the height of the mast and saw only the sea. There was nothing left to discover, Cook realized, for the Dutch had already explored to the west and this was the Continent's end. And so, although Cook had taken possession of parts of eastern Australia already, he "once more hoisted English Coulers [sic] and in the Name of His Majesty King George the Third took possession of the whole Eastern Coast from the above Latitude down to this place by the name of *New South Wales*, together with all the Bays, Harbours Rivers and Islands" (ibid.: 387-388). Three volleys were fired; they were answered by three from the ship.

Alex knows his books. We're standing on the peak, looking at the ocean, and he points out the significance of Cook's actions for future Australia. Cook's instructions, like those of British voyagers before him, insisted that possession be taken only with the "Consent of the Natives" (Beaglehole 1955: cclxxxiii). But, neither here nor elsewhere did Cook elicit indigenous consent. Rather, we sense his relief when local people simply left the visitors to their own devices: "From the appearence [sic] of these People we expected that they would have opposed our landing but as we approachd [sic] the Shore they all made off and left us in peaceable possession of as much of the Island as served our purpose" (ibid.: 387). To read

Cook's journal is to imagine beach landings and ceremonies all along the eastern seaboard, acts of possession linked for the benefit of the Admiralty and the Crown, and metropolitan readers. It's a sweeping gesture that takes in everything from here to there, a vast mental dot-to-dot. Our perspective, in contrast, is all local – we're dazzled by the surf, the beach, the scrubby bush, the anthills, the sight of the ship at anchor, the insects, and the heat. They are experiences that cannot be located on any map.

With the hint of an offshore breeze, we're woken at four for sail handling. We discover, in a way that Newton would have appreciated, what it means to get a stationary ship moving. One whole watch is ordered to the anchor. Chickens in their coop and the wardroom "windows" – a shallow but heavy greenhouse box – have to be moved and the hole in the deck covered with a grating. It's over this grating that we climb when we come to turn the capstan. Then the capstan is assembled: wooden spars are inserted into a spindle like a giant cotton reel. A dozen or more people power the capstan by pushing in pairs, now slowing, now speeding to avoid a spar in the back, ducking and hopping to avoid sails, ropes, and other clutter on the deck. Orders are sung out, "Walk forward slowly on the capstan", then "capstan, avast!" There's no shantying, no "What shall we do with the drunken sailor?" At best there's the telling of vulgar jokes, at worst, a low muttering. Finally, there's no sound at all, just shuffling and resting.

The messenger cable, a thin rope that communicates with the unwieldy anchor cable, feeds round the spindle and two men with mallets are given the task of "fleeting". They squat under the turning capstan like truculent children and hammer coils of messenger cable up to the top of the spindle. Another pair squats on the deck near the rough-tree rail and "tails" the messenger by pulling coils off the top of the reel. With a fat and greasy rope in their laps, this job is just plain dirty. As it feeds off the capstan, the cable is carried by a chain of hands back through the waist of the ship to the foredeck where it's flaked out. Since the end of the messenger is attached to an anchor cable roughly twice its size in diameter, the two cables have to be tied together. Here, we learn the etymology of a familiar word. "Nippers", pieces of rope about a meter long, bind the messenger to the anchor cable. As the capstan spools the messenger, so reeling up more anchor cable, a line of people in the waist hands off their nippers. When the nipper reaches the end of the line, it is untied and a sailor runs it back to the foredeck where it is reaffixed by wrapping it around the two cables with a little twist. In this way, the messenger rope hauls up the cable, not so much conveying, as enticing, the anchor out of the sea. The excess cable, wet, sometimes sandy and covered in marine life, is then fed into the forepeak hatch. Two dwarfish but powerful people must creep into this hole and wind the anchor cable around another squat spindle. The cable is wider than a man's arm, weighing maybe 20 pounds a foot, and thick with coagulated tar and silt. It's trollish work. The second mate, meanwhile, hangs off the front of the bowsprit and reports the progress of the anchor to the captain. Bells signal the number of shackles, or forty-foot lengths, that have yet to be taken up. Finally, the anchor stock and flukes clear the water. It's all yelling and ringing and hauling and more yelling.

While one watch tends the anchor, others are assigned to sail handling. The captain passes general orders to the first mate, who gives orders to the captains o' the top and an upper yardie, who goes aloft to remove the rolling tackle. The captains o' the top translate the orders into terms we can understand. So far, I've grasped only the fact that the rigging is arranged in pairs so that port will be easing and controlling, while starboard hauls. The clews, bunts, and reefs, mizzen tops'l bowlines and main topmast stays'l halyards still look to me like a hempen mess. I heave but without wit, a litotic kind of sailor.

We're on a parabolic course to the old Batavia. Today, however, marks the real start of the navigators' navigating and, without the use of GPS, the beginning of some circuitousness. They're using a French map that dates from 1756. We wonder why Cook used a twenty-year-old French map when the Dutch knew so much about these waters. Whatever the reason, Vaugondy's map is the one we're reenacting. Our library also includes volumes by Beaglehole, Banks, Dalrymple, Dampier, Hawkesworth, a bird book, Parkin's volumes on the *Endeavour*, two *Lonely Planet* guides, a collection of sea shanties, and Cherry-Garrad's *The Worst Journey in the World*. We can't help feeling that, even with all the resources available to us, we're less informed than Cook and, consequently, we make a poor job of identifying, classifying, and steering. For about a week the navigators use dead reckoning. This plots our net course over a four-hour period as a vector sum that factors in leeway and corrects for magnetic variation and the curvature of the earth. Our course is tracked on the traverse board, a round piece of wood marked with a compass rose and holes that correspond to the hours and half hours of the watch. Each half-hourly change in course is plotted with a peg in the compass rose. This Parcheesi-like affair is supplemented by the lunar distance method to establish our position. Moonbeam's task this morning is to record the altitude of the sun and perform mathematical feats with his observation. But he's in a tizzy by the afternoon when he finds that his two-hour calculation puts our position a hundred miles inland. Perhaps this is what Cook meant when he said that, although longitude could be worked out quite easily with the help of the nautical almanac and astronomical ephemeris, the lunar distance calculations are laborious and discouraging to beginners.

Inside the Barrier Reef there was little bird and animal life: we saw a sea snake and then for more than a week, nothing. Now that we're in the Timor Sea, there's a good deal more marine life. At dusk a flock of small birds swarms us, darting through the rigging and wheeling about the ship. They're an incandescent blue with long paradisiacal tail feathers. With each fly-by their iridescent wings catch the last glimmers of light; then they're gone. There're also fish. We're overjoyed that our salt beef and sauerkraut will be supplemented with fresh food when the fishermen finally haul in a large mackerel and barracuda. Cook had no trouble finding fish but our fishermen have been defensive about their inability to keep us provisioned. They explain it this way and that – the season, the ship's speed. It seems to me, though, that these waters are probably overfished.

In the morning, the captain musters us on the quarterdeck to tell us that we can be happy we're in the "safest place in the world". By this he means to tell us that the World Trade Center and the Pentagon have been attacked. The captain's speech is so confusing we think it's a hoax staged by the BBC as part of our reality TV ordeal. But then someone starts weeping and real reality intrudes. Still it's hard to fathom. I think this means there'll be war. Not everyone agrees.

The Americans on board are given permission to use the satellite phone. We run, all of us, to the Great Cabin and wait to call. Everyone's family is safe, even JB's, whose mother works on Wall Street. I worry that my father might have been on an eastbound flight but I get through to him and he's ok. We have a brief conversation interrupted by dropouts in the line. "Are you still going up?" he says. At cross-purposes, I think he means aloft, but realize later he means north, to Indonesia, where anti-American sentiment is strong. Then I get through to my partner. Her voice is thin and frail, as though she were speaking with great effort about unspeakable things. I long to be at home rather than stuck in this time warp, and, not for the first time, I feel that being on the ship cuts us off from a world that won't be the same when we return.

We hold a memorial service and lower the flag to half-mast. We sit on the quarterdeck and the captain says the Lord's Prayer. It's an odd choice and the prayer is only haltingly repeated. Then the Maori start to sing and this is a little more comforting. The director films it all – the singing, the crying, the stricken and dazed faces. Then he comes to interview the historians. What's there to say? When Cook got to Batavia he learned that there had been an uprising in Poland, supported by the Turks; Carteret's ship *Swallow* had returned from the South Seas some two years earlier. They are historical parallels of the most banal sort. There's no meaningful comparison to be drawn either between our isolation and Cook's, or between our strife and his. We can't say much about the devastation in New York either. Our capacity to interpret and create meaning seems to be diminished at the moment we need these faculties most. Perhaps that's what Adorno meant when he said no poetry was possible after Auschwitz: it wasn't a moral prohibition so much as an intellectual failure.

I'm reduced by a loss of purpose. This 18th-century charade made sense while it contributed to the possibility of political reconciliation. I thought that being ignorant of history was, potentially, to repeat it, and I weighed the responsibility of playing the past against possible mis-tellings of the story. Now, I wonder what lessons the 18th century can possibly hold. Our experiences seem only to sever us from what came before. We're people of the "now", alive only to the immediate need for food, rest, and distraction.

In the days to come, the first mate orders a rigorous program of cleaning and maintenance – painting and scraping and swabbing – that keeps everyone busy. Rations increase; discipline relaxes a little. We're made to play games. The watches have to compete against each other and are rewarded with food. When we're not on watch or doing maintenance we talk about eating. Alex reads aloud from the *Lonely Planet Guide* to Java. We discuss rambutans, durians, mangosteens, and soursop. Will the fruit be in season? Will we be able to take a ripe mangosteen home, as Queen Victoria once desired? We choose restaurants in Jakarta. Shall we eat at Lan Na Thai, one of the city's posher establishments? What about Café Batavia in historic Kota, where the food is also excellent, if pricey? Or maybe we should get our first meal of *gado gado* and *sate* from a *kaki lima*, a street vendor.

But we're in the doldrums now. Our world is monochromatic, the sea and sky utterly blue. There's nothing to distract the eye, and somehow this reduction in sensory input gnaws at the imagination. We're given little news, but still I fixate on home – people jumping out of windows, the coming war. We have another three weeks at sea and I don't know how I'll cope with the isolation. Jonathan returns to Banks and Cook. They knew homesickness, Jonathan says, and looks up the passage in Banks's journal: "The greatest part of them [the sailors] were now pretty far gone with the longing for home." It was called "nostalgia" then and Banks thought the only effective remedy was "constant employment for [the] mind" (Beaglehole 1962: 145). Cook set the seamen to picking oakum and making spun yarn.

I'll not be picking oakum or spinning yarn but I do take some comfort from the sea. Washing on deck in the morning, I see a school of fish clear the waves like a flock of small birds. I remember seeing flying fish as a child traveling by ship from South Africa to Australia. In my mind's eye the flying fish were bigger, their "wings" positively avian. Forster's drawing of a flying fish looked like a miniature coelacanth, ready to grow legs and scuttle onto the land. These creatures, though, are still more aqueous than terrestrial. Aside from flying fish, we see an abundance of phosphorescence. This is the sole compensation for night watch – the sight of sparkling water being thrown up by the bow and a trail of shimmering light left in our wake. There are wet hessian bags on deck and, as we come off watch, we stand around shaking and smacking the bags and marvelling at the lightshow.

We're in the homestretch now and I'm cheered by the prospect of land. Cook had been anxious to avoid all contact with the Dutch and had bypassed Kupang, making instead for the neighboring island of Savu. Savu was barely marked on the charts and Cook wasn't sure whether it was a Dutch or a Portuguese possession, or whether it could still be claimed for Britain. Banks described it as an island of low, sloping hills. There were no visible signs of cultivation, just a few houses and land cleared around stands of coconut palms. Since the crew was suffering badly from a lack of fresh food, lieutenant Gore was sent immediately to trade for fresh provisions. He learned of a harbor and a town – the islanders drew a map in the sand – where they might purchase sheep, hogs, fruit, and fowls. On the leeward side of the island, Cook mounted a proper expedition and, for the first time in three years, the sailors spotted European dress – blue frock coats, white waistcoats, and laced hats. Were these people Portuguese, Banks wondered? At the leeside bay of Seba, they found their answer: colors were hoisted and three volleys fired. It was the Dutch, whom they'd been trying so hard to avoid.

Cook's trading delegation was introduced to the local raja, who was prepared to sell them everything they wanted, but only if they received permission from the Dutch East India Company. Before any goods could change hands, they must apply to the only white resident on the island (Beaglehole 1962: 152). After years spent trading with indigenous peoples, Cook had forgotten this kind of protocol. He was used to establishing his own market regulations: he would demarcate and fortify a trading place, nominate a trader, and try to control value by limiting the supply of commodities. In the islands of central and western Polynesia, Tierra del Fuego, and even along the Australian coast, he had generally managed to set the terms. Only occasionally was he thwarted by native restrictions on the alienability of their own goods. Here, however, gestures of hospitality did not lubricate trade in the familiar ways (Agnew 2004a). Taking sailors hostage on shore, the raja and the Company official went to dine on the ship where they were presented with various gifts – a "spying glass", one of Banks's greyhounds, a sheep, and sufficient mutton and alcohol for the aftereffects to be felt the next day. Cook soon disagreed over the terms of trade: Were the goods to be bought for money, as he wished, or must they be bartered for precious ship commodities?

I, too, am curious about the island's market. We run the pinnace onto the beach and wade ashore. The ro-ro ferry from Kupang is being unloaded, and bags of rice and cement are piled high on the jetty. Small fishing boats, crammed with people and goods, are unmooring. Along the jetty, clusters of people, all staring at us, are sitting on their haunches with their wares laid out in front of them. I try to exchange some of my batteries for what I presume is betel nut. The batteries had been intended as "domestic" trade goods but none of the *Endeavours* is interested in batteries and, anyway, they have nothing to offer in return. So I fish out a few batteries and gesture for a bit of betel. Soon there is a group of people around me, proffering this and that. Thrust into my hand is a great wad of betel and some long green pods. A small, youngish woman, with a mouth reddened by the nut and teeth eroded almost to the gum, steps forward to explain. By signs she shows me how to combine the *pinang* or dried betel (*Areca catechu*) with *ceris,* the long green pod, which is snapped in half and dipped in a white powder. I'm a bit leery of the powder, which someone produces in a plastic bag, but I shove the concoction into my mouth anyway. It tastes vile – bitter and sloppy – and, to my disappointment, I don't notice much of anything. Later I start to feel lethargic and find myself gaping, open-mouthed at a wall, in a state of forgetfulness. Maybe it's fatigue or heat stroke and not the betel, but I don't much like the feeling and spit out the last of the betel juice. I'm offered a sort of chaser in the form of tobacco, which I'm encouraged to chew although it scorches the throat. I suppose the tobacco might energize one after the soporific effects of the betel and lime but I'm done with these experiments and set off for the market in the main street.

Open-fronted shops offer cheap clothing, packaged foodstuffs, and household wares, and people squat with their produce by the roadside. I'm eager to know whether the market offers some of the same kinds of things that Cook and Banks were able to buy – what spices now grow in the once-famous Spice Islands? Although there's an atmosphere of market-day excitement, people are offering only the smallest quantities of goods for sale – a handful of bananas and peanuts, a few chillies, a pair of tomatoes. I know there will be little produce until the rains have come, but still I'm surprised by how little the people have. Indigo, ginger, cinnamon, tobacco, *gula lempeng* or palm sugar, and a delicious sweet cake – that's about it. I also buy a stick from the *Cinchona* tree that's sold as an antimalarial. It works, the woman tells me, but not very well.

A dilapidated truck stops in the market and I'm hauled aboard by some of the *Endeavours*. Twenty minutes later, we arrive at a cluster of houses, where women have slung bolts of hand-woven blue and brown cloth, or *ikat*, around the perimeter of a dusty clearing. A group of gong players and drummers taps out a tattoo; people hang around, the odd fowl and goat skitter off into the palm stands. The camera crew wanders off to reenact one of Banks's collecting excursions and I'm introduced to a teacher called Ovidius and his pupils, who press around in communicative silence. Our interaction is cut short by the start of some dancing – first a wedding dance, performed by men and women dressed in black and russet-coloured *ikat* and sporting headdresses made of frilly rattan. Then there's a rice-winnowing dance and, finally, a dance in which we all participate, the *pedoa*. The dancers have small palm receptacles filled with pebbles attached to their feet, which they stomp and shuffle in the dusty ground as the leader calls out in a nasal, high-pitched tone.

After the dancing, I head back to the beach, riding pillion on Ovidius' motorbike. We whip through the dry rice paddies and groves of fan palms, skirt goats, donkeys, and chickens, and are halted on the road by a herd of buffalo, which regard us with dopey suspicion. Ovidius shoos them aside and we careen towards town. Across the paddies lies his house. He invites me to visit but the ship is waiting and, already in the distance, the pinnace is being rowed out to collect us. Ovidius waves, "I will remember you forever." "And I you." On this island, we have found less than Cook found – less vegetation, less productive land, less water – but needier people. We have also found more of the very thing we need most – the generosity of strangers at a time when the world is divided against itself.

The voyage is at an end and I'm finding the transition from the wooden world to the real world difficult. Like a hypothermic person, I feel I ought not be warmed too quickly. On shore, I'm as weak-legged and sensitive as an infant. Rather than being overjoyed by the reintroduction to flowers, butterflies, and the scent of frangipani, I want shielding from excess sensations. My hotel room is fitted out in colonial retro style and for a few minutes I'm awed by the possibilities. Then I make tea and shower and realize that, although the *Endeavours* have talked relentlessly about food, hygiene, and bodily functions, I've neither washed properly, been alone, nor looked in a mirror in almost two months. Ship-life imposes a regime of physical as well as emotional self-alienation, and when private and public selves are forced into conflict, it is the inner life that shuts down. I set off with Jonathan in search of a hairdresser and so begins the process of reentering the world. It is, in a sense, our first autonomous act, an act of reclaiming ourselves from the Benthamite ship.

For me, our historical reenactment became frivolous, even unethical after what happened in New York. But in other ways, too, the wooden world strikes me as wrong – wrong in its rejection of the wider world, wrong in asserting its superiority over society at large, and wrong in its neglect of civility. It is a world of force and brutality, one that derides care, intimacy, and gentility. Our director, in contrast, sees the sailors' life as one of rough but jolly fraternity. He's convinced that our voyage from Cairns to Bali was closely allied with the historical one. The historians disagree and discuss how the voyage might best be characterized at home. This is a trope familiar to all travellers. Still, I find it necessary to figure out for myself the distinction between voyage and representation, experience and reflection. Jonathan says he'll call the voyage "marvellous"; I call it "sublime", a volatile mixture of fear and pleasure. I also come to question the old chestnut about history, thinking that it is, in fact, those who repeat history who are doomed not to understand it. And so our journey delivers us home: We find that experience has not brought us closer to the past. From now on, when we want to "feel like" Cortés or Cook, we'll have to settle for translation and metaphor. History's "pure serene" remains what Keats always said it was – the product of skilled reflection.

References

Agnew, Vanessa. 1998. "Red Feathers, White Paper, Blueprint: Exchange and Informal Empire in Georg Forster's 'Voyage Round the World'." PhD Thesis. Cardiff: University of Wales.

Agnew, Vanessa 2002. "What Can Re-enactment Tell Us about the Past?" http://www.bbc.co.uk/history/programmes/programme _archive/theship_history_reenactment_01.shtml (accessed 2 Apr 2010).

Agnew, Vanessa. 2004a. "Exchange Strategies in Cook's Second Voyage." *Cross-Cultural Encounters and Constructions of Knowledge in the 18th and 19th Centuries: Non-European and European Travel Exploration in Comparative Perspective. Interkulturelle Begegnungen und Wissenskonstruktionen im 18. und 19. Jahrhundert. Außereuropäische und europäische Forschungsreisen im Vergleich.* Eds. Philippe Despoix/Justus Fetscher/Michael Lackner. Kassel: Kassel University Press. 163-196.

Agnew, Vanessa. 2004b. "Introduction: What Is Reenactment?" *Criticism* 46.3: 327-339.

Beaglehole, John C., ed. 1955. *The Journals of Captain James Cook on His Voyages of Discovery: The Voyage of the Endeavour 1768–1771*. Vol. 1. Cambridge: Published for the Hakluyt Society at the University Press.

Beaglehole, John C., ed. 1962. *The Endeavour Journal of Joseph Banks 1768–1771*. Vols. 1 and 2. Sydney: The Trustees of the Public Library of New South Wales in Association with Angus and Robertson.

Cook, Alexander. 2004a. "Sailing on 'The Ship': Re-enactment and the Quest for Popular History." *History Workshop Journal* 57: 247-255.

Cook, Alexander. 2004b. "The Use and Abuse of Historical Reenactment: Thoughts on Recent Trends in Public History." *Criticism* 46.3: 487-496.

Lamb, Jonathan. 2001. *Preserving the Self in the South Seas, 1680-1840*. Chicago: Chicago University Press.

Lamb, Jonathan. 2008. "Historical Re-enactment, Extremity, and Passion." *The Eighteenth Century* 49.3: 239-250.

McCalman, Iain. 2004. "The Little Ship of Horrors: Reenacting Extreme History." *Criticism* 46.3: 477-486.

Nugent, Maria. 2009. *Captain Cook Was Here*. Cambridge: Cambridge University Press.

Schwartz, Anja. 2007. "'Not This Year!' Reenacting Contested Pasts Aboard 'The Ship'." *Rethinking History* 11.3: 427-446.

The Ship (GB 2002, Chris Terrill).

Terrill, Chris. 2001. "Why I did it." http://ww.bbc.co.uk/history/programmes/theship/about_01.shtml (accessed 19 Oct 2009).

"Little Families":
The Social Fabric of Civil War Reenacting

GORDON L. JONES

The Quest

At its core, reenacting – whether Civil War or any other time period – is about making a past visible. It is about seeing something that isn't there: a vacant wind-swept field now filled with armies and pageantry, blood and smoke. It is about the human desire to transform imagined images of the intangible past into a tangible present, not unlike the way a painter paints or a sculptor sculpts. But reenacting is more ambitious: its aim is not merely a visual transformation of space, but a physical transformation of a landscape by incorporating the past directly onto the human body, which then creates a three-dimensional and constantly changing performance. A little feather here, a home-made quilt there, some yellow or red trim, and your completely authentic Civil War soldier appears in the flesh. What's better, he is joined by hundreds or thousands of others, all moving about as part of a grand spectacle, the likes and feel of which cannot be duplicated by toy soldiers, colorful maps, or movies. Reenacting begins with the sense of sight, but eventually stimulates all the senses, attempting to create a feeling of real experience for participant and spectator alike. By so doing, it asks: What did it look like? How did it feel?

The supreme mission for reenactors is answering those very questions, the end result of which, if done properly, is both a cathartic rush for themselves and a commemorative punch for spectators. For participants, reenacting is all about achieving a 'rush'. A rush can come during a 'battle', it can happen around a campfire, and it is especially likely to occur on a cold night camping in the mud with your fellow sufferers: the sublime moment of 'being there', or 'time-tripping', a transcendent burst of intense emotional connectedness when the Civil War seems not just real, but tangible. Sharing that moment is also the source of endless discussion and bonding among reenactors, nearly all of whom have their own pet theory on why they feel the way they do, and why they share this strange, emotional, and seemingly inexplicable fascination with the Civil War.

The path to achieving the ever-elusive rush is never as simple or straightforward as reenactors would wish. For one thing, since the 1961 ban on reenactments on battlefields owned by the National Park Service, reenactors in the United States usually have to look beyond original battle sites for their battles; so today, less than one-fifth of all Civil War reenactments take place on such 'sacred' ground. Fortunately for reenactors, however, almost any rural landscape can be made into a temporary commemorative space – where there are no original battlefields, a battlefield can be imagined. Unlike Colonial Williamsburg and other 'permanent' living history sites, sacred ground in reenacting is as portable as the individuals who embody it: transported in cars, created in a field, and abandoned when the weekend is over, not unlike an old-fashioned Baptist tent revival. Far more difficult to construct – and control – is the human element. The reenactors' quest for an emotional time-trip is never a solitary journey; they must rely on their comrades not only to people their temporary fantasy landscape, but to play in it with them. Ay, there's the rub: Who gets to play? What should they look like? How should they behave? And, perhaps most significant: Who decides?

Social Building Blocks

To understand how Civil War reenactors populate their faux historical landscapes, an understanding of the inner workings of the small local organizations, better known as 'units' is required. Usually comprised of somewhere between ten and thirty regular participants, units are the basic social building blocks of the Civil War reenacting hobby. They are roughly analogous to the basic social building blocks of real Civil War armies: the 'mess', comprised of five to ten soldiers who shared a campfire and cooked their meals together. Civil War historian Bell Wiley coined the term "little families" to describe the bonds of camaraderie among Union and Confederate mess mates. He might just as well have been describing today's reenacting units.

Almost without exception, reenactors participate as part of a unit. Of the 350 reenactors I surveyed in three countries, only one claimed no unit allegiance at all. Reenacting's 'little families' are tight-knit semi-fraternal organizations with members closely bound to one another by common socio-economic backgrounds, intense fascination with military history, and shared experiences. Their camps become a place of refuge into which middle-aged white men [who constitute 90 % of all reenactors] can retreat for a weekend, there to blow off steam with others like themselves. Sometimes, 'little families' are just that: fathers, sons, parents, children, brothers, and sisters often participate together, forming either the whole or the core of a particular unit. Sometimes single individuals within a unit take on an informal internal role as a father figure, or a family matriarch. Here is the experienced old-timer, the person who has done the most research, or has the most charismatic personality, and the one that the younger or less experienced members trust for leadership and advice.

Indeed, it is here within the 'little family' that individual reenactors find the practical support needed to begin participation; it is also here that most decisions about their scope of participation are contemplated, debated, and decided. It is the 'little families' who shape individual and collective notions of historical 'fact', authenticity of performance, and intensity of emotional engagement. Although reenactors frequently remark that they entered the hobby for fun, education, or for the experience of an emotional 'rush' connecting them to the Civil War, it is this sense of camaraderie and family that keeps them coming back for more. It is the most powerful glue in the reenacting hobby.

Civil War reenacting is largely the domain of white men, most of whom are celebrating their imminent arrival at portly middle-age with a fresh growth of whiskers. For better or for worse, the Tubby Bearded Guys (or T.B.G.s as they are called in the hobby), make up the vast majority of 'soldiers' in the reenacting hobby. According to my survey data, the average Civil War reenactor is a white man, about thirty-eight years old, living a comfortable middle-class existence as a skilled tradesman or white-collar professional. He is married, and although his wife does not participate with him, other male relatives do. He attended some college but never quite made it to graduation; instead he fills his library with Civil War books in an attempt to educate himself. He tends toward middle-right political conservatism, usually voting Republican, though his conservatism is tempered by a secular outlook on life. Our average T.B.G. is in many ways the direct descendant of T.J. Jackson Lears's antimodern malcontents yearning for something more than (sub) urban material abundance. His is the quest to find a better past, with better men (Lears 1981).

In honor of that supposed better past, most Civil War reenactment units name themselves after an actual Civil War company or regiment, such as Company B of the Second South Carolina Volunteer Infantry (originally thirty to one hundred soldiers). Others, seeking a more realistic scale (five to ten men), portray an actual mess, to which is assigned a real or imagined 1860s nickname such as 'The Lazy Jacks Mess'. Members of this unit then shape their dress, equipage, arms, and other aspects of their impressions to match or resemble that which they understand to have been used by the original unit at some point(s) in the war.

Deciding which original regiment, company, or mess to portray is often a matter of geography (a regiment formed in the same area as the reenactors live), fame (a regiment that played some conspicuous part in one or more battles), ancestry (reenactors descended from members of that regiment), or mere personal preference based on any or all of the above. While there are no rules for this sort of thing, the majority of reenactment units choose to portray a regiment from their home state, a decision often prompted by members' theoretical allegiance to their state and its cause during the war. Thus, as might be expected, the former Confederate states tend to yield more Confederate reenacting units and vice versa in former Union states. Reenacting units in places without a direct local tie to the war often pick the more famous regiments. Thus, there are plenty of 26th North Carolinas and 20th Maines in all parts of the country (both played conspicuous roles at Gettysburg, the latter made famous by the 1974 novel *The Killer Angels*).

Reenacting's 'little families' adopt historical designations not unlike motorcycle gangs adopt 'colors': unit members try to distinguish themselves as a group, starting with visual symbols of solidarity. Most units, no matter how small, adopt a flag of some sort. It might be a great sweeping green flag with a yellow harp on it for members of the Irish Brigade, or it could be a small homemade Confederate battle flag with your unit's name painted into the center. Distinctive uniforms are the most common means of showing your colors. Confederate units might adopt a particular style jacket in a distinctive shade of gray. Union units, though admittedly more limited in their uniform choices, might elect to go with jackets or frock coats instead of the usual fatigue blouse. Hats are another vehicle for promoting unit identity. The 42nd Pennsylvania 'Bucktails' are the fellows with the fur tails pinned to their forage caps; members of an Iron Brigade regiment have the distinctive black Hardee hats with all the plumed trimmings. Often, attaching bright brass numbers and letters to caps signifying regiment or company identification is sufficient, all of this in spite of the fact that these visual methods of self-identification are invariably exaggerated far beyond historical precedent.

Similar to its Civil War predecessors, a reenacting unit's campfire is its communal altar. It is here that members of the 'little family' gather to chat, cook their food and generally hang out. At night the campfire becomes both a sacred space as the focus of bonding, and a profane space as the focus of drinking, singing, and storytelling. The nighttime campfire is the seat of unit camaraderie, where you see your friends at their best (partying) and worst (waking up the next morning). Here is where you learn about your friends, your hobby, and your past. Here is where information is shared, opinions expressed, and prejudices aired.

"The main thing I like about reenacting is the atmosphere", says Tom. "I can get away from it all. There's no phones, beepers, faxes, nothing. There's anonymity to it. Nobody really cares what you do in your private life... You come here and be a soldier, you don't have to be a husband or father" ("Tom" 1999: CH-1A: 20, 53).

For its participants, much of the appeal of the hobby lies in a sort of nostalgic return to their youth, an idyllic time before the ensnaring responsibilities of adulthood. That immersion, though seldom achieved physically, is often achieved mentally by common consent among the members of a unit. Around the campfire you seldom talk at any length about your work or your life beyond reenacting because nobody wants to hear about it. Instead you have to talk about something else – usually sports, movies, books, history (especially ancestry) or reenacting (especially internal politics). As a result, reenactors tend to define each other less by their occupations or other worldly status, and more by their weekend performances. If you are considered a good reenactor with a decent impression and convivial manner, it matters little what you do the rest of the week.

Just as normal class differences are relaxed around the campfire, so are social boundaries and the daytime requirements for authenticity. What would normally be unacceptable in front of a public audience – loud farts and deep belches for example – are not only accepted, but even encouraged, not unlike children at recess. Participants who normally do not or cannot sing – do so around a campfire. Raucous songs that cannot be sung anywhere else – like Barnacle Bill the Sailor – are sung around the campfire. It is the same for dirty jokes and stories. The campfire essentially works like an escape valve for conservative white men, allowing them a private space where politically-correct social no-nos simply do not exist.

Normally buried emotions may also bubble up at night around a campfire. Here, ordinarily reserved men may reach out to their comrades, give them a hug, and make teary-eyed toasts to their unit, their ancestors, and the causes for which they fought. Singing songs or listening to music (usually, but not always from the Civil War period) goes hand-in-hand with campfire culture, producing its own sort of period rush for participants. "[...] in the evening, the camp was ours alone", writes Steven Gallacci, an Air Force veteran experiencing his first event, "And we enjoyed the soldierly camaraderie that I hadn't realized I'd missed so much from my time in service. I was lullabied to sleep with the sounds of a fiddler playing tunes more than a century old. I departed Leavenworth [Washington] profoundly moved by my experience... I felt changed by it all" (Gallacci 1998: 8).

Part of the appeal of Civil War reenacting is its collective insistence on 'real' experience – such as the duty of suffering through rain, cold, heat, and dust. Unlike real Civil War soldiers, Civil War reenactors always have the option to simply pack up and go home when the weather gets miserable. But it is the familial bonds developed around the unit campfire that encourage (and coerce) individuals to stick it out and actually go through with such intentional suffering. Reinforcing these familial bonds is the sense of inclusion and importance afforded each individual unit member. To not attend a particular event is to risk missing some (mis)adventure that everyone else will be talking about for the next year. Once I was planning to drive to a nearby event on a Saturday morning, but changed my mind when it started to rain Friday night. Knowing my comrades would be soaked to the bone, I immediately jumped into my car and drove to the event that night so I would be soaked to the bone, too. Otherwise, I would miss all the 'fun' and never hear the end of it. One of my shivering rain-sodden fellows lamented, "I could be at home in a warm bed with a warm woman instead of out here freezing. I'm dangerous. I ought to be locked up" ("Joel" 1994: 56). Suffering ennobles, but it also functions as a rite of passage within your 'little family'.

Family Crises

Despite the fraternal bonds of its members – or perhaps because of them – the 'little family' can also be a seething cauldron of controversies, petty jealousies, and political intrigue. Despite initial loyalty to a particular unit, most reenactors eventually go through at least two or three family crises within a unit during their time in the hobby, at which time they often switch units or form their own new units. Issues such as who should be in charge, what levels of authenticity to maintain, women participating as 'soldiers', and how to balance history and politics are powerful enough to break otherwise unbreakable bonds of friendship. At an average reenactment event in the U.S., there may be fifty or sixty units present, each with basic similarities in appearance and performance, but always with slightly different traditions and philosophies toward the hobby.

The most basic philosophical differences between units involve self-imposed levels of authenticity in the camp setting. At stake is the definition of reenacting itself: is it a hobby for fun or is it a tool for experiential learning and mystical quests? On one hand the argument for 'fun' goes something like this: "I'm not really in the army and so if I want to have an ice chest hidden in a wooden box that only I know is there then I will do that. I draw the line at what the public sees and perceives" (Yu 1995: 22:07). Here, the emphasis is on achieving enough visual authenticity to make the unit's 'authentic' camp somewhat believable. On the other hand, the argument for authenticity is as follows: "I just don't like seeing all the coolers hidden in wooden boxes, the wife and kids in a big old tent. If I'm going to spend all this time and money, I want to feel a little bit of what they might have felt. Having a home cooked meal every night – they would've had hardtack" ("Todd" 2000: OV-2A:192). In this case, the emphasis goes beyond visual authenticity to encompass a rigid internalized standard of dress and behavior meant for the intellectual and spiritual edification of the individual. These two competing visions of authenticity define virtually all units in the hobby. Those that fall into the first category are known derisively as 'campers' or 'farbs', while those that fall into the second are known derisively as 'campaigners' or 'hardcores'. Everyone else falls somewhere in between.

Fig. 1: Family camp: reenactors welcome their visitors,
Olustee, Florida

Photograph: Gordon L. Jones

In 'camper' units, also known as 'family' units, men play soldiers while their younger children and wives play civilians in the same camp area. These literal 'little families' emphasize the importance of the hobby as a means of building family unity by spending quality time together. Parents also see the occasion as a healthy way to educate their children. Family units usually focus their off-battlefield hours on cooking (by the women), playing games (for the children), telling stories (sometimes from the Bible), and singing (often with instruments). Their spacious camps, while adhering to the spirit of authenticity by using only period items, are filled with chairs, tables, cots, lanterns, fire irons, cook pots and other period ephemera, much of which is considered necessary for the comfort of children. Their coolers, not always carefully hidden inside their tents, are usually filled with soft drinks, eggs, milk, and sandwich meats. This is the sort of camp wherein a total stranger will be invited by a smiling well-dressed lady to sit down and partake of a plate of beef stew and cornbread, with a piece of coconut cake for dessert.

In a campaigner unit, only males are allowed; civilians, even wives and children, are relegated to a separate camp some distance away (that is, if they even attend at all). These units emphasize the campfire as a place to get away from their real families for a weekend for some good old-fashioned male bonding amid a common quest for the transcendent period rush. Campaigners focus their off-battlefield hours on cooking period rations, telling war stories and dirty jokes, and taking long naps, sometimes after sipping a little whiskey. Their tiny disorganized camps usually consist only of blankets, lean-tos, and a campfire (sans tents, coolers or other ephemera). For campaigners, authenticity is a round-the-clock experience, with few exceptions made for nighttime parties. A stranger is not likely to even find a campaigner camp, situated as it is off in the woods well away from the other participants. If by chance he stumbles upon it, the stranger will be greeted with uncomfortable stares from its lounging residents until such time as he takes the hint to leave.

Fig. 2: Male bonding: messmates share their rations after "battle", Babenhausen, Germany

Photograph: Gordon L. Jones

The 'little families' on the extreme ends of the authenticity spectrum invariably define themselves in opposition to each other. Camper units condemn the campaigners for being too extreme and too exclusive; campaigners condemn campers for being inauthentic or farbs. Meanwhile, the vast majority of units define themselves as occupying the righteous middle ground in opposition to all others.

These 'mainstream' units are visually distinguished by the placement of their white canvas tents in orderly rows along army-regulation 'company streets'. Each street is an open grassy space about eight or ten feet wide enclosed by two rows of tents facing each other. This open space, surmounted by the campfire at one end, becomes the temporary home and nighttime gathering place for each unit, while the tents form a visible boundary line separating one unit from another, thus serving to reinforce each unit's sense of internal cohesion. Like the campaigners, mainstreamers emphasize male bonding and the quest for a rush, but like the campers, their camps are filled with tents, chairs, and other ephemera. Their coolers, generally hidden inside their tents, are usually filled with beer; otherwise, members bring more easily concealed bottles of whiskey. In a mainstream camp, authenticity rules generally cease to apply at dusk when the parties begin. In the daytime, a stranger walking into this kind of camp is likely to find no one in it. Its residents are usually attending drill or roll call, going shopping on sutlers' row (merchants selling period reproduction items), or buying their lunch at a hotdog stand. But at night, everyone is welcome to sit around the fire, hoist a brew, and sing Civil War songs (without coconut cake).

Typically, most individuals start out in the reenacting hobby as part of a family or a mainstream unit. As 'newbies', their philosophical views on authenticity are defined by their 'little family': uniforms and gear deemed 'period correct' by the group (especially by its father figure) are so deemed by its individuals, regardless of any historical evidence to the contrary. Over the next couple of years, those views are further internalized through the bonds of campfire camaraderie, such that they become practically sacred and inviolable. Yet there are a few individuals (often young and usually single) for whom the camaraderie never quite sticks. Favorably impressed by the uniforms, gear, and camping habits of the hardcore units, the initial bonds with their family or mainstream unit may weaken and crumble. Individuals or groups of individuals begin to feel that their unit's seemingly lax attitudes on authenticity are preventing them from pursuing a deeper and more meaningful emotional experience. Meanwhile, other members of the 'little family' consider such talk a sign of disloyalty, or even a personal insult. And so the factions form. Eventually, the disaffected break ties with their parent family and either join another or form their own, usually with stress, frustration, and hurt feelings all around. Individual evolution in authenticity is usually a one-way process: campers may become hardcores, but hardcores seldom become campers.

Fig. 3: Hardcore camp: a lone sentry guards the blankets in an almost-invisible camp, Elmira, New York

Photograph: Gordon L. Jones

The participation of women – either on or off the battlefield – is an especially emotional issue for mainstream units. Dominated as they are by Tubby Bearded Guys engaged in pseudo-military style bonding, most such units do not exactly encourage women to participate. "If you know a woman is present", chuckled a California man, "it makes it kind of tough to act like you would around just a pure male group... it's always nice not to have to worry about being politically correct and things around a campfire" (Yu 1995: 36:26). Of course most women – especially single women – are not exactly attracted to all-male shenanigans. Needless to say, no campaigner unit would even consider having a woman as a member – if she could find one willing to talk to her. But there are exceptions among the mainstreamers. Like the presence of African American men, the presence of women in a unit camp is often seen as evidence of the generously inclusive nature of the hobby. In such instances, however, women are usually portraying cooks, washer-women, or refugees – the very women (aside from prostitutes) commonly encountered in Civil War camps of the 1860s. Usually these are spouses or girlfriends of the members, who, because of their willingness to 'rough it' with the men, are the ones most likely to find acceptance within the 'little family'. Though many single men still resent any female presence as historically inaccurate, as long as women know 'their place' in the 19th century, their acceptance by the majority of male reenactors is generally assured.

It is only when women assert 'their place' as 20th century social equals and attempt to enter the male ranks dressed as soldiers that most men – and many women as well – draw the line on grounds of historical authenticity. Speaking on behalf of his comrades, a California geologist stated simply, "There is no way a woman could get in the regular army at that time" (Yu 1995: 31:56). Although there were documented cases of women who served as Civil War soldiers disguised as men, such cases were extremely rare (Blanton/Cook 2002).

Fig. 4: Women in the ranks: a married couple at their dinner table, Taminick, Australia

Photograph: Gordon L. Jones

Nevertheless, women who dress as Civil War soldiers at reenactments are increasingly common, especially among family units whose female members are looking for something more to do in the hobby than cook, take care of children, and watch the battle from the spectator line. What makes this issue so controversial for many participants is that the hobby cannot serve as a refuge for traditional white male values or an outlet for male bonding if it is to be infiltrated by the multi-cultural and female present. The supreme irony of this controversy lies in reenacting's outward claim of providing healthy fantasy escape for anyone of any race or gender who cares to participate. According to this logic, a three-hundred pound maintenance worker from New York can be transformed by a costume into a gaunt, ragged rebel; a California school teacher can suddenly take on the persona of an Irish immigrant; and anyone who owns a horse and has a feathered hat can be J.E.B. Stuart. So why, some women say, can they not assume similar roles?

Aside from authenticity in camp settings, the other great point of controversy in the Civil War reenacting hobby is the matter of political activism. Here, too, the very definition of the hobby is at stake: is this a private venue for fun, camaraderie, and time-tripping, or is this a public venue for promoting historical-political views? The vast majority of reenactors like to think of their hobby as a community of like-minded history-conscious people, an extension of their 'little families', with all reenactors bound by similar conservative values and mutual respect for the soldiers of 1861-1865, no matter for which side they fought. This notion of national or family community is the ideological descendant of the reconciliationist tradition that has overwhelmingly dominated Civil War memory in the United States (Blight 2001).

For those units in this political mainstream, uniform colors are as transient as an actor's costume; blue or gray is merely a temporary external identity quite apart from personal preferences for one side or the other. Most reenactors (especially the more experienced) regularly change their uniforms and participate as soldiers of the other side, a practice known as 'galvanizing'. "Actors that go on TV or movies, they do whatever the role calls for", remarked an Ohio 'Confederate'. "If you're a reenactor, you're basically the same thing. If you take it any further than that... in my opinion, that's too far. You're over the line, or it's more than reenacting to you" ("Jim" 2000: OV-4A: 25). As a result, many units actually sport two impressions: the primary one, for which the unit is named (the 20th South Carolina Infantry for example) and a secondary one, which is generally a 'galvanized' impression (the 13th United States Infantry). The new member is first expected to acquire the uniform and gear for his primary impression, and then, as time and money allow, to build his 'galvanized' impression.

But for activist units – neo-Confederates primarily, but also neo-Yankees and Afro-Yankees – reenacting is but one of many occasions to literally embody their regional and racial identities by using their blue or gray uniforms as political bumper stickers. Hence they cannot and will not galvanize; indeed, to wear the color of the other side would seem an insult to their ancestors. A Southern-born California reenactor claimed, "I would rather die before I'd put on a Yankee uniform. Now that's a strong statement, but I feel that strongly about the Southern cause..." (Yu 1995: 15:33). White neo-Yankees refuse to wear gray out of similar respect for their birthplace, their ancestors, and what their ancestors fought for. Bill, a middle-aged Miami man explains: "I remember my dad telling me a few years ago when I was a little kid, why we don't dress like the rebels. He said son, your great, great grandfather would turn over in his grave if we put that uniform on" ("Bill" 2001: OL-1A: 255).

Afro-Yankees are by far the smallest minority in reenacting, with numbers nationally probably not exceeding 250. Unlike white reenactors who divide themselves between political mainstream and activist factions, black reenactors by virtue of their small numbers and their (at least in this context) conspicuous skin color are almost always activists. As counter-weights to reenacting's strong neo-Confederate presence, they invariably use the hobby as an opportunity to embody and advertise the emancipationist memory-stream to all who care to listen. "It's an important mission of ours to remember the African-Americans who served in the Civil War", explains a sergeant of the all-black 54th Massachusetts, "Our mission [is] to spread the word and relive and honor their sacrifices" ("Joe" 2001: OL-2A:003).

Fig. 5: Mainstream camp, activist unit: African American reenactors relax along their company street, Olustee, Florida

Photograph: Gordon L. Jones

As with white activist units, black units see their hobby primarily as an educational outlet. "I do this mainly for one reason: to educate", remarked an African American reenactor at Olustee, "history class in high school did not mention a black man in uniform in the Civil War. I'm out here to inform all the public, black and white, because before I started this hobby I was ignorant as to our involvement" ("Stan" 2001: OL-2A: 133, 140). As gray uniforms are for neo-Confederates, so are blue uniforms for Afro-Yankees: symbolic advertisements for a larger message of heritage and race pride.

The challenge for activist units is that nearly all of the behavioral norms in Civil War reenacting cater to the political mainstream, hence discouraging partisan or extremist expressions. Battle performances are planned so that, if at all possible, each side gets to 'win' at least once during the weekend. For example, at the 'Raid on Lexington' event near Columbia, South Carolina, in March 2001, only Sunday's battle was actually supposed to be the 1865 'raid' in which Sherman's Union army overwhelms Confederate defenders. The previous day was the 1864 Battle of New Market, Virginia, a Confederate victory. Campsites at reenactment events are also arranged with impartiality in mind. In order to suggest historically-accurate settings, event organizers require that Union and Confederate troops pitch their tents in often widely-separated parts of the site. In reality, each campsite is carefully chosen so as to be equidistant from common parking, concession, and 'battlefield' areas; to do otherwise risks an accusation of sectional favoritism, a charge especially sensitive in such a self-consciously reconciliationist atmosphere.

Mainstream units struggle to differentiate their public image from that of activist units. The problem is that many reenactors (even mainstreamers) use the same clothing, flags, and pseudo-military organizational structure for both reenactments and other commemorative events, hence giving the public the same visual cues for each. Lee, an outspoken advocate of keeping Confederate symbols in public places and at the same time a self-professed 'hardcore' authentic, told me, "I cringe whenever I see somebody wearing a [reenactment] uniform at a flag rally. I tell everybody 'Don't wear your uniform! It makes us look bad'" (Lee ____ 2001). When the annual Confederate Hero Day commemorations on the grounds of the Texas capitol building became a "forum for battle flag and southern heritage spokesmen to advance their political agendas", Phil McBride and his Confederate unit refused to participate. "I will continue to reenact Civil War battles as a Confederate soldier", the Texas school administrator concluded, "and political correctness be damned... I'm real glad that I was born into the US of A where racial equality is actively promoted, and where on weekends I can freely play the role of a nineteenth-century armed secessionist" (McBride 2002: 64). And yet for many observers, there still appears to be something paradoxical about this attitude. Can you really favor racial equality while wearing a Confederate uniform? Which says more: the words you speak or the symbols you wear?

For precisely this reason, the political mainstream's claim on reconciliationist history is inevitably controversial. Many black reenactors will take offense that there is neither an explicit condemnation of slavery nor a direct linkage to current-day racial injustices; many white reenactors will likewise smell a politically-correct rat when either slavery is cited as the chief cause of the war or (especially) if the South is blamed for slavery. Both groups may take offense when the bitterness and divisiveness of the Civil War is deemphasized in favor of overly reconciliationist or patriotic rhetoric. And, at the same time, those who take that rhetoric seriously will no doubt be offended that anyone else takes exception to their claim. As a result, conservative white and more liberal black reenactors, whose views on the Civil War stand at opposite ends of the political spectrum, both represent themselves as persecuted minorities.

The Lava Lamp Effect

Unit allegiances, like family loyalties, can and often do shift the longer you stay in the hobby. I estimate the average existence for any unit at about five years, though some have existed in some form upwards of twenty years (not without generating their share of splinter groups). In the end, the reenacting hobby is like a giant lava lamp: units form, exist for a few years, then split into factions that then either re-form into larger units or themselves collapse.

Long-time veterans of Civil War reenacting insist that unit strife was never as bad in the old days. They recall the supposedly halcyon years of the 1970s and early 1980s when the hobby was still small, when everyone knew each other and it felt like a real family. The trouble, they say, started when their family grew so large that its members stopped knowing or caring about each other. Then, when the old leaders stepped down, their 'underlings' began grabbing for power. "You've got two people who want to be big dogs", lamented one, "When that happens, that's when the politics comes into play" ("George" 2001: LX-2A: 366).

Of course, there was never a time when the 'little families' were immune from the personalities and philosophies that create family crises. The same sorts of disputes within units and their umbrella organizations have been repeated time and again with hundreds of variations. Many disputes involve women, uniform regulations, or galvanizing too often. Some involve drinking, Christian values, or a seemingly over-obsessive leader. Some are over something as simple as pets in camp or as dire as an extramarital affair. Nearly all disputes involve questions of authority, authenticity, politics, and personal autonomy in a larger struggle to define modern social boundaries in a hobby that draws its inspiration from the outmoded but still honored values of the Victorian past. Reenacting's 'little families', like the actual regiments and the states they supposedly portray, define themselves through conflict. But at the end of the day, reenactors have too much emotion invested in their hobby to simply walk away. Most would rather leave their unit than leave the hobby; units are but temporary arrangements in a larger social and political containment zone: a giant lava-lamp.

References

Blanton, DeAnne/Lauren M. Cook. 2002. *They Fought Like Demons: Women Soldiers in the Civil War.* New York: Vintage Books.

Blight, David W. 2001. *Race and Reunion: The Civil War in American Memory.* Cambridge: Harvard University Press.

Gallacci, Steven A. 1998. *Notes from the Field: My First Year in the Great Conflict.* Seattle, WA: Thoughts and Images.

"Joel" [pseudonym]. 1994. *My Life as a Re-enactor for the Last Twenty Years, or How to Shoot Yankees for Fun and Profit.* Unpublished manuscript in author's possession.

Lears, T.J. Jackson. 1981. *No Place of Grace: Antimodernism and the Transformation of American Culture, 1880-1920.* New York: Pantheon Books.

McBride, Phil. 2002. "Uncle J.J., Levi Miller, and Me." *Camp Chase Gazette* 29.4: 62-64.

Men of Reenaction (USA 1995, Jessica Yu) .

PERSONAL INTERVIEWS

"Bill" [pseudonym]. 2001. Battle of Olustee event, Olustee, Florida. 17 Feb 2001. OL-1A: 214-295.

"George" [pseudonym]. 2001. "Raid on Lexington" event, Lexington, South Carolina. 25 Mar 2001. LX-2A: 320-411.

"Jim" [pseudonym]. 2000. Ohio Village event, Columbus, Ohio. 14 Apr 2000. OV-4A: 010-085.

"Joe" [pseudonym]. 2001. Battle of Olustee event, Olustee, Florida. 18 Feb 2001. OL-2A: 001-088.

Lee _____. 2001. Personal communication, Atlanta History Center, Atlanta, Georgia. 21 Jul 2001.

"Stan" [pseudonym]. 2001. Battle of Olustee event, Olustee, Florida. 18 Feb 2001. OL-2A: 133-176.

"Todd" [pseudonym]. 2000. Ohio Village event, Columbus, Ohio. 14 Apr 2000. OV-2A: 178-205.

"Tom" [pseudonym]. 1999. Battle of Chickamauga event, Catoosa County, Georgia. 18 Sep 1999. CH-1A: 001-060.

Ventures into History

REGINA LOFTUS/PAUL RÖLLKE/VICTORIA TAFFERNER

Ventures into History is a series of projects working with children where visualizations and interactive situations are developed through a framework of simulated historical conditions. We understand these visualizations and situations to be the carriers of historical information, and in this paper we will demonstrate the methods of transfer used in the process, as well as give an account of the children-related content which is conveyed by and through these projects. By combining the staging of events and interaction of the participants, a situation analogous to real life can be conjured up in which a previously 'other' historical world becomes comprehensible. Our experience has confirmed that even complex historical conditions can be understood and enacted by children in these situations.

At this point we would like to say something about the terminology we use to describe this project. The original German term 'Historische Spiele' (Baier/Frei 1990) translates literally into English as 'historical games'. We believe, however, that this English term is misleading when used to describe our projects. We have therefore chosen 'Ventures into History' which we believe provides a more accurate description of what we do, and we shall use this term throughout this paper.

A reconstructed historical environment provides a unique opportunity for the stimulation of cognitive processes and the comprehension of history. The tasks and challenges undertaken in the context of a Venture into History rest primarily on a number of scripted, imagined yet historically plausible scenarios which are constructed and guided by the historical knowledge of a team of variously skilled adult participants whom we refer to as 'teamers' and who perform and teach crafts, lead small groups of children, and represent civic authorities within the framework of our simulated history.

For the period of one week, up to a hundred children and approximately twenty-five teamers immerse themselves in a reconstructed 'historical' world. The surroundings are composed of an arrangement of buildings loosely resembling historical examples in which workshops, administrative centres, and clerical institutions have been installed, and to which the participants are allocated. They remain in their allotted groups for the entire week and assume active roles within the historical situations which occur, and in which they have the possibility of exercising active influence and agency.

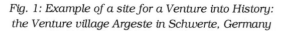

Fig. 1: Example of a site for a Venture into History:
the Venture village Argeste in Schwerte, Germany

Photograph: Regina Loftus / Paul Röllke

The basic framework of a Venture into History is a script that defines the historical time-line and the theoretical basis upon which the actions are developed. Additionally, aims and objectives for the venture at hand are formulated, defining the general direction the project should take. Set against this structural framework, the teamers are also able to create historical identities for themselves. The role of the teamers within the larger framework is extremely important. Teamers create a certain historical atmosphere through their interaction in various situations and, through the impressions they give, relate basic historical information. In this way the teamers have a great influence on the development of the venture and serve as models of historical identities for the participating children. The important positions that they assume in the community groups make them conveyors of the action and initiators of events. The interaction between the teamers themselves and their historical identities within their prescribed milieus allow for historical living conditions to emerge and unfold. In this way situations of every day medieval life can be intimately experienced. Much of the cognitive understanding which occurs at a Venture into History is fuelled by the creative and imaginative involvement of the teamers, and as such the role requires extensive historical research, preparation, and training.

The ventures are set in the context of a medieval environment, and begin as soon as the participants enter the (re-)constructed site, their temporary historical 'village' (cf. Kärgling 2009: 141). The children usually start the venture with very little previous know-ledge about the historical context, and enter as strangers into an unknown cultural environment, where they are ritually introduced to their community groups and become acquainted with the rules and customs of this 'new world'. The children are required to adapt to their surroundings through observation, following instructions and carrying out their responsibilities and tasks. Furthermore an historical name, a costume and their assumed status in the historic community enables them to develop an identity of their own as an historical person. As their historical identity develops their percep-tion of the historical situation in which they find themselves also evolves.

Fig. 2: Citizens talking politics watched
and listened to by children

Photograph: Regina Loftus / Paul Röllke

Their involvement in the venture includes participating in the meet-ings of the town council as representatives, working as craftsmen in workshops, representing their trade in the guild, working as maids or bondsmen in the households, conversing with neighbours in their sparse leisure time and attending church when the bell rings.

Fig. 3: Meeting of the town council

Photograph: Regina Loftus/Paul Röllke

In accordance with their tasks and responsibilities, the participants are not treated as children. Rather, they assume the status of young medieval adults and are correspondingly treated as such by all participants. Inherent to their status they are required to take responsibility for their actions during the venture, and are encouraged to acquire an increasing sense of independence and self confidence in the performance of their tasks.

Fig. 4: Attending mass

Photograph: Regina Loftus/Paul Röllke

Authenticity as an Historical Expression?

The past is irretrievably gone and can not be revived. However, we assume that history can be 'recaptured' and reconstructed in our ventures through the encouragement of cognitive processes that result from active involvement and increasing understanding of the framing historical context. Traditionally, a preoccupation with history requires working with written sources and material legacies. However, their mere material presence transmits none of the attached information from past circumstances, which must be identified by researchers, and placed in context. A very important foundation for this work process is the identification of a source or an object as belonging to the particular historical period in question. Being judged 'as authentic' and hence historic, such artefacts often serve as the basis of historical understanding. Statements concerning historical circumstances are constructed from the small units of information that the objects and sources are credited with. In the various forms of 'staging the past' in the public sphere, the term authenticity is frequently used in this sense as a material understanding which, when adhered to strictly, provides performative history with a particular status and entrenches a sense of meritocracy within the community.

The representation of historical conditions, using reconstructions which by virtue of their manufacture and use are defined as historically authentic, implies the closest possible approximation of historical circumstances. Notably in the case of the hard-core form of reenactments, and in some forms of museum theatre, the equipment used is considered of central importance in the presentation of historical conditions and events. In these rather elaborate formations of living history, the actors rely on the reassurance that their actions are solidly based in a scientifically researched framework enabling them to justify the contents they enact. This approach is not to be criticized as it does serve in many cases to paint a credible picture of a past material culture, and in doing so aids in the creation and understanding of an historical period and environment. It is obviously of considerable importance for the protagonists to reconstruct the material culture in minute detail, since no unworthy substitutes can be used to recreate that historical 'feeling'. It is therefore conceivable that reenactors who pursue this level of accuracy and authenticity are able to achieve a feeling of historical 'closeness' through the process of procuring or manufacturing their equipment in the most authentic way possible. However, it needs to be pointed out that the scale for the proximity to historical reality is relative and even if differences between grades of approximation are quantitatively measurable, there is no way in which proximity could possibly merge into identity – at best, what is achieved is a token form of isomorphism (Hochbruck 2005: 46; Handler/Saxton 1988: 243).

That this isomorphism can create problems, even where for all events and purposes the intention is the transmission of historical knowledge, becomes evident from an essay on iron-age Celtic living history by Jörg Bofinger and Thomas Hoppe (2006). Under the heading "Originaltreue und Esotherik",[1] they claim a controlling quality for good living history as different from esoteric beliefs about the Celts:

"Letztlich werden damit den gerade im Bereich der prähistorischen Kulturen wild wuchernden esoterischen Sehnsüchten Grenzen gesetzt und ein wichtiger Beitrag zur Vermittlung archäologisch–historischen Fachwissens geleistet."[2] (Bofinger/Hoppe 2006: 87)

At the same time, in their opinion living history is simultaneously part of a history as construction and a method for the distillation and presentation of plausible, believable and logical metaphors and models of what history might have been like (Bofinger/Hoppe 2006: 83). Good living history is when

"neben dem rostigen Klumpen in der Vitrine die silbern glänzende Eisenfibel am Gewand eines lebenden Kelten, eines Interpretatoren, zu sehen ist und er genau erklären oder gar vorführen kann, wie sie gemacht ist und wer sie wann und in welchem Gebiet getragen hat, seine Frau daneben den Stoff dazu herstellt und den Besuchern das Weben nach prähistorischer Art beibringt."[3] (Bofinger/Hoppe 2006: 87)

In our opinion history is reconstructed in its entirety, and not partly, by science. The sudden appearance of a living Celt among the visitors of an event seems to contradict a statement made by the same authors only a few lines earlier, in which the limits and dangers of living history reconstructions and interpretations are pointed out:

---

1   "Fidelity to originals and the esoteric" (translation).

2   "Ultimately, the esoteric yearnings rampant especially in the field of prehistoric cultures can be curtailed, and an important contribution is made to the conveyance of archaeological and historical expertise" (translation).

3   "...next to the rusty lump in the showcase (author's note: That is how it looks in the museum!) one can see the shining iron fibula on the cloak of a living Celt, of an interpreter who is able to explain or even demonstrate exactly how it was made, and who wore it when and where, his wife beside him producing the appropriate fabric and instructing the visitors in prehistoric weaving" (translation).

"Gerade weil lebendig gemachte Vergangenheit so bildhaft prägnant wirkt, kann sehr leicht einem einseitigen, romantisierenden Geschichtsbild Vorschub geleistet werden."[4] (Bofinger/Hoppe 2006: 87)

In our opinion, if the claims made with respect to the historical credibility of 'living history' and 'reenactment' are to be maintained, it is at least equally important to research the historical, cultural mentality in question alongside the material culture.

Living History, Reenactment and the Audience

Generally speaking, museum visitors and spectators at a reenactment can be assumed to have a general interest in historical circumstances and living conditions. Out of the wealth of information offered them, whether it be three-dimensional, textual, or staged and depending on their inclination and educational background, they will be expected to process the information independently. For the most part this will be successful. However, the transformation of this acquired knowledge into historical perceptions of the past is probably a difficult task for many. From the efforts in the area of museum pedagogy to assess visitor data and in view of the proliferation of living history and reenactment events (though not, as yet, museum theatre programmes), it is rather obvious that many visitors prefer an easier and more vivid access to history. Evidently these visitors are not prepared to acquire the information laboriously but would rather enjoy presentations and staged environments to extend their historical knowledge through a form of 'experience'.

Living history thematises the past as a human expression. Through representing historical situations by means of clothing, utensils, crafts, or entertainment, actors create a picture of the past in which museum objects can be recognized in their functional context. The linguistic and active transmission of historical knowledge within the framework of living history is embedded in an atmosphere of an experienced sensuous 'pastness'.

The observer does not need prior knowledge to recognize this image as historical. The presence of 'Celts' creates for him the impression of experiencing a historical situation. This manifestation, which the performing living historians facilitate, allows the observer to experience the performance as reality, effectuating the insight: "That's what it was like!" However, neither the visual perception in association with explanations by the living historians, nor even the

---

4   "Precisely because the animated past concisely conveys a pictorial image, one can easily foster a one sided and romanticized historical impression" (translation).

offer of active involvement – usually meaning that members of the audience can handle instruments, or try to use them for a brief period themselves – release the observers from their generally consuming role. Even if they are emotionally responsive to human content in the presentation, they remain spectators, outsiders dissociated not altogether from an experience, but from the living environment.

If the mediation is quite explicitly designed to address the emotional world of human beings, one must keep in mind that the absorption of historical information in this way will stimulate a much more intensive subjective interpretation of the past in the mind of the recipient. This process, however, cannot be implemented with participants of events such as those under consideration here, because they require a particular manner of presentation using reconstructed historical situations. One can not expect an otherwise uninformed audience to think scientifically and demand of them that they critically analyse the form of presentation they receive.

Emphasis in performance is placed on the creation of a visual atmosphere and on the possibility of an emotional approach on the side of the audience. To achieve this, it is not initially necessary to employ authentic materials. Rather, as Cornelius Holtorf makes clear in his contribution to this volume, certain key information to encourage the spectator's thought processes to follow a certain direction are sufficient. Performances must and usually do assume that visitors have some rudimentary knowledge with regard to history. Confronted with a ruin or an archaic looking object, no matter what its real age, it will be inferred by the framing narrative that the object has a story to tell. The object is thus attributed with 'pastness'. The same phenomenon also occurs when historical situations are depicted. The appearance of a person clothed in unusual and assumedly historical attire, and the accompanying circumstances surrounding the appearance, elicit the impression of an encounter with an historical character. This allows a direct interaction, and the visitor becomes emotionally accessible for the historical context which brings him or her closer to the living historians who in turn imagine themselves in a historical situation.

In this context it is important to note that at this point within the context of a historical scenario, participants will begin to recognize their ability to assess the nature of formally alien objects. If they acquire confidence in this new ability, they will also gain confidence in their negotiations with the unknown. Curiosity will guide them on, and it becomes of less relevance whether the experience is based on originals, on authentically reproduced material objects or even on objects only serving the same function as the originals, since the primary aim is rather to awaken an idea of an historical situation and environment. Given the situational context a good copy can transmit the intended information just as well as an authentic original. If the quality of the copy is such that only experts will be able to tell the difference, it might as well be noted that the stimulation of emotion and thought through a well produced copy has been employed over decades if not centuries in tourism and has been exploited in the furniture and art industry as well (Semmel 2000). Extrapolations show that the number of 'original' objects annually exported from Egypt exceeds historical probability. Obviously the copy can be quite as charming and evoke equally well the feeling of antiquity and history in the buyer. The sensuous experience of pastness apparently may be as appealing or even supplant the intellectual experience of authenticity.

The concretization of pastness in living history and reenactment takes place compactly in an array of depicted images, through which vivid and descriptive information is made directly tangible in an historical context. In this way the observer is able to assimilate historical knowledge, make comparisons and utilize them as a basis for individual assessment. The audience is served with edited historical knowledge, so to speak, and by interpreting this information correctly is able to draw their own conclusions. In this manner interaction with the historical material acquires a sensual aspect resulting in an emotionally satisfied visitor, which appeals not only to the visitor's intellect but satisfies an emotional need to engage with the past. This subjective experience will undoubtedly aid in the retention of historical information. It will be clearly and vividly fixed in memory.

History in a Plastic Bucket

The plot of a Venture into History requires the appropriate environment. The site is equipped with stylized historical surroundings and requisites. It sets the scene for the storyline of the historical period and provides points of reference for all participants, enabling them to move and interact within the simulated 'historical' era. Initially the designed venue serves to provide an emotional opening for the participants and for the tasks they are to undertake in the 'other' world. For the participants, it soon becomes both mentally and emotionally clear: I have left my modern-day life behind and find myself in a historical setting. At the same time, they realize that life in the historical setting confronts them with very different demands than the ones they have known so far. Typical questions like "Was there such a thing in the Middle Ages?" make it clear that even the first steps the participant takes in a venture promptly lead to encounters with historical situations that provoke confrontations.

Original objects are not used. All equipment, requisites, costumes and tools are of modern origin. To facilitate their association with an historical era, their appearance and function have the essential character of historical examples. On the level and for the purposes of the Venture into History it is not really of particular relevance whether the costumes the children wear were sewn with a machine or by hand. Sewing itself does imbue the clothing with historical information only where and when the actual sewing process is thematised, and where additional relevance can be drawn from the manufacture of a garment as a series of manufacturing steps. Material matters where historical relationships can be inferred from its properties. "Clothes make the man" indeed, but their manufacture is seldom of interest. It is of rather more importance how they appear, and what their effect is on others. Essentially the garment's appearance indicates the affiliation to an era and the status of its wearer.

The modern hammer, like its medieval counterpart, is made of wrought iron and a wood handle. Depending on its weight and on the strike capability of the user an effect is created on a glowing piece of iron that is worked on by an anvil. Industrially produced tools with a material composition similar to the historical model yield in their usage the same information as those that are handmade. Another example: in some scenarios, plastic buckets are used out of concern for modern hygienic conditions. They have nothing to do with the middle ages – not materially, anyway. However, the plastic material undergoes a 'metamorphosis' to a medieval bucket in the light of its major function as an important piece of equipment for water transport in the community. For the water carrier it is simply a vessel to convey water from the well to the house. The historical situation is not evoked through the bucket, it comes about through the work and imagination of the participants living out the venture.

In the context of the venture, the focus is generally on function, process, and activity, rather than on materials. Accurate reconstructions are not essential: the costumes and equipment as well as the buildings are able through their usage to produce obvious and tangible information. The shape of tools and equipment which differ only slightly in appearance from their historical equivalents does not imply that one could easily imagine oneself in a historical setting. Their use in a staged historical context, however, transforms them into carriers of historical information. Within the framework of reconstructed historical relationships, it is the user who senses the historical moment. Emotionally and mentally they behave like historical persons absorbed in a historical work process. As a matter of course they make use of all available tools, without individually questioning each one. As far as they are concerned, the tools are merely the means of production necessary for their work processes – which are historical.

In our opinion and as far as we have been able to observe, in this process even the individual's transformative powers of the imagination are of secondary importance. More will depend on the planning, design, and scope of previously prepared tasks for the historical situation. The storyline and its implementation by the entire group serve as starting point for all ensuing activities. These are structured during preliminary research. At every stage of the venture it is left to the teamers to embellish the different elements of the story within their hierarchical framework of historical knowledge. The resulting manifestation is interwoven in social, political, religious and personal relationships and is a pictorial representation of derived historical information.

The teamers are equipped with broader practical and historical knowledge in general, and specifically for the storyline they act as catalysts and instigators, ensuring an adequate historical depiction. They enable the participants in momentary situations to absorb and process historical information. This learning process continues throughout the venture but goes largely unnoticed. Instead, the individual participant becomes increasingly part of the venture. Children – and teamers – report that they experience shifts and alterations in their modern-day thinking. Within the venture, they become more confident in the assessment of historical information, which in turn enables them individually to form their 'historical' thinking and actions. These are continuously synchronized with the reactions and expressions of other children and fellow teamers.

In living out an 'historical' person teamers are often individually affected by the different manifestations of the venture. They act and interact in the venture as an historical person and independently seek solutions to problems or ways and means to shape the historical world. At the same time they are constrained by social norms and regulations. In this way historical information is created and passed on. The individual interpretations are incorporated and become part of the fabric of the venture.

The blacksmith's role in the medieval community serves to underline the historical interdependence between guilds and citizens. A product such as an iron knife must adhere to particular quality standards determined by guild decrees and market laws, so that in the production of a knife the demands and constraints of the community also play an important role. The blacksmith and his apprentices can expect visits from the guild master to scrutinize the quality of the production. Should the blacksmith or his apprentices not fulfil their contracts, they may expect severe penalties and sanctions which may lead to their workshop being closed. This example illustrates how the organization of work within a community structure transmits not only historical information about production processes, but also how these processes are embedded in the community itself. Through production, purchase and the exchange of wares, a system of monetary circulation evolves, which includes wages for the apprentices, tax dues, and costs of living. The successful and above all profitable sale of their products on market day serves to give the apprentices a feeling of accomplishment.

A bustling public life characterizes a Venture into History. The participants are continuously exposed to a plethora of different social experiences and interactions. Prayers and daily visits to the church by every inhabitant serve to demonstrate the intense religious pervasion of medieval society. The meetings of the town council are held in an open-air enclosure. In this way, the reigning hierarchy of the society can be conspicuously demonstrated. It also allows the town inhabitants to follow the council's discussions and decisions which will directly affect them. Proposed tax levies and rising interest rates will of course have an effect on every citizen's purse. The consequences may be far-reaching and have detrimental effects on work and daily life. Threats endangering the community, whether external or internal, can only be resolved or overcome through mutual consent or joint action.

As already indicated above, we consider a Venture into History a designed 'othered' environment. In order to make this environment comprehensible and be able to shape it, the participants, the teamers in particular, have to prepare themselves by doing intensive research and training in getting acquainted with certain historical roles or rather the individual characters they are supposed to represent. For them it becomes necessary to be able to operate functionally and believably within a set of norms, values and rules different from their 'normal' life. In order to achieve this it is essential to have access to the reasoning and emotions of historical figures. This is only possible if the external historical circumstances are known and the contemporary mentality is investigated. The preparation of the venture for the teamers therefore places special emphasis on investigating the historical figures they are going to represent. A work template that we call "action space" is used to deal with specific aspects of the individual's life history (Röllke/Loftus 2008: 18).

Presenting an historical figure within a venture does not merely mean enacting a role. It is not a stage performance (at least not in the more limited sense) and it is not the intention to depict scenes for spectators. The character manifestations of the 'historical' persons serve on the one hand to convey information to one another and on the other hand to shape and structure the flow of the venture. In this they are somewhat similar to Bertolt Brecht's theory of the *Lehrstück* (Brecht 1967; cf. Hochbruck 1997: 104). The action in the game is purely situational and demands of the teamers a great deal of communication and emotional involvement as well as extensive knowledge. Only in this way is it possible for the teamers to comprehend the historical figures they represent, and as such to contribute actively to the venture. Costumes and staged historical situations promote this process. As a participant, I interact in an 'othered' world together with others manifesting characters of equal strangeness. The more intensely the venture can be shaped by the historical figures, the more credibly their actions, statements and expressions will affect their fellow participants. The intensity of the experience of historical life is thus greatly enhanced.

In workshops the teamers explore the effects of individual behaviour patterns on their fellow teamers, which in turn provide feedback for shaping their own individual historical characters. Experimentation is vital for the teamers' training and their role in providing structure within the historical setting.

The majority of the participants, children and young people, are introduced differently to their historical identity. They are acquainted with the venture's storyline and know that they will be entering into an othered historical world. The outward appearance of the staged venue for the venture is sufficient to evoke the feeling that they are entering an historical world. By means of ritual enrolment in community groups they are enabled to identify with their environment. The groups provide for their orientation and their need for security in this new world. The groups are entrusted with duties that are integral in the social, political and religious life of the venture's society. In this way they are able to absorb information and patterns of behaviour which serve and help them to develop their own 'historical' identity. Through observation and personal experience, participants quickly notice how their duties are associated with the manifestation of their historic personality and begin to assess which behavioural patterns are appropriate for them and which position or standing can be assumed. Constraints and social relationships within their community groups are experienced on a personal level. The strong identification with their community group and its duties and the intense emotional outbursts that occur can be cited as evidence of the seriousness with which they adapt to their role as 'historical' figures in the venture. With increasing insight into the theme of the venture and with improving craft skills their ability to assess the historical period chosen as the basis for the venture expands. This personal experience facilitates in forming a direct relationship to history and its development. All relationships within the venture are based on deduced historical contexts and are recognized and interpreted as intrinsic necessities of the venture.

Historical Information and its
Productive Use in the Venture

Generally in a venture, we pursue the idea that the storyline is acted out in an adult world, and within it the children occupy a special position. The children are treated as adults and respected accordingly. Under these circumstances the children experience changes of identity. On the one hand, they are confronted with responsibilities that ensue from their interaction as a historical figure, on the other hand they experience an increased sense of excitement in shaping life as an adult. They are obliged to carry out typical adult tasks. Within this order of interaction they are compelled to deal with and comprehend historical circumstances in order to make individual decisions and take actions. For example, acting as members of a delegation negotiating a peace treaty at the end of the Thirty Years' War in 1648, they have to grapple on the one hand with the demands of their opponents, and on the other hand formulate their own position.

Political action, however, requires that the participants have perceived and understood the historical circumstances. When French and Imperial envoys, using a map of middle Europe, dispute over the balance of power, they must be able to articulate their historical claims. It soon becomes very obvious how complex the exchange of information concerning money, land and power can be in this process. Young members of the delegation are not expected to behave as passive participants, but to use the circumstances to become actively involved, using their newly acquired historical knowledge. The task as a member of the delegation is to judge the statements made by one's opponents, to appraise them and reach a decision in the interests of one's Lord.

Within the venture, the transfer of historical information is not reduced to reading and observation. On the contrary, quite the reverse is true. The transfer is achieved by literally grasping the situation and actively intervening. The young participants are not abandoned in this situation. In the necessary discourse with the members of their own delegation the exchange of historical information generates further aspects for more possible solutions. In addition to the intellectual pre-occupation with historical information, the emotional processing of the 'historical' circumstances also plays a major role.

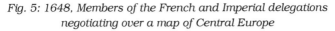

Fig. 5: 1648, Members of the French and Imperial delegations negotiating over a map of Central Europe

Photograph: Regina Loftus / Paul Röllke

Soldiers attacking the city walls, for example, armed of course with wooden weapons only and equipped with rudimentary armament, still feel the excitement and thrill of military aggression. The defenders often experience feelings of uneasiness and threat, which in some cases can lead to tears. The representation of armed conflict is felt to be real and immediate. Situations such as these are resolved within the venture without resorting to a direct contact between the parties – the children are often so intensely immersed in the action that they could physically hurt each other even with wooden weapons. Children of an anxious disposition are looked after and accompanied by the teamers during such precarious situations.

Since human aggression has shaped a large part of history, it is addressed within the ventures time and time again. Disputes are carefully and thoroughly prepared, so that each participant understands the basics of the event and is able to assess it. Important to note in this process is the insight that human intentions are equally responsible for situations of conflict and peace.

Our experience indicates that historical events shaped by intense emotional experiences remain deeply imprinted in the mind. As one child remarked: "On 19 September 1622, the Spanish occupied my hometown Svierte. I know why, I was there!"

Observations on the Social Aspects
of Ventures into History

A variety of social relationships can be observed evolving and developing between participants over the course of a venture. The life and work in well-defined groups and the historical family structures serve to provide a secure framework in an 'othered' world in which to position oneself. The previously mentioned basic structure and the interaction in an adult world ensure from the outset that the venture is meaningful for the children. If the venture achieves its pedagogical aim, the children gradually learn to see themselves as part of a community, and their work and its manifestation ensure that the community can provide for itself and sustain itself within the larger historical context. The tasks they undertake and fulfil are recognized as a necessary part of the community life. The more clearly they realize how important each person is for shaping the life in this 'historical' society, the more seriously they will perform their tasks. The moral and historical-legal involvement in working and living conditions creates a relationship of trust between them and the leaders of the teams, and the leaders of the historical community on the whole. The latter particularly demand goods and services which are rewarded and which in turn encourage and promote work and cooperation in the fulfilment of duties. To the best of their capabilities the children try to meet these requirements, provided that the insights they gain are based on understanding (rather than coercion). No participant is admonished for not meeting requirements; instead, they are given the best possible support. In this way the children develop relationships, making them increasingly self-confident. Many are able, already after a short time, to master and independently practise a craft, and are self-confident enough to build relationships and socially interact with strangers in the community. In time they become involved in political and social activities, such as guild organization and town councils in the medieval city, or they might even act as commanders of a military unit.

The interaction and success in their tasks and duties make it increasingly clear to them that they really can act and interact like adults, which enables them to reflect how their behaviour affects other players and the ongoing interaction. It is not always possible within the time available in the venture for the children to process all the information necessary to enable them to respond in an appropriately historical way in all respects. Modern ideas for the solution of problems continuously crop up. However, a teamer can often react and construe a historical solution without breaking out of the time-frame and, so to speak, returning to the present. During a discussion of the town council in the thriving town of Svierte, the question was raised as to how the town could become wealthier. A young member of the council proposed attempting to boost tourism. The mayor took up his proposal and construed a historical solution: he commented that the proposal was good, because it would certainly attract more merchants and craftsmen if the town could offer more amenities and opportunities.

As citizens and residents in the 'historical' society all participants are involved in the political, social and religious life. Shaping this life requires all participants to contribute opinions and form judgements towards solutions for problems. Such contributions are taken seriously in discussions and meetings, and integrated into the subsequent interaction. The participants recognize that they are regarded as valued and responsible members of society capable of handling complex situations and achieving satisfactory results. All this reflects on the success of the community as well as the entire venture and each participant. In addition to their special treatment during the venture the younger participants often encounter social relationships that have in many cases disappeared from their contemporary modern world. These are not superimposed, but rather manifest themselves as a necessity in the venture. The food, which is prepared entirely by the young participants over an open fire, is eaten together in the community group. Dealing with open fire is done self-consciously and mindfully, as is chopping wood or working with sharp tools. These examples demonstrate quite clearly to the young participants that the teamers trust them. In the majority of cases precise instructions and explanations for the work at hand are quite sufficient to enable them to perform the task independently and responsibly on their own.

We regard the ability to participate in a different culture, interacting in a responsible fashion, as an important prerequisite to discovering and revealing the nature of relationships in different cultures, whether they be remotely similar or very foreign. If in addition to the theoretical knowledge of historical circumstances a venture can facilitate a perceptiveness about life in other cultures we believe that cross-cultural associations and perspectives can be cultivated in this way, and that these new perceptions will be conducive for the children in the life that they later lead.

A Venture into History is a journey into an 'othered' culture, involving participation in social, political and religious interactions. The manifestations of this world are interpreted and lived within the framework of the venture, and in doing so historical circumstances can be genuinely experienced and serve later as counterpoints to the everyday modern world. We believe that transcultural perspectives are significant for the development of insights into the nature and structure of other cultures and their traditions.

References

Baier, Eberhard/Alfred Georg Frei. 1990. *Geschichte spielen. Ein Handbuch für historische Stadtspiele*. Pfaffenweiler: Centaurus.

Bofinger, Jörg/Thomas Hoppe. 2006. "Echt keltisch? Eisenzeitliche Geschichtsdarstellung. Möglichkeiten und Grenzen." *Lebendige Vergangenheit. Vom archäologischen Experiment zur Zeitreise.* Ed. Erwin Keefer. [Archäologie in Deutschland. Sonderheft 2006.] Stuttgart: Theiss. 83-87.

Brecht, Bertolt. 1967. "Zur Theorie des Lehrstücks." *Gesammelte Werke 17. Schriften zum Theater 3.* Frankfurt am Main: Suhrkamp. 1024-1055.

Gustafsson, Lotten. 1998. "The Play about the Plot. History on Stage and at Stake during the Medieval Week in Visby." *Ethnologia Europaea. Journal of European Ethnology* 28.1: 17-26.

Handler, Richard/William Saxton. 1988. "Dyssimulation: Reflexivity, Narrative, and the Quest for Authenticity in Living History." *Cultural Anthropology* 3.3: 242-260.

Hochbruck, Wolfgang. 1997. "Between 'Living History' and Pageantry. Historical Reenactments in American Culture." *Beyond the Mainstream.* Ed. Peter-Paul Schnierer. Trier: wvt. 93-105.

Hochbruck, Wolfgang. 2005. *Geschichtstheater. Dramatische Präsentationen historischer Lebenswelten.* Remseck: GTG.

Kärgling, Karl-Heinz. 2009. "Die Megedeborch. Ein Historisches Spiel im Kulturhistorischen Museum Magdeburg." *Karfunkel Codex 7 [Aufbruch in die Gotik].* 140-141.

Röllke, Paul/Regina Loftus. 2008. *"Das Mittelalter fängt montags an": Handbuch Historisches Spiel.* Schwerte: Ruhrtalmuseum Schwerte.

Semmel, Stuart. 2000. "Reading the Tangible Past. British Tourism, Collecting, and Memory after Waterloo." *Representations* 69: 9-37.

Playing Ethnology

ANJA DRESCHKE

"I've long thought that teaching and learning
anthropology should be more fun than they
often are. Perhaps we should not merely read
and comment on ethnographies, but actually
perform them." (Victor W. Turner 1982: 89)

First Contact

One of my first contacts with the Cologne Tribes *(Kölner Stämme)*
was when I visited the summer camp of the Hun Horde of Dünn-
wald *(Dünnwalder Hunnenhorde)*. On a public green on the outskirts
of a suburb of Cologne, about fifteen tents had been built in a semi-
circle around a large wooden table. At this table, seated on lavishly
ornamented thrones, the rulers of the Hun Horde were holding
court, dressed up in elaborate robes made of leather, rivets and fur,
looking quite terrifying with scars and wounds painted all over their
faces. A second group, the 1st Mongolian Horde of Cologne *(1. Kölner
Mongolenhorde)*, wearing colourful silk clothing and caps paced
gravely across the lawn, accompanied by the soundtrack of a Hollywood historical movie. When they arrived at the table, the chairman of
the visiting club, a Genghis Khan impersonator, stepped forward to
greet Attila, the leader of the hosts, with a solemn exchange of gifts.
This impressive ritual recurred throughout the day, as the Hun Horde
welcomed numerous fellow 'tribes', ranging from historically accurate representations of Romans and gladiators in chariots, Vikings,
Scots and North American Indians to 'cannibals' with fantasy costumes, grass skirts, and bones in their hair.

Despite the intimidating impression that the Huns provoked
during these welcoming ceremonies, they were very polite towards
outsiders like me who came to visit the camp. A woman, who introduced herself as Amalasuntha, Queen of the Ostrogoths, attentively
showed me around the camp, which was supposed to be the reconstruction of a habitation of Huns during the lifetime of Attila. They
had been camping for two weeks now, she told me, renouncing all
forms of modern comforts, and submerging themselves in the his-

toric environments of their role models. I was impressed by the opu-
lently furnished tents, luxuriously decorated with various kinds of
animal skulls, stuffed birds, weapons, brass goblets and oriental
carpets; although these carefully staged conglomerates of flea market antiques and home-made objects reminded me more of a curiosity cabinet, or a film setting, than of the dwelling of an Asiatic no-
mad. In response to my question concerning the choice of decora-
tions, Amalasuntha explained that, once infected with the 'Hun vi-
rus', it's like being possessed; one develops a kind of 'Hunnish gaze'
which enables one to discern what is Hun-like and what not. She
further explained: "All of the possessions are loot that was acquired
during raids. And since the Huns were nomads and conquered all,
anything can be Hunnish." When I finally asked her what fascinated
her most about this hobby she answered, to my surprise, "You can
really play ethnology here."[1]

The Tribes of Cologne

The ethnographic example I am going to discuss in this article concerns the Cologne Tribes, an association of more than 80 societies
with over 3,500 members from Cologne who imitate a great variety
of historic epochs and/or 'foreign' cultures such as Romans, Vikings, North American Indians, Africans, etc. and notably Huns and
Mongolians, as a leisure time activity.[2] The average society comprises about 30 members. Most groups consist of extended families,
friends, neighbours and co-workers, who spend their weekends reenacting the lifeworlds of their role models.[3]

This article is based mainly on the field research I conducted on
the Cologne Tribes from 2003 to 2009 accompanying selected societies, participating in their activities, attending their club meetings

---

1   In the following I will use the term 'ethnology' in the sense of *Ethnologie* as
    it is used in German for 'cultural anthropology'.
2   The data was given to me by a spokesman of the Cologne Tribes. It is diffi-
    cult to figure out how many people actually practice the hobby. Firstly, be-
    cause a division exists between 'inactive' members who just support their
    club financially and 'active' members who regularly take part in the imper-
    sonations and role playing. Secondly, the phenomenon is spreading into
    the surrounding area of Cologne. New societies are founded all over the
    region and even abroad: In 2007 the first Hun society was founded in the
    Netherlands. Not all of these societies have been included here.
3   There are small 'clans' with just three or four members and large societies
    with about 70 members.

and interviewing them at home.[4] So far there has been almost no other research or publications on the Cologne Tribes, except a coffee table book illustrating this extraordinary hobby with elaborately staged photographs (Hartmann/Schmitz 1991).[5]

The main activity of the Cologne Tribes consists of the organisation of so-called summer camps: In summer almost every society holds a camping event located in a public park within the city or in the suburbs of Cologne that can last from between one weekend to two weeks. These camps appear to be a startling fusion of theatre performance, living history museum, world exhibition, fun fair, and camping ground. During the daytime, the club members conduct guided tours around the camps to educate all kinds of visitors – either fellow hobbyists or 'civilians' (i.e. people who are not dressed up) – on the culture they are imitating. In this case, they do first person impersonations comparable to the performances known from living history museums. More theatre-like are the elaborate role playing events that stage the life at the court of an historic ruler. In addition, various kinds of rituals are performed by so-called shamans including initiations for new members and inaugurations for prospective rulers, as well as initiation rites for children and teenagers, or matrimonial rites. Thus, a wide range of rituals and ceremonies has been invented, combining local traditions with ritual practices deriving from various religious contexts, for example Catholicism and Siberian or Mongolian shamanism. To many club members, these rituals are of great personal and even spiritual importance.[6] Thus, it is surprising that within short distance from these ritualistic per-

---

4   The main focus of my research is situated in the field of visual anthropology, see also my ethnographic documentary *Die Stämme von Köln (The Tribes of Cologne)*.

5   Edited by photographers Petra Hartmann and Stefan Schmitz, this book was not only the first and sole publication on the Cologne Tribes to give a comprehensive overview of all societies in their grand diversity, but it probably also established the term "Kölner Stämme" (which is the title of the book). Its publication in 1992 was accompanied by an exhibition at the Museum of East Asian Art in Cologne and a major event organized in cooperation with a regional broadcasting station (WDR) at the *Tanzbrunnen* in Cologne, where all the societies presented themselves to the public together for the first time. This resulted in the foundation of an umbrella organisation for all societies, the so-called O-Team *(Organisationsteam)*, that henceforth organised a triennial gathering of all societies, the 'tribal camp' *(Stämmelager)*. Thus the book was and still is of particular significance to the corporate identity of the societies.

6   Spirituality and shamanism are of significant importance to the Cologne Tribes as I will explore in "Possession Play. On Trance Rituals and Impersonation Among the Cologne Tribes" (Dreschke forthcoming) and my PhD thesis on the Cologne Tribes.

formances most summer camps provide a 'commercial area' with a beer stall and a barbecue, and sometimes a DJ is hired to entertain visitors. With this fun fair atmosphere the societies hope to attract a larger number of visitors, not only to increase their prestige, but also to finance their hobby with the money they earn by selling drinks and food. In the evening, after the 'civilians' have left, the atmosphere of the event changes even more into that of a camping ground: The club members gather around a campfire to celebrate together on a more casual level. Some even swap their robes for tracksuits because 'modern' items, forbidden during the day, are now allowed. Thus, one can regard these summer camps as multi-purpose themed environments.

In the following paragraphs I will introduce my case study in the context of the local carnival tradition and power-relations of Cologne, and in the context of historical and 'ethnic' reenactments as a leisure time activity. I will then turn to the strategies of popularisation and appropriation of not only historical, but also ethnological knowledge among the Cologne Tribes.

At the beginning of my research, I was surprised how frequently members of the Cologne Tribes referred to the term 'ethnology'. As Christoph Antweiler has pointed out, the discipline of ethnology or *Völkerkunde* is not widely known to the German public and non-academics usually have only a vague idea of its contents. Instead, a fascination with the allegedly 'exotic' topics of the discipline rather than an interest in ethnological theories or methods draws the attention of non-academics (Antweiler 2005: 17-18).

Nevertheless, mass media have contributed to the popularisation of certain ethnological representations of 'foreign' cultures or cultural 'otherness' that have become obsolete, or at least have been called into question within the discipline with the so-called Writing-Culture-Debate (Clifford/Marcus 1986) since the 1980s. Critical discussions on how ethnologists constructed their 'objects' through 'othering' have changed the discipline. But in popular representations, these 'out-dated' ethnological perspectives on 'foreign' cultures still prevail and influence our perceptions of cultural 'otherness'.

Anti-Carnival

Almost every society of the Cologne Tribes originated from the carnival, which is an important if not defining feature of the local identity. The Cologne carnival, like other carnival traditions, is a dynamic cultural practice of hybridisation, constantly absorbing 'other' traditions and inventing new ones. Critique of political and social circumstances is formulated by inversion and parody. Each carnival season sees new masquerades inspired by all kinds of current events from political discussion to popular TV programmes. Thus, the Cologne carnival is constantly shaped and changed by various influences from popular culture to politics, either local or global.

In this context, however, the tradition of the Cologne Tribes can be traced back to the 19th century when the impact of globalization and colonialism caused a profound interest in 'exotic' people in general, an interest that also influenced the carnival. In 1885, for example, the motto of the famous carnival parade on Rose Monday was "Prince Carnival as Colonist" *(Held Karneval als Kolonisator)* and all participants of the procession were masked as Africans in what can be judged as a reaction to, and political comment on, the occupation of Germany's first colonies in Africa. Afterwards, an ongoing 'Africa fever' was to be noticed in Cologne, which led to the foundation of several carnival clubs (cf. Brog/von der Bank 2008). Another important impact on the ethnic masquerades in the Cologne carnival in the 19th and early 20th century were the so-called *Völkerschauen* – exhibitions of 'exotic' people in the Cologne Zoo. These displays of cultural otherness were integrated into the carnival parades (Frohn 2000: 125).

After WWII, another popular source had an important effect on the adaptation of 'exotic' costumes in the Cologne carnival: US-American historical movies. In 1958, the 1st Hun Horde of Cologne – which is the oldest and most established society of the Cologne Tribes – was founded out of fascination with Douglas Sirk's film *Sign of the Pagan* (1954) which had Jack Palance play the role of Attila the Hun. With furs, bedside carpets and rivets, the members of the 1st Hun Horde of Cologne imitated the costumes of this and other popular Hollywood films, and thereby created a kind of 'carnivalesque hun style' that still prevails. Though several other carnival societies referring to ethnic groups or historical epochs were established through the impact of historical movies, none of them became as popular as the Huns or other Asiatic nomads like Mongolians. Today almost every neighbourhood of Cologne has its own Hun or Mongolian 'tribe'.[7]

Even though most of these 'tribes' were originally founded as carnival clubs and many take part in various parades, their relation to the established carnival societies is marked by ambivalence. To understand this ambiguity one has to take into account the great social, political and economic importance of the carnival in Cologne.

---

7   Also influenced by Hollywood was the foundation of several other 'tribes' like Vikings, Romans, gladiators or pirates. And, of course, numerous Indian societies were founded inspired by the film adaptations of the books of Karl May that became very popular in Germany in the 1960s.

Most of the traditions that shape the current carnival – above all the parade on Rose Monday which still remains the highlight of each carnival season – were 'invented' in the early 19th century by the Festival Committee of the Cologne Carnival *(Festkomitee des Kölner Karnevals)*, a collective of upper class citizens. The idea was to establish a structure that would reorganize the so-called street carnival that was threatening to vanish under the French occupation. The newly invented carnival, however, became a means of expressing anti-Prussian sentiment after 1817 with the city now occupied by the Prussians. The members of the first carnival club, founded in 1823, dressed up in uniforms and marched in an affected dull and clumsy manner, thus mocking the military drill of the Prussian occupants (Euler-Schmidt/Leifeld 2007: 19-20). But what was initiated as a parody of the Prussian military has today become a kind of conservative, 'old boys' network. Some members of carnival societies are powerful players in local politics and economics, and outsiders even accuse them of being a driving force behind the *Kölsche Klüngel* (a local euphemism for nepotism and corruption).[8] The festival committee not only organises the Rose Monday parade but also claims to be the guardian of carnival traditions, and justifies the exclusion of the Cologne Tribes from the parade on grounds of them not being part of the tradition.

In return, the Hun societies of the Cologne Tribes refer to the legend of St. Ursula as a means of legitimizing themselves as part of the local tradition. The legend has it that St. Ursula and 11,000 virgins were killed by the Huns when they besieged the city of Cologne. Their martyrdom saved the city from being plundered and destroyed by the Huns.

As mentioned above, the established carnival societies are not accessible for everybody, but are restricted to the upper classes by means of high membership fees and personal networks. The members of the Cologne Tribes, however, belong to the lower-middle or lower class, hence for most of them membership in the established carnival societies is almost impossible. Their identification with the hostile Huns of the legend of St. Ursula might then be seen as a protest against the traditional carnival societies or as a kind of anti-carnival. In line with what Victor Turner (1987) has stated, carnival can be characterized as a liminal space where traditions can be inversed as well as established. The alternation of structure and anti-structure is also characteristic for the relationship between the traditional carnival societies – which are organised in the Festival Committee of the Carnival of Cologne *(Festkomitee des Kölner Kar-*

---

8   On the historical and social development of the *Kölsche Klüngel* in relation to the Cologne carnival, cf. Klauser (2007: 181ff.).

nevals) – and the Cologne Tribes. Therefore, the summer camps of the Cologne Tribes can be seen as an extension of the liminal space of the winter carnival, a space where the established carnival traditions are reversed and reinvented.

Amateur Ethnology

The Cologne Tribes can be described as embedded in the local situation and traditions of Cologne, but they are also a particular form of a more common phenomenon. The staging of other time-periods as a leisure time activity has become extremely popular over the last decades. Besides commercialized forms, such as theme parks and 'medieval' fairs, a prospering scene of hobbyists has developed, searching for access to history through corporeal performance. These hobbyists refer to their activities as reenactment or living history. Although the terms are often used synonymously, the first actually describes the often site-specific re-staging of particular past events, notably military encounters, as a public spectacle, while the latter denotes more generally the collective experience of historical life worlds, like the Middle Ages through immersion or empathy (Arns 2007: 39-40). The Cologne Tribes are distinguished from other historical reenactment communities by the fact that they not only reconstruct past time periods, but explicitly 'foreign' cultures. Whereas in most cases people re-stage historical epochs that they assume to be of their 'own' cultural heritage, within my case study it is foremost the fascination with 'other' or 'foreign' cultures or ethnic groups. This phenomenon has been characterized as "ethnic drag" (Sieg 2002) or "cultural masquerade" (Broyles Gonzalez 1989), with regard to Indian hobbyism or Indianism, that is "groups of enthusiastic amateurs who study and re-enact, on European soil, their specific version of nineteenth-century Native American life by producing replicas of artifacts and clothing and wearing these in homemade settings reminiscent of living history museums" (Kalshoven 2005: 66).[9] During her field research among European Indian hobbyists, Petra Kalshoven has observed how some of them have gained a remarkable knowledge regarding the material culture of the historical Native Americans and "consider their involvement as a dedicated form of amateur ethnology" (ibid.: 69). This notion of amateur ethnology also applies to some clubs of the Cologne Tribes. There has been a relation to ethnology since the formation of the first club in the 1950s: The 1st Hun Horde of Cologne *(1. Kölner*

---

9   Indian hobbyism is not restricted to Europe. Similar phenomenona can be found in the US (cf. e.g. Deloria 1998).

Hunnenhorde) chose the predicate 'Society for Ethnology' *(Verein für Ethnologie)* right from its foundation in 1958. Though in the beginning, their interest was mainly inspired by historical dramas from Hollywood, over the years some club members started to research the history behind the ethnic groups they imitated by studying historic and ethnographic literature in an attempt to become more 'authentic' with their costumes and performances. Today one can discern two different, if not opposed tendencies: a fancy-carnivalesque approach that can roughly be connected with the 'Huns', on the one hand, while on the other, the 'Mongolians' prefer a more 'authentic' approach based on ethnographical and historical knowledge.

When the 1st Mongolian Horde of Cologne *(1. Kölner Mongolenhorde)* was founded in the early 1980s, the appearance of the costumes did not differ much from the fanciful-carnivalesque 'Huns'.[10] This changed in the early 1990s, when some club members started travelling to Mongolia on a regular basis and brought back original Mongolian costumes and entire yurts furnished with beds, ovens, etc. Gradually, the members of the Mongolian societies established contact with Mongolian migrants living in Cologne and some 'real' Mongolians became club members.[11] So another kind of engagement with Mongolian culture was initiated which now also includes exchange with contemporary Mongolia and Mongolian people.

To gain further knowledge on Mongolian history and culture, the club members drew on various kinds of media sources such as academic literature, travelogues and tourist guides, historical dramas and TV-documentaries, public slide shows or museum exhibitions. In 2005, a museum invited the 1st Mongolian Horde of Cologne to take part in an exhibition of Mongolian history and culture. They not only gave one of their yurts as a loan to be displayed in the con-

---

10 Similar to the Hun hordes, the members of the Mongolian clubs ascribe the idea to start their hobby to the influence of popular culture. In their case, it was a song called *Dschingis Khan* (Gengis Khan), interpreted by a band with the same name, which became very popular in Germany in the late 1970s and participated in the Eurovision Song Contest for Germany in 1979. Where the Huns refer to St. Ursula, the Mongolian societies, too, have a kind of origin myth to explain and legitimise their appropriation of the Mongolian culture. They relate to the Franciscan monk Arnold von Köln, a missionary who travelled to China and Mongolia in the early 14th century. Referring to this, the Mongolian societies jestingly claim to be the descendants of the Mongolians that Arnold von Köln could possibly have brought back to Cologne.

11 Another important impact of change was the Expo 2000 in Hanover. After the Mongolian societies visited this world exhibition they began designing their summer camps according to the example of the Mongolian pavilion that was displayed there.

text of the exhibition, but also performed in their Mongolian costumes and gave information on Mongolian history and culture to the visitors.[12] In turn, this collaboration initiated another change in the way the society designed their representations: After they had been invited by the museum, the 1st Mongolian Horde of Cologne decided that their activities should become more educative. They arranged a so-called culture camp to celebrate the traditional Mongolian *Naadam* festival with wrestling and archery. For this occasion they converted a yurt into a museum of artefacts, either from Mongolia or self-made reproductions of Mongolian artefacts such as *Tsam* masks.[13]

Even though most members of the Mongolian societies have become experts on Mongolian history with regard to dates and genealogies, a rather ahistoric view on sociocultural aspects still prevails. They share the opinion that the people in the steppe of Mongolia still live as they did in the 12th or 13th century, only having been 'spoiled' in recent years either by the Soviet government or the

---

12 Ironically, on a poster advertising this exhibition it was announced that "Every Sunday from 12 to 6, Mongolians demonstrate life in a yurt, explain the traditional rules of hospitality and introduce their games and songs." It showed a picture of a couple dressed in Mongolian costumes who were obviously not from Mongolia. Actually, the couple came from Italy to Germany as migrant workers in the 1970s. Among the Cologne Tribes they are highly respected because of their expert knowledge. They study all available literature on Mongolia and have travelled there. To be able to read literature in Mongolian, they decided to study the Mongolian language at the University of Bonn, but were rejected for lack of the adequate high school degree *(Abitur)*. When I first met them, they were very sceptical about me because of this negative experience with academia – especially when it turned out that their knowledge about the Mongolian culture far exceeded mine.

13 Another example for this kind of exchange between the Cologne Tribes and museums is the collaboration between a museum in Cologne and an Indian Hobbyist. The latter's interest in North American Indians had been spurred by an exhibition in this very museum when he was a child. Among the Cologne Tribes, his approach is considered extreme, as he became a kind of dropout, dedicating his whole life to Indianism. Like most members of the Cologne Tribes, he comes from a working class background and has no high school degree that could have enabled him to go to university. Despite this lack of formal education, and although he has never visited the USA, he has gathered a vast knowledge on North American Indians by way of literature and, more importantly, by producing replicas of their material culture. For him, this has not only become a source of income, but also one of practical expert knowledge that is required in the handling of objects in the museum context. Accordingly, the museum asked for his assistance in correctly building a teepee for an exhibition, since he was the only available person who could provide these practical skills.

threats of modernisation in general. They regard it as their duty to preserve the cultural heritage of Mongolia from extinction. This mirrors an ethnological perspective that has been constitutive for the discipline, and obviously had a great influence on popular perceptions of 'foreign' cultures. I would argue that the representations and performances of the Cologne Tribes can be considered a popularization of the anthropological agenda which mirrors ideas that have in recent years become out-dated in the discipline but that had great influence on common world views in the past and still linger on today.

Play vs. Authenticity

Finally I would like to return to the scene I depicted in the introduction concerning the idea of ‚playing ethnology'. As Petra Kalshoven has pointed out, the term 'play' is contentious among Indian hobbyists: There are many "(usually implicit) interpretations and appreciations of 'play' among Indianists: for example, play as a learning tool, or as something that requires skill and expertise, or play as something disrespectful or unworthy of respect. One Indianst's play may not be another Indianist's play" (Kalshoven 2005: 83). With reference to Gregory Bateson (1972), she suggests that in the context of hobbyism there exists no clear framework that signals "this is play." The boundaries between play and seriousness are constantly called into question and at least for outsiders it is difficult to distinguish role playing from everyday behaviour, as she experienced in her own field research. Thus, it appears to be more suitable to pose the question "Is this play?" (ibid.: 68). In the case of the Cologne Tribes, the notion of play is just as ambiguous. Some use the term 'play' in describing their activities in order to avoid being taken too seriously. For example, when I first introduced myself as an ethnologist, most of the members of the Cologne Tribes were surprised that I wanted to do research on them. Since what they did was "just play", they suggested that I should travel to foreign countries and study 'real' foreigners instead. Some of them even felt sorry for me that I had to 'settle for' doing research on them, the 'fake' tribes.

Others, however, reacted in a negative way when I referred to their activities as play. They were so convinced of the seriousness of their re-staging that they assumed I had contacted them in order to study the foreign or past cultures they had revived by means of their reenactments. They themselves used the term 'play' in a pejorative way to describe fellow 'tribes' whom they considered as not behaving or dressing authentically. Thus, the concept of 'play' is drawn in stark opposition to the concept of 'authenticity'.

Among the Cologne Tribes, the notion of 'authenticity' is of great importance and discussions on how 'authentic' or playful the hobby should be are essential to almost every club member I talked to. Ideas of authenticity are closely related to visibility: Modern items like watches, mobile phones or cigarettes, for instance, are allowed, as long as they are invisible. They should be hidden under the clothes or in bags. Making a phone call or smoking a cigarette is tolerated, as long as you hide behind your yurt. Many tents possess a hidden partition where modern camping equipment is kept, sometimes even a refrigerator. Nevertheless, modern items are a matter of discussion. There have been debates about buying objects imported from Mongolia, which some 'hardliners' reject as 'modern' and mass-produced. These hardliners consider only hand-made objects 'authentic' and carefully reconstruct the material culture, copying historic artifacts they have found in ethnographic books or museum displays. Some even demand that the tools for making the items have to be 'authentic' as well, and costumes should not be made with a sewing machine but only by hand-stitching. The methods of reconstructing the material culture have become akin to those of experimental archaeology, where armaments are made out of bones without the use of modern tools in order to figure out how people in the past could possibly have produced such objects. These opinions hold only for a small group of 'extremists', however, who complain that the rules concerning historical accuracy have become too lax. They nostalgically conjure up the old days when people were sentenced to the pillory for wearing sneakers.

To confirm the 'authenticity' or historical accuracy of their performances, some members draw on academic ethnographic literature. The display of expert knowledge is a major means by which members increase their prestige and power within the societies. An example of this practice are the Mongolian clubs' shamans who hold the position of experts and often are consulted in questions on culture and history. Some of them refer to scholarly ethnological writings to develop role playing and rituals. In particular, an ethnography on religious beliefs in ancient Mongolia by Erika and Manfred Taube (Taube/Taube 1983) is used for this purpose. The rituals described in this book are imitated during performances, and sometimes prayers and invocations of gods are literally quoted from it during rituals. Among the Cologne Tribes, it is therefore referred to as "The Bible of the Shamans".

This performative approach to ethnographic literature parallels the methods of theatre anthropology in the 1970s: In order to provide students and audience with a more hands-on or performative access to ethnographic literature, anthropologist Victor Turner and theatre director Richard Schechner had experimented with the dramatisation of ethnographies (Turner 1982). This approach can be considered a return to the early days of ethnographic research, when Franz Boas, one of the founding figures of the discipline became well known for performing the *Hamats'a* ritual of the *Bella Coola* himself at the United States National Museum in 1895 (Kort/ Hollein 2006: 180). Even though these hands-on methods have become more or less obsolete in current anthropological research, the central method of ethnology itself, participant observation, is still a more experience-based approach to dealing with knowledge when compared to historical source study.

Conclusion

Marvin Carlson suggests that hobbyist reenactment should be read as an "unofficial 'folk' living-history movement" that has grown "alongside the official living history movement developed by established museums, the government, and foundations" (2000: 243). According to Carlson the main difference between these two ideas of living history consists in observation vs. participation:

"'Official' living history, insofar as it involves performance, operates much like traditional theatre. An audience comes to a performance space to observe in a relatively passive manner performers who assume imaginary personae. In the 'folk' living history there may still be an audience, but the emphasis is upon direct participation." (Carlson 2000: 243)

Thus Carlson calls into question the common differentiation between amateurs/hobbyists and academics/professionals in the context of living history or more generally in the context with dealing with the past:

"Historians, and for that matter anyone involved in remembering or recounting past events, have always visited their records, their documentary sources, even their own memories, as 'anthropological fieldworkers', visitors from another culture, and they have always, consciously or not, participated as imaginative performers in their historical reports by applying to the data they have selected for study the strategies of reflexivity, narrative, interpretation and imaginative reconstruction. We, historians and laymen alike, have always recreated the past in terms of our own needs, hopes, and physical and mental modes of being in the world." (Carlson 2000: 246)

As I experienced in my case study on the Cologne Tribes, the community of people who practice this hobby is not a homogenous group. The motivation ranges from educational interests and social aspects to the pure pleasure of dressing up. Equally diverse are the approaches concerning the authenticity of the performances: On the one hand, one finds the strict historical accuracy of an historian doing first person impersonations, while on the other hand, one has role players who freely make use of the whole repertoire of popular representations of history to create their individual 'patchwork past'.[14] I do not, however, consider these contradictory concepts as standing in direct opposition, but rather as two ends of a continuum, with the academic turning into an actor in search of a more hands-on access to history on the one side, and the amateur trying to confirm her acting out of past events with scientific knowledge on the other. Both – the historically correct impersonator and the fantasy role player – attend the same reenactment events, and they can even be members of the same clubs; only insiders will recognize the difference, if at all. Moreover, the attitude of reenactors towards their practices can change in the course of their 'career', more often from fantasy to authenticity, but also from authenticity to fantasy.

As my research on the Cologne tribes has shown, most of the participants start their hobbyist 'career' with a fascination with popular cultural or fictional representations of the past or of 'foreign' cultures, for example adventure novels or historical movies. These representations seem to elicit the desire of bodily experiencing these imaginings of the past, in order to deepen their historical and anthropological knowledge of past times and foreign cultures. In drawing on all accessible media resources such as fiction films, TV documentaries, novels, ethnographies, historical literature and museum exhibitions, the members of the Cologne Tribes blur the differentiation between academic and popular forms of historical and anthropological representation.

Nevertheless, discussions and conflicts about how to practice reenactments are not only daily occurrences, but seem to be driving forces in the hobby that often lead to splits and the foundation of new groups who develop their own way of reenactment. Thus, controversies and discussions result in permanent changes. I would therefore not agree with the widespread assumption that reenactors imitate past events in a rather naive or affirmative way, or that their aim is merely to escape from the complexities and ambiguities of the postmodern world into a past that they idealise for its simplicity and

---

14 Here I would also include the phenomenon called fantasy role play or live action role play (LARP). LARPs can either be based on history or on fantasy settings. I would include both since even role playing based on fantasy literature usually refers to elements of medieval imagery. And since we are talking about the staging of other time periods, the science fiction set role playing can also be taken into account – as a staging of the future. Thus, I would also consider the *Star Trek* fandom as described by Wenger (2006).

stability.[15] Quite to the contrary, the Cologne Tribes show various forms of creative appropriation and performance of historical and ethnological knowledge.

References

Antweiler, Christoph. 2005. *Ethnologie. Ein Führer zu populären Medien.* München: Dietrich Reimer Verlag.

Arns, Inke. 2007. "History Will Repeat Itself. Strategien des Reenactment in der zeitgenössischen (Medien-)Kunst und Performance." *History Will Repeat Itself. Strategien des Reenactment in der zeitgenössischen (Medien-)Kunst und Performance.* Eds. Inke Arns/Gabriele Horn. Frankfurt am Main: Revolver. 38-63.

Bateson, Gregory. 1972. "A Theory of Play and Fantasy." *Steps to an Ecology of Mind.* New York: Ballantine Books.

Brog, Hildegard/Matthias von der Bank. 2008. "Karneval und Kolonialismus." http://www.kopfwelten.org/kp/ereignisse/karneval/index.html (accessed 2 Apr 2010).

Broyles Gonzalez, Yolanda. 1989. "Cheyennes in the Black Forest: A Social Drama." *The Americanization of the Global Village: Essays in Comparative Popular Culture.* Ed. Roger Rollin. Bowling Green, OH: Bowling Green State University Popular Press. 70-86.

Carlson, Marvin. 2000. "Performing the Past: Living History and Cultural Memory." *Paragrana* 9.2: 237-248.

Clifford, James/Georg E. Marcus. 1986. *Writing Culture. The Poetics and Politics of Ethnography.* Berkeley: University of California Press.

Deloria, Philip Joseph. 1998. *Playing Indian.* New Haven: Yale University Press.

Die Stämme von Köln (Germany 2010, Anja Dreschke).

Dreschke, Anja. 2010. "Possession Play. On Trance Rituals and Impersonation Among the Cologne Tribes." *Trance Media and New Media.* Eds. Heike Behrend/Anja Dreschke/Martin Zillinger. New York: Fordham University Press (forthcoming).

Euler-Schmidt, Michael/Marcus Leifeld. 2007. *Der Kölner Rosenmontagszug 1823-1948.* Köln: J.P. Bachem Verlag.

Frohn, Christina. 2000. *Der organisierte Narr. Karneval in Aachen, Düsseldorf und Köln von 1823 bis 1914.* Marburg: Jonas Verlag.

Hartmann, Petra/Stephan Schmitz, eds. 1991. *Die Kölner Stämme: Menschen, Mythen, Maskenspiel.* Köln: Vista Point.

---

15 For this kind of critique, cf. for example Arns (2007: 31–32).

Kalshoven, Petra Tjitske. 2005. "'Is This Play?' Reframing Metaphoric Action on Indianist Playgrounds." *Kroeber Anthropological Society Papers* 91: 66-91.

Klauser, Helene. 2007. *Kölner Karneval zwischen Uniform und Lebensform*. Münster: Waxmann.

Kort, Pamela/Max Hollein. 2006. *I like America. Fiktionen des Wilden Westens*. München: Prestel.

Sieg, Katrin. 2002. *Ethnic Drag. Performing Race, Nation, Sexuality in West Germany*. Ann Arbor: The University of Michigan Press.

Sign of the Pagan (USA 1953, Douglas Sirk).

Taube, Erika/Manfred Taube. 1983. *Schamanen und Rhapsoden. Die geistige Kultur der alten Mongolei*. Leipzig: Koehler & Amelang.

Turner, Victor W. 1982. "Dramatic Ritual/Ritual Drama. Performative and Reflexive Anthropology." *From Ritual to Theatre. The Human Seriousness of Play*. New York: PAJ Publications. 89-101.

Turner, Victor W. 1987. "Images and Reflections: Ritual, Drama, Carnival, Film, and Spectacle in Cultural Performance." *The Anthropology of Performance*. Ed. Victor W. Turner. New York: PAJ Publications. 21-32.

Wenger, Christian. 2006. *Jenseits der Sterne. Gemeinschaft und Identität in Fankulturen. Zur Konstruktion des Star Trek-Fandoms*. Bielefeld: transcript.

LIST OF CONTRIBUTORS

Vanessa Agnew is Associate Professor of German Studies at the University of Michigan, Ann Arbor. She studied music at the University of Queensland in Australia, received her MA in Germanistik from New York University, and a PhD in European Studies from the University of Wales, Cardiff (1998), with a dissertation on Georg Forster and the British exploration of the Pacific. She was a participant consultant on the *The Ship* (BBC 2001) which retraced part of Cook's first voyage on a replica tall ship. She now researches and teaches on the cultural history of music, 18th-century travel writing, natural history, and historical reenactment. Her books include *Settler and Creole Reenactment,* coedited with Jonathan Lamb (Palgrave 2010) and *Enlightenment Orpheus: The Power of Music in Other Worlds* (Oxford University Press 2008), which won the Kenshur Prize for Eighteenth-Century Studies and the American Musicological Society's Lewis Lockwood Award in 2009. She is a series coeditor on reenactment for Palgrave and is currently working on an edited volume on *Affective Cognition.*

Anja Dreschke studied Cultural Anthropology, History of Arts and Theatre, Film and Television Studies at the University of Cologne. She is a research fellow at the University of Siegen, Forschungskolleg Medienumbrüche, in a project called "Trance Media and New Media". She is also a lecturer for Visual Anthropology and Media Ethnology at the Department of Social and Cultural Anthropology at the University of Cologne and works as a filmmaker, curator, and journalist in the fields of anthropology, film/media and art. Her PhD project on the Cologne Tribes *(Kölner Stämme)* combines text, video and photography.

Joy Hendry is Professor of Social Anthropology at Oxford Brookes University, Oxford, England where she was also the founder of the Europe Japan Research Centre. She received her DPhil in 1979 from Oxford University, and is a Senior Member of St. Antony's College, Oxford. She has carried out long-term fieldwork in Japan, Canada and Mexico, but has recently visited all five continents to examine global movements in tourism, alternatives to museums, and other forms of cultural display. Her publications include *Wrapping Culture: Politeness, Presentation and Power in Japan and Other Societies* (Oxford University Press 1993), *The Orient Strikes Back: A Global View of Cultural Display* (Berg 2000), and *Reclaiming Culture: Indigenous People and Self-Representation* (Palgrave 2005).

Wolfgang Hochbruck is Professor of North American Philology and Cultural Studies at the University of Freiburg, Germany. A navy veteran, former journalist and director of a Living History Theatre Group, he received his doctorate from the University of Freiburg in 1990, taught for a year at the University of Osnabrück following the fall of the Iron Curtain, and wrote his habilitation at the University of Stuttgart on the cultural memory of the American Civil War. After several years as a professor of American Literature at the Technical University of Braunschweig, he followed a call back to his old *alma mater* and now resides in Waldkirch with his family. He is the head of the research project "Theatrical (Re-)Constructions of North-American History" and one of the directors of the Centre for Security and Society at the University of Freiburg.

Cornelius Holtorf is Associate Professor (Docent) and Head of Archaeology and Heritage Studies at Linnaeus University, Kalmar, Sweden. Born and raised in Germany, he emigrated to the U.K. in 1993 and moved on to Sweden in 2002. After gaining his PhD in 1998 from the University of Wales, Holtorf was employed at the Universities of Gothenburg, Cambridge and Lund as well as at the Swedish National Heritage Board in Stockholm before moving to Kalmar in 2008. His research interests and the topics of numerous publications include the portrayal of archaeology and archaeologists in popular culture, the significance and meaning of heritage in modern society, and the archaeology of contemporary zoos. He is also the director of archaeological excavations at Monte da Igreja near Évora in southern Portugal, and co-ordinator of an interdisciplinary scholarly network investigating "Places as Stories".

Gordon L. Jones is the Senior Military Historian and Curator at the Atlanta History Center in Atlanta, Georgia, where he is responsible for the care, exhibition, and research of approximately 11,000 American Civil War artifacts. He was the writer and curator of the 9,200 square-foot permanent exhibition "Turning Point: The American Civil War", which opened in 1996, as well as temporary exhibitions addressing southern regional culture. In 2007, Jones completed his PhD in the Graduate Institute of the Liberal Arts at Emory University in Atlanta, specializing in Civil War popular culture and the processes of remembering, commemorating, and recreating the past. He also holds a BA in History from Furman University in South Carolina and an MA in Public History and Museum Studies from the University of South Carolina. Jones has been involved as both participant and observer in Civil War reenacting for almost 30 years.

Regina Loftus studied Archaeology, Geology and Ethnology at the University of Cologne and finished her Master in 1986. Apart from creating exhibitions for museums, she works freelance in the field of museum paedagogy in schools and museums in Germany and is one of the main organizers of a project called "Ventures into History". She is the author of the historical novel *Die Fäden des Schicksals* (Novum 2009) and lives in Schwerte near Dortmund.

Scott A. Lukas is Professor of Anthropology and Sociology at Lake Tahoe Community College. He received his PhD in Cultural Anthropology from Rice University in 1998. In 2005 he was the recipient of the Oxford University Press/American Anthropological Association Award for Excellence in Undergraduate Teaching of Anthropology. His research focuses on the consequences of cultural remaking. He is the author/editor of *The Themed Space: Locating Culture, Nation, and Self* (Lexington 2007), as well as *Theme Park* (Reaktion 2008), *Fear, Cultural Anxiety, and Transformation: Horror, Science Fiction, and Fantasy Films Remade* (Lexington 2008), *Recent Developments in Criminological Theory* (Ashgate 2009), and *Strategies in Teaching Anthropology* (Prentice-Hall 2010). He is the founder of the Gender Ads Project (www.genderads.com). In 2008, he was the keynote speaker for the Storytelling, Architecture, Technology, and Experience conference sponsored by the Theming Entertainment Association at Walt Disney World. He once worked as a theme park trainer at Six Flags AstroWorld.

Carolyn Oesterle is a research fellow at the English Department of the University of Freiburg, Germany, and member of the DFG-Research Group 875: "History in Popular Cultures". She studied English and American Studies, Sports Science, and German Philology at the University of Freiburg, Germany and Washington University in St. Louis, USA. After several years of editorial work in an academic publishing company and print media agency, she now works as an assistant in the research project "Theatrical (Re-)Constructions of North American History". Her research interests are 20th-century American literature and culture and theater and performance studies. Her dissertation focuses on performative appropriations of history and their functions in North American living history projects.

Paul Röllke studied Archaeology, Geology, and Ethnology at the University of Hamburg. For twenty years, he has been working for the History Museum in Hamburg-Harburg and the Museum of Ethnology in Hamburg in the field of museum education, and he is one of the initiators of a project called "Ventures into History". He now lives in Basel, Switzerland, and works with schools and other educational institutes.

Amos S. Ron is a Senior Lecturer in Tourism Studies at the Department of Tourism and Hospitality Studies at Kinneret College on the Sea of Galilee, Israel. He received his doctorate in Cultural Geography from the Hebrew University of Jerusalem in 2001 on the subject of spatial commemoration of pioneers in the Sea of Galilee region – using the methodology of landscape interpretation. His research interests are in tourism & leisure studies, cultural geography, and geography of religion. Parallel to his academic studies, he worked as a tour guide, for the most part with English-speaking Christian pilgrims. He has published articles and book chapters on Christian and Muslim pilgrimage, agricultural leisure activities, and Jewish pioneer heritage in Israel. He is currently engaged in co-authoring a book on contemporary Christian travel.

Noel B. Salazar is a Marie Curie Fellow and Fellow of the Research Foundation – Flanders at the University of Leuven, Belgium. He received his PhD in Anthropology from the University of Pennsylvania, USA. Salazar's research interests include cultural (im)mobilities, the local-to-global nexus, discourses and imaginaries of Otherness, cultural brokering, and cosmopolitanism, while his geographical focus is on Indonesia, Tanzania, Chile, and Belgium. He has published widely, in various languages, and is the author of *Envisioning Eden: Mobilizing Imaginaries in Tourism and Beyond* (Berghahn Books 2010). His current research focuses on how dominant European imaginaries of travel to and from the "global South" are (dis)connected, and he is on the editorial boards of *Annals of Tourism Research*, *International Journal of Tourism Anthropology*, *Mondes du Tourisme*, and *AIBR – Revista de Antropología Iberoamericana*, and on UNWTO's and UNESCO's official roster of consultants.

Judith Schlehe is Professor of Social and Cultural Anthropology at the University of Freiburg, Germany. She received her PhD in 1987 and finished her habilitation in 1997. She was professor of Anthropology *pro tempore* at the University of Bremen and the University of Mainz. Since 2002, Schlehe has held a chair in Anthropology at the University of Freiburg. She has published widely on the topics of cultural globalization and intercultural issues, gender, religious dynamics, the anthropology of disaster, popular forms of representing cultures, and new approaches to transnational collaboration against the background of diverse academic cultures. A current research project is on images of 'the West' in Indonesia ("Beyond Occidentalism"), another on "Staging Historical Lifeworlds in Theme- and Culture-Parks: Reflections of Self and Other in Asia and Europe". Her regional specialisation is on Southeast Asia, and she has carried out long-term fieldwork in Indonesia and Mongolia.

Victoria Tafferner is presently completing a Master in British and American Cultural Studies at the University of Freiburg. She received a Bachelor of Music from the University of Cape Town in 1999 and a Diploma from the Musikhochschule Freiburg in 2003, and she is an active chamber and orchestral musician. Her academic interests include performance and history, book history, class, culture, and political activism. Her master's thesis explores the performativity of class in living history and reenactment.

Martine Teunissen is director and owner of the company 'Beleef Het Verleden'/'Experience The Past' (Historical Events & Consultancy). She received her M.Phil in February 2008 at Leiden University after completing her thesis on the representation of the past in public spheres. Examining the different examples of European and American open-air museums, with a main focus on Colonial Williamsburg, inspired her to bring this knowledge into practice. Having founded her company in May 2008, she – together with a team of live interpreters from several countries – now provides live interpretation for several museums, schools, castles, and heritage centres to recreate history in an enjoyable and educational way. She is developing a computer game that will provide school children with an interactive learning opportunity with regard to the past.

Michiko Uike-Bormann is a research fellow at the Institute of Social and Cultural Anthropology at the University of Freiburg, Germany. She studied Cultural Anthropology, Japanese Studies, and German Philology at the University of Cologne and at Ritsumeikan University in Kyōto, Japan. After working as a research assistant at the CITS (Center for Inter- and Transcultural Studies) at the University of Cologne, she became a member of the DFG-Research Group "History in Popular Cultures" in 2007 where she is working as a research assistant in the anthropological project "Staging Historical Lifeworlds in Theme- and Culture-Parks: Reflections of Self and Other in Asia and Europe". Her PhD thesis focuses on Japanese cultural theme parks.

Mark Wallis has been involved in professional costumed interpretation since 1977 when he received his first paid commission for co-producing an historical event celebrating the oldest bridge over the River Thames – he can thus claim to be among the first to have used costumed interpretation professionally in the UK. Wallis holds a BA in Costume Design and an MA in Theatre History – the latter gained in America where he lived and worked for nine years, bringing history to life on a massive scale with the Living History Centre's Elizabethan and Dickensian festivals, and – on a more purist level – with the Colonial Williamsburg Foundation (for which he remains a consultant). While at Williamsburg he founded Past Pleasures Ltd, and on moving back to Britain in 1987 set about employing costumed interpreters in historic sites. His expertise was acknowledged recently when the Association for Heritage Interpretation made him a Fellow, whilst for some years he was also a director of the International Museum Theatre Alliance (Europe).